Indigenous Literatures from Micronesia

The New Oceania Literary Series

Series Editor: Craig Santos Perez

The New Oceania Literary Series publishes thematic anthologies that highlight the diversity and complexity of Pacific literature. These volumes present creative writing, literary scholarship, and pedagogical materials written by an intergenerational network of authors, scholars, and educators from Polynesia, Micronesia, Melanesia, and the global Pacific diaspora. This series is committed to creating thought-provoking books for the classroom and the community.

Indigenous Literatures from Micronesia

Edited by Evelyn Flores and Emelihter Kihleng

University of Hawai'i Press

HONOLULU

"Fino' Finakpo' / Final Words," (2008), "Manotohge Hit / We Stand" (1996), and "I Tinituhon (The Beginning)" (1996) © by Leonard Z. Iriarte.

Printed in the United States of America

24 23 22 21 20 19   6 5 4 3 2 1

Library of Congress Cataloging-in-Publication Data

Names: Flores, Evelyn, editor. | Kihleng, Emelihter S., editor.

Title: Indigenous literatures from Micronesia / edited by Evelyn Flores and Emelihter Kihleng.
Other titles: New Oceania literary series.
Description: Honolulu : University of Hawai'i Press, [2019] | Series: The new Oceania literary series | In Palauan, Chamorro, Chuukese, I-Kiribati, Kosraean, Marshallese, Nauruan, Pohnpeian, and Yapese, with some English.
Identifiers: LCCN 2018037462| ISBN 9780824875411 (cloth : alk. paper) | ISBN 9780824877460 (pbk. : alk. paper)
Subjects: LCSH: Micronesian literature. | Micronesian literature—Translations into English. | Micronesia—Literary collections.
Classification: LCC PL6195 .I53 2019 | DDC 899/.52—dc2'
LC record available at https://lccn.loc.gov/2018037462

Maps of Micronesia, Guam and the Northern Mariana Islands, Central Caroline Islands, Chuuk Lagoon, Republic of the Marshall Islands, and Palau by Mānoa Mapworks, Inc.

Interior art: "Unicorns are Real on Guåhan II" blockprint by Monica Dolores Baza.

Cover art: "Guåhan Pugua" block mixed media by Monica Dolores Baza.

University of Hawai'i Press books are printed on acid-free paper and meet the guidelines for permanence and durability of the Council on Library Resources.

We dedicate *Indigenous Literatures from Micronesia*

to Teresia Teaiwa

What keeps us here?

Islands in an ocean.

What makes us leave?

Islands in an ocean.

What calls us back?

Islands in an ocean.

—Teresia Teaiwa,

from "No One Is an Island"

Contents

Resistance

Remembering

Identities

Voyages

Family

A New Micronesia

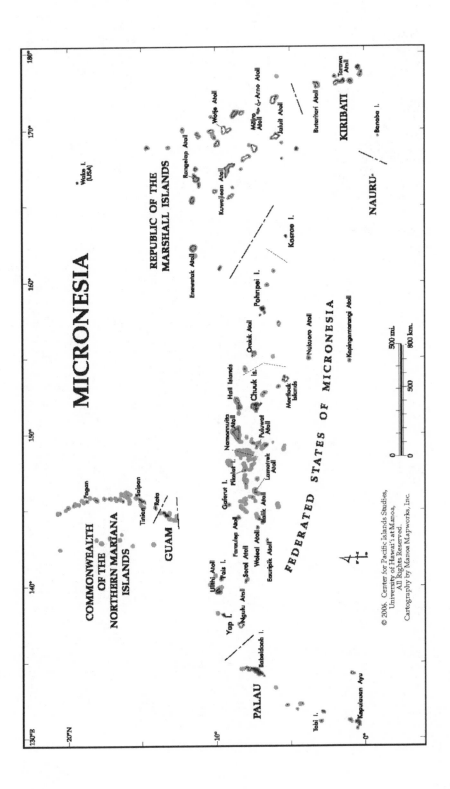

MICRONESIA

COMMONWEALTH OF THE NORTHERN MARIANA ISLANDS

REPUBLIC OF THE MARSHALL ISLANDS

FEDERATED STATES OF MICRONESIA

GUAM

PALAU

KIRIBATI

NAURU

Wake I. (USA)

Pagan
Saipan
Tinian
Rota

Rongelap Atoll
Wotje Atoll
Kuwajlean Atoll
Majro Atoll
Jaluit Atoll
Arno Atoll

Enewetak Atoll

Kosrae I.

Pohnpei I.
Oroluk Atoll

Nukuoro Atoll

Kapingamarangi Atoll

Butaritari Atoll

Tarawa Atoll

Banaba I.

Ulithi Atoll
Fais I.
Yap
Sorol Atoll
Ngulu Atoll
Faraulep Atoll
Woleai Atoll
Eauripik Atoll
Ifalik Atoll

Gaferut I.
Pikelot I.
Namonuito Atoll
Hall Islands
Chuuk Is.
Lamotrek Atoll
Puluwat Atoll
Mortlock Islands

Babeldaob I.

Tobi I.
Kepulauan Ayu

500 mi.
800 km.
500

130°E   140°   150°   160°   170°   180°

20°N

10°

0°

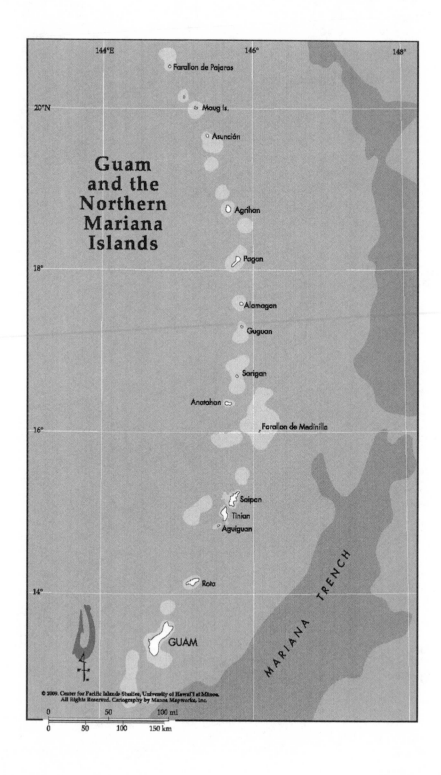

**Guam
and the
Northern
Mariana
Islands**

144°E   146°   148°

○ Farallon de Pajaros

20°N

◐ Maug Is.

○ Asunción

◑ Agrihan

◐ Pagan

18°

○ Alamagan

○ Guguan

○ Sarigan

Anatahan ◌

Farallon de Medinilla

16°

Saipan
Tinian
Agviguan

Rota

14°

GUAM

MARIANA TRENCH

0	50	100 mi

0	50	100	150 km

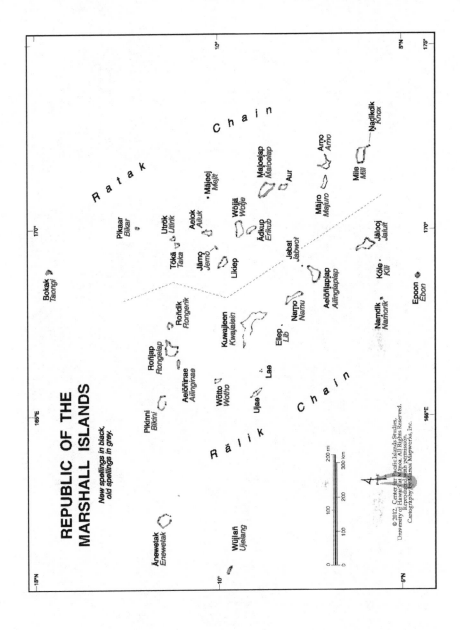

REPUBLIC OF THE MARSHALL ISLANDS

*New spellings in black;
old spellings in grey.*

Ānewetak
Enewetak

Wūjlañ
Ujelang

Pikinni
Bikini

Roñlap
Rongelap

Aelōñinae
Ailinginae

Roñdik
Rongerik

Wōtto
Wotho

Ujae

Lae

Ralik Chain

Bokak
Taongi

Pikaar
Bikar

Utrōk
Utirik

Tōkā
Taka

Jāmo
Jemo

Likiep

Aelok
Ailuk

Mājeej
Mejit

Wōjja
Wotje

Adkup
Erikub

Kuwajleen
Kwajalein

Ellep
Lib

Naṃo
Namu

Jebat
Jabwot

Ratak Chain

Maļoelap
Maloelap

Aur

Mājro
Majuro

Arṇo
Arno

Mile
Mili

Naḑikdik
Knox

Jālooj
Jaluit

Aelōñḷapḷap
Ailinglaplap

Kōle
Kili

Naṃdik
Namorik

Epoon
Ebon

200 mi

300 km

15°N

10°N

5°N

165°E

170°

175°

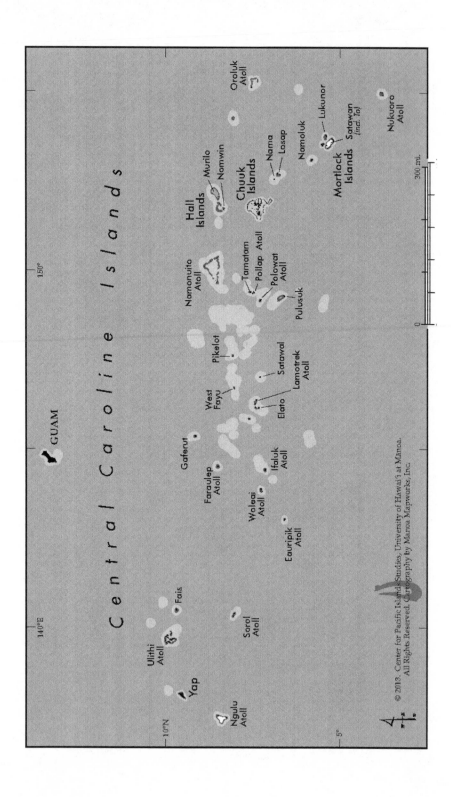

Central Caroline Islands

GUAM

Ulithi Atoll
Fais
Yap
Ngulu Atoll
Sorol Atoll
Eauripik Atoll
Woleai Atoll
Faraulep Atoll
Ifaluk Atoll
Gaferut
Elato
Lamotrek Atoll
West Fayu
Satawal
Pikelot
Namonuito Atoll
Tamatam
Pollap Atoll
Polowat Atoll
Pulusuk
Pulap
Hall Islands
Murilo
Nomwin
Chuuk Islands
Nama
Losap
Namoluk
Nomoi
Mortlock Islands
Lukunor
Satawan (incl. Ta)
Oroluk Atoll
Nukuoro Atoll

140°E
150°
10°N
5°

0   300 mi.

© 2013. Center for Pacific Island Studies, University of Hawaiʻi at Mānoa.
All Rights Reserved. Cartography by Mānoa Mapworks, Inc.

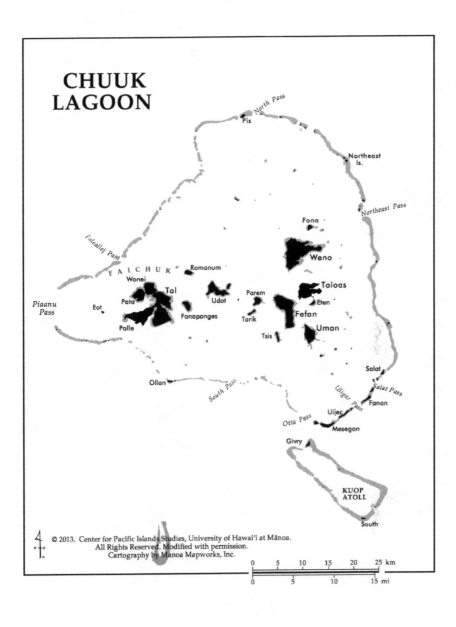

CHUUK
LAGOON

North Pass

Pis

Northeast
is.

Northeast Pass

Faleallej Pass

Fona

Weno

F A I C H U K

Romanum

Wonei

Tol

Toloas

Pata

Udot

Parem

Eten

Piaanu
Pass

Eot

Fanapanges

Fefan

Tarik

Polle

Uman

Tsis

Salat

Ollan

South Pass

Salat Pass

Uligar Pass

Fanan

Otta Pass

Uijec

Mesegon

Givry

KUOP
ATOLL

South

0   5   10   15   20   25 km

0   5   10   15 mi

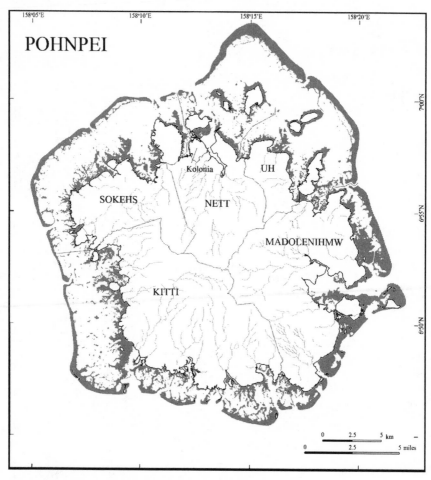

POHNPEI

Kolonia

UH

SOKEHS

NETT

MADOLENIHMW

KITTI

0   2.5   5 km

0   2.5   5 miles

Map by Island Research & Education Initiative (iREi).

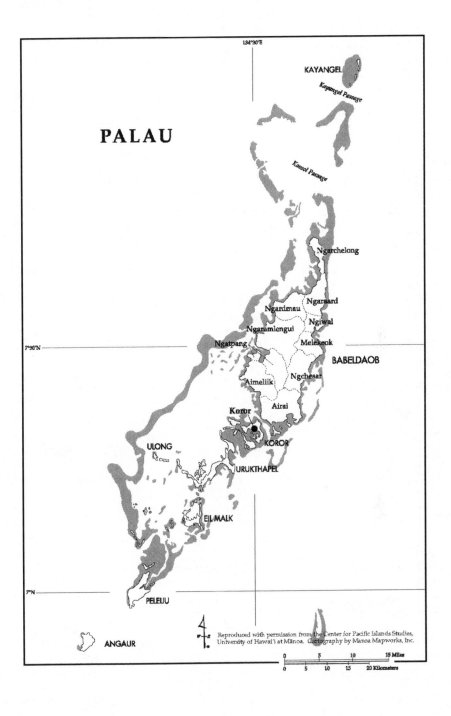

PALAU

134°30'E

KAYANGEL

Kayangel Passage

Kossol Passage

Ngarchelong

Ngaraard

Ngardmau

Ngiwal

Ngaramlengui

Melekeok

Ngatpang

7°30'N

BABELDAOB

Aimeliik

Ngchesar

Airai

Koror

KOROR

ULONG

URUKTHAPEL

EIL MALK

7°N

PELELIU

ANGAUR

Reproduced with permission from the Center for Pacific Islands Studies,
University of Hawai'i at Mānoa. Cartography by Manoa Mapworks, Inc.

0   5   10   15 Miles

0   5   10   15   20 Kilometers

Preface

Born in the cradle of post–World War II reconstruction, I grew up in the thick of both persistent Chamoru struggles for equal rights and intense Americanization. The Chamoru language was outlawed in the schools; there was no such thing in the curriculum as Guam history or any kind of history, for that matter, about our Pacific region; there was nothing in our textbooks by a Pacific writer, much less a Chamoru one. Everything we learned in those years in school was knowledge imported from the continental United States.

My parents spoke to us children in English and to each other in Chamoru. They understood the message being sent by the American administration: English was to be *the* language of education; to speak English well meant to excel in school, and to excel meant moving up in this brave new world. Our "mainland" friends urged them to send us off to the "States" for a quality college education. Of course, wanting only the best for their children, they sacrificed and waved good-bye to us at the airport, one after the other. When it was my turn, amid tears, layers of leis, and lots of nervous excitement, I boarded the plane and joined the diaspora of thousands of Chamoru whose swelling numbers have resulted in more of us living in California and Washington than in our homeland. Meanwhile, back on Guam, resistance warriors were waging cultural and language battles to hold endangered ground. I knew little about these struggles, isolated as I was from them.

At thirty-two, I literally awoke with a start one morning in the middle of eastern Oregon's high desert, thousands of miles from Guam, to the shocking realization that George Washington was not my forefather and I didn't know who was. This deeply troubling thought launched me on a journey to find out where I could possibly have lost something as important as my foreparents. I didn't yet understand that they'd been stolen from my generation and buried beneath huge mounds of Western textbooks, curricula, classrooms, libraries, and media or sunk in the deepest parts of oceans of indifferent, official discourses. I just knew they weren't there.

Finally returning home with my husband and two children after a thirteen-year absence, I was sure we'd find shelves and shelves of books written by Chamoru, featuring Chamoru children involved in Chamoru adventures. There were none. The public and university libraries were as bare for them as they had been for me. Out of a sense of outrage, I wrote and published three picture books in the space of a year. These cultural treasures, along with others written and being written, continue to build a positive self-image in our island's children.

Still questing for my ancestors as were others of my generation, I left Guam again, this time to pursue a doctorate at the University of Michigan. Respected scholars from various fields of diversity handed me valuable tools for excavation and guided me to a dissertation that helped me understand that my culture had gotten buried, superseded by the determination of Americanization. In 2000, I returned to my teaching at the University of Guam and made EN333, Literature of Guam, Micronesia, and the Pacific, my excavation headquarters. This academic site provided me a place to launch not just my culture-founded pedagogy but my projects to preserve indigenous history and literature. My students read, talked, researched, and wrote about Hawaiian, Fijian, Ni-Vanuatu, and Māori literature, among others, but most importantly, they were brought home to their own Chamoru literature. Their gratitude, awe, and amazement when they found themselves in the literature we'd read energized my efforts. Seventeen years and four hundred graduates later, I know that at least eight thousand high school students' lives have been changed by these teaching apprentices going out to return Chamoru culture to those who own it.

This anthology is the continuation of this recovery and assertion process. The work remains of breaking down myths and building up re-visioned ones that empower rather than demean. It remains to tell new stories that are really ancient ones, persisting in our blood, paradoxically and endearingly both familiar and breathtakingly novel, stories that deconstruct the lies and half-truths that we've come to believe. This purpose has never changed. We must bring those narratives, our histories and imaginations, home. We must return our children to their foremothers and forefathers.

Evelyn Flores

This anthology means a great deal to me as a Micronesian and, more specifically, as a Pohnpeian woman poet, born and raised on Guam, as well as in Pohnpei and Hawai'i. It means that my and Dr. Evelyn Flores's dream, wthich we first began pursuing as colleagues in the English Department at the University of Guam almost ten years ago, will become a reality. Most importantly, the publication of this anthology means that Micronesian voices will finally be heard on the page, and we will no longer have to justify a gap in the literature of Oceania. For teachers of Pacific, postcolonial, and/or world literatures, it means that there is now a collection from our part of the world that features the creative and scholarly writing of the indigenous people of Micronesia as opposed to stories written about us by outsiders. For the writers featured in this volume, it means recognition in a groundbreaking work, and for those Micronesian writers not featured, the collection can provide inspiration and perhaps a sense of community.

When I first started writing, the only collection of poetry by a fellow Micronesian that I had read was by the late Banaban/I-Kiribati/African American Teresia Teaiwa, *Searching for Nei Nim'anoa* (Mana Publications, 1995). I could identify with her voice, and I loved how beautifully she wove the personal with the political in her poetry. The only other work that I saw my reflection in during that time was the Samoan Sia Figiel's novel *Where We Once Belonged* (Pasifika Press, 1996). It is crucial that all people, including Micronesians, have writers in whom we can see ourselves. Pasifika scholars such as Albert Wendt, Vilsoni Hereniko, and Selina Tusitala Marsh have written about how essential it is for the survival of our Pacific cultures to see ourselves reflected in our art. This is why it is so critical for us to perpetuate our art forms, including our indigenous literature.

Smallness is truly a state of mind for those of us who call Micronesia home. For us, this region is far from small: it is our universe. Our Micro is indeed Macro, and this is clearly demonstrated in *Indigenous Literatures from Micronesia*. It is not perfect, of course: we still have a way to go in terms of representing all of the islands in the region, and certain islands are represented much more than others, but it is a beginning. All of us in Oceania have reason to celebrate this publication. I celebrate this text as one of the editors, as a poet, and as an intellectual, but most of all as a proud Micronesian.

Emelihter Kihleng

Acknowledgments

This ocean journey toward an anthology of indigenous writing from Micronesia has been one marked by *i minagof yan i biaheru*, by happiness and adventure—happiness for a work finally getting done and for meeting new writers and learning about pioneer ones, by delight in seeing them all in the same room, by adventure in discovering tremendously moving pieces that had not received coverage previously, and by joy that now they will. The passage has been buoyed by stories from knowledgeable and generous guides who stepped up to help us read the stars and the currents and to make landfall. It gives us great pleasure to present the roll call of those who have been of such invaluable assistance.

We extend a special lei of gratitude to Brandy Nālani McDougall, Native Hawaiian author, editor, and publisher, for the critical insights she provided as our outside reviewer.

To Craig Santos Perez, we say Dångkalu na saina ma'åse' for the generosity of his continuing belief in the project and its value, his guidance and advice during the search for a publisher, and his singular drive as we neared the finish line.

At the start, we sought the advice of friends, colleagues, and mentors who had experience editing anthologies. They included Sāmoan author and emeritus professor of English, University of Auckland, Albert Wendt; Māori scholar and editor Reina Whaitiri; poet and professor of English, Mills College, Juliana Spahr; and poet and translator extraordinaire Jen Hofer.

In the important task of locating twentieth-century iconic writers and their work, there were several who were key. Lee Perez Cruz alerted us to the work of Fred Quinene, an officially appointed Guam poet laureate. We located copies of Yapese statesman John Mangafel's work, plus biographies and photos of him, through the combined efforts of Bill Jaynes of *The Kaselehlie Press*; Letitia Hickson, formerly the Outreach Coordinator at Center for Pacific Islands Studies, UH Mānoa; Dr. Monique Storie of the Micronesia Area Research Center (MARC); and Lynette Furuhashi of Hamilton Library, UH Mānoa.

We thank English majors Liezl Roxas, Jayne Jasmin, Alex Kerr, Alana Kerr, and Eleanor Heacock for searching the library and bringing the "goods" back to the office. Their research yielded Belauan Hermana Ramarui's and Isabelle Asang's material. Yoichi Renguul, director of the TRIO Programs here at the University of Guam, gave us contact information but also a strong lead to another story. "You ought to read Asang's 'Moon Sickness,'" he urged. Getting our hands on the evasive "Moon Sickness" piece led us through labyrinths of archives that began with Dr. Storie, who connected us with Paul Drake, who recovered the dissertation from UH Mānoa's archives. Between human and internet technology, we were able to finally see "Moon Sickness" glowing on our screens.

Our research assistants also discovered at MARC the work of Valentine Sengebau, published by the Northern Marianas Humanities Council in Saipan. Then, desperately searching for Nauruan authors, we were almost ready to board a plane for Nauru when we stumbled via the internet onto a report written by Dr. Alamanda Lauti. It proved to be a gold mine. Not only was Dr. Lauti's report filled with statistics but it also contained stories of courageous Nauruan women who had lain down in front of airplanes and who had braved male scorn to break down the doors of parliament.

Guampedia's extensive archive of authors' biographies helped us to fill in some more puzzling blanks. We thank *Guampedia*'s staff for giving us permission to use their materials. And then of course there was—and is—the University of Guam College of Liberal Arts and Social Sciences, and Dean James Sellmann's faithful support of our project. Hearty thanks go to him for providing time allocations for research, the use of equipment and space, travel grants for conferences to discuss the project, and funding for research assistants.

Through all these many networks converging, this important anthology has come together; through many hands paddling, our sakman (ocean-going vessel) has at last crossed this previously uncharted blue.

To all of you who helped propel us forward to completion, and finally and most importantly to the brave writers who have graciously shared their voices with us, we say Dångkalu na saina ma'åse' (Chamoru), Kalahngan (Pohnpeian), Ke mesulang (Belauan), Kammagar (Yapese), Ko rabwa (I-Kiribati), Kommol tata (Marshallese), Kinisou chapur (Chuukese), Tubwa (Nauruan), Kulo malulap (Kosraean), and Thank you.

Introduction

Thousands of years ago, our seafaring ancestors charted the stars, navigated across the ocean, and arrived at the thousands of small, uninhabited atolls and volcanic islands that are our home today. They planted their crops, built houses, chanted songs, buried the dead, and birthed generations. Over millennia, we developed unique cultures and complex societies in our sea of islands.

Europeans named the vast waters "Mar Pacifico," or "The Pacific Ocean," and divided the Pacific into three geographic areas: Micronesia, Melanesia, and Polynesia. The name "Micronesia" means "tiny islands," and refers to the two thousand small islands (comprising a total land area of a thousand square miles) in the Western Pacific. There is little that is tiny about the region's span, however. The total ocean area of Micronesia covers nearly three million square miles.

Micronesia includes four main island groups (the Caroline Islands, the Gilbert Islands, the Mariana Islands, and the Marshall Islands), plus the islands of Nauru and Wake. The indigenous islanders of the region included in this anthology are Chamoru (Chamorro), Belauan (Palauan), Pohnpeian, Kosraean, Chuukese, Yapese, Marshallese, Nauruan, and I-Kiribati. While there are many cultural similarities, we all speak different languages and have our own unique customs, identities, arts, and histories.

Western nations began colonizing Micronesia in the sixteenth century. The largest island in the region, Guåhan (Guam), was Magellan's first recorded landfall in 1521. Over four hundred years of colonization followed, with Spain using the island as an important transit point for the lucrative galleon trade route between Acapulco, Guåhan, and Manila. By the mid-seventeenth century, the Spanish empire had colonized the Mariana Islands and by the mid-nineteenth century, the rest of Micronesia. During the late 1800s, other nations began to claim ownership: the British moved to take control of the Gilbert Islands; the Germans claimed Nauru and the Marshalls, Caroline, and Northern Mariana Islands. It was with the Spanish–American war of 1898 that the United States became one of the top players in the region, taking control of Guåhan and Wake Island.

Germany's territories were seized in World War I and these later became League of Nations mandates. Nauru became a mandate of Australia, while the other formerly German colonies became mandates of Japan. During World War II, Japan invaded and seized Guåhan and Nauru, thus expanding its imperial territory in Micronesia. After Japan's defeat in 1944, Guåhan once again became a territory of the United States, while the other mandated islands became a United Nations Trusteeship, administered by the U.S. and known as the "Trust Territory of the Pacific Islands."

After the war, the political tides of Micronesia changed dramatically. In 1950, Chamorus on Guåhan were granted American citizenship. Nauru gained national independence in 1968, and Kiribati followed in 1979. A covenant to establish the Commonwealth of the Northern Mariana Islands in union with the U.S. was approved in 1976. In 1986, the U.S. signed into law the Compacts of Free Association with the Federated States of Micronesia, which included Pohnpei, Yap, Chuuk, and Kosrae and the Republic of the Marshall Islands. In 1994, the Republic of Palau also entered into a Compact of Free Association with the U.S. Today, Guåhan remains the only island in Micronesia that has not been given the opportunity to exercise its right to self-determination.

The islands of Micronesia attracted the West primarily for their strategic location on the global capitalist trade routes between Europe, the Americas, and Asia, but there was also the large incentive for soul-saving. From the start, wherever the flag of Spain went, missionaries followed close after. Additionally, the islands became "laboratories" for archaeological, scientific, ecological, medical, and anthropological research. But most of all, they became (and continue to be) strategic sites for U.S. militarism in the Asia-Pacific region.

Micronesia was devastated during the Pacific Theater of World War II, as the U.S. and Japan vied for control of the region. During the Cold War, the U.S. and Britain conducted numerous nuclear weapons tests in the Marshall Islands and Kiribati, which not only caused devastating environmental damage but also displaced many people from their homes and poisoned generations of Marshallese with nuclear radiation.

Today, Guåhan is one of the most important American military locations, often referred to as the "Tip of America's Spear," with a third of the island covered by military bases. The Northern Mariana Islands are used by the U.S. military for military training, live firing ranges, and bombing exercises. The Ronald Reagan Ballistic Missile Defense Test Site is an important missile test range, located in the Marshall Islands. Militarization in Micronesia has caused environmental destruction, indigenous displacement from ancestral land and fishing grounds, economic dependence on military spending, and increased incidences of sexual assault. Micronesia has also become a "military recruiter's paradise," with a large number of indigenous Micronesians joining the U.S. armed forces.

The colonial relationships in Micronesia have opened new routes of migration during the past fifty years. Micronesians from the Freely Associated States have migrated to Guåhan, the Northern Mariana Islands, Hawai'i, and many places in the continental United States. Chamorros from Guam and the Northern Marianas have also migrated to Hawai'i, the continental United States, and even Puerto Rico. Nauruans and I-Kiribati have migrated to Fiji, Australia, and New Zealand. The major reasons for Micronesian migration include employment, education, health care, and military service. Today, there are Micronesians who have larger populations living away in migrant communities than in their home islands. Like other diaspora sojourners, many of these twenty-first-century travelers have often faced the traumas of migration, including discrimination, homesickness, cultural disconnection, native language loss, poverty, homelessness, and incarceration.

Recently, Micronesia has made global news because of the existential threat of climate change. Rising sea levels are threatening low-lying atolls and islands in Chuuk, the Marshall Islands, Kiribati, Yap, and Nauru. Severe typhoons and flooding, along with extreme heat and drought, have become common throughout the region. Ocean warming and acidification have devastated coral reefs and the marine life that the reefs support. If trends continue, climate change may make many Micronesian islands uninhabitable, forcing our people to relocate and become climate change refugees.

Despite the overwhelming imperial forces that have impacted Micronesia, we indigenous peoples continue to protest the ongoing exploitation of our region; we continue to revitalize and nurture our cultures and languages, and advocate for demilitarization and environmental sustainability. We persist in fighting for disarmament of nuclear weapons, the decolonization of our countries, and the indigenous rights of our peoples. Even when we migrate far from our ancestral homelands, we form strong diasporic communities to ensure that we are able to migrate with dignity, and many Micronesians abroad have achieved educational and economic success. Considering our entire history, Micronesians exemplify resilience.

A powerful expression of our steadfastness is our literature, the oral, visual, and written. Micronesians have a rich and vibrant legacy of chants, tattoos, songs, artwork, genealogies, and oral storytelling. Our literature is a vessel of memory, culture, history, identity, politics, and geography. Our earliest texts were skin and barkcloth, which we tattooed, painted, and wove designs on. Written literature in the Western sense of pen on paper is a more recent form of creative Micronesian expression. We have authored numerous plays, film scripts, poems, short stories, novels, memoirs, political speeches, legends, biographies, and even comics. Some Micronesian authors have gained international acclaim.

Even though there is a growing body of Micronesian literature, there has never been a significant anthology that has presented the range, diversity, and complexity of Micronesian literature. Moreover, Micronesian literature has often been marginalized and ignored in discussions about Pacific, indigenous, post-colonial, migrant, and international literatures. In the summer of 2009, we launched this project with a general goal to produce an anthology of indigenous literatures from Micronesia. As scholars and writers, we had grown tired of hearing that Micronesia "lacked" a written literature when we knew that this was not, in fact, the reality. As both poets and scholars, we knew that Micronesia was like a literary volcano erupting, with brave, young voices joining more seasoned ones, changing the literary scape with their challenges to centuries-old reductive representations.

After many years of work, the *Indigenous Literatures from Micronesia* anthology is born. Bringing together poetry, short stories, critical and creative essays, chants, and excerpts of plays, this groundbreaking anthology reflects a worldview unique to the islands of Micronesia, while also resonating with the larger issues facing Pacific Islanders and indigenous peoples throughout the world. The anthology's reach is broad as the region itself. It spans all of the island groups of the area and the diaspora with over seventy authors and over 120 pieces. It showcases nine of the thirteen basic language groups of the region, which has as many as twenty spoken languages, including Belauan, Chamoru, Chuukese, I-Kiribati, Kosraean, Marshallese, Nauruan, Pohnpeian, and Yapese. Some of the authors chose to translate their work into English, while others chose not to translate. Since several of the languages have contested orthographies, we have respected how the different authors have chosen to represent their indigenous language.

To help readers navigate this anthology, we have provided maps of Micronesia as a whole, as well as maps of the island groups. Along with each author's name we have included the island from which they trace their roots. Some authors also include footnotes to explain references or provide contexts. For the excerpts of plays and novels, we have included brief summaries of the work as a whole.

The anthology is organized into seven thematic sections. "Origins" explores creation, foundational, and ancestral stories; "Resistance" includes work responding to colonialism and militarism; "Remembering" captures diverse memories and experiences; "Identities" articulates the complexities of culture and notions of self; "Voyages" maps stories about migration and diaspora; "Family" delves into interpersonal and community relationships; and "A New Micronesia" gathers experimental, liminal, and cutting-edge voices.

We've blessed our ocean-going vessel and sung the songs of the great Micronesian navigators and, with ceremony, launched it. We hope that it will journey into classrooms across the world, break past boundaries into global print and internet communities, inspire and empower other Pacific voices, raise awareness about the uniqueness of our islands and cultures, and celebrate our survival and resilience.

Garlanding

Teweiariki Teaero (Kiribati)

i woke up and went east
this early dawn
before the eastern sky becomes light
to pick bwabwaku from tabwakea's land
from the top of the uritangaroa tree
flowers that are nice and better than all others
wrapped in the fragrance and
newness of dawn

i weave
flowers that are second to none
using the songs of the itibwerere

i anoint them
with the ngeaiarabo
to be your garland
your garland that is beautiful
your garland your taranga
your garland while you read here
turning the pages of this our book
going over and scrutinizing
the many ideas
in peace

i am putting on you
your garland
the irauea the korotabuki the nimwaereere
your taranga to look after others with
health peace and prosperity
you and i too
here

Previously published, *On Eitei's Wings*, Pacific Writing Forum, 2000.

ORIGINS

I Tinituhon/The Beginning

Leonard Z. Iriarte (Guåhan)

Gi tinituhon, i tinituhon,[1]
Ge'halom hinasson i Yahululo',
Manetnon i hinafa siha,
Taihinekkok yan taichi,
Ge'halom hinasson i Yahululo',
Ge'halom hinasson, ge'halom hinasson i Yahululo',
Hui![2] Taihinekkok yan taichi,
Hå!

Gi tinituhon, i tinituhon,
Annai tåya' tåno' yan tåya' hånom,
Manetnon i hinafa siha,
Taihinekkok yan taichi,
Annai umadingan si Saina, manhuyong hulu,
Ya milalak i hinasso-ña,
Manmåtto talangan hulu
Manmåtto talangan hulu,
Manmåtto talangan hulu,

Chumiche' si Pontan,
Ya ha tungo' na maolek,
Magof si Fo'na lokkue',
Ya ha tutuhon lumålai,
Kalang i manglo', uma'gang gui',
Annai hiningok gui' as Pontan,
Ha tutuhon mangguifi

Language consultants, Mark A. Santos and Jeremy N. C. Cepeda
1. *I Tinituhon*, "The Beginning," is a song (typically sung and performed by women) derived from the indigenous creation story. It is a reference to the initial human settlement of the Mariana Archipelago. It is therefore viewed as an oral title to the land.
2. The vocalizations *Hui! Hå!* and *Hoi'!* are used to convey a deeper, underlying semantic sense. They are calls ritualistically used as a bridge to the supernatural realm.

Ha tutuhon i guinifi,
Ha tutuhon i guinifi,

Manli'e' gui' sagan taotao,
Ha li'e' i fama'iyan,
Guaha meggai na lina'la' tåsi,
Måtmo haggan yan guihan,
Ya annai makmåta gui',
Ha ågang i che'lu-ña,
"Hånao mågi yan ekungok,
Sa' ti åpmam måtai yu',
Sa' ti åpmam måtai yu',"

"Chule' i agaga' na odda',
Yan yalaka gi inai yan hånom,
Fa'tinas i palao'an,
I fine'nana na håga,
Fa'tinas i lahi lokkue',
I fine'nana na låhi,
Na'etnon siha på'go,
Yan na'huyong i taotao siha,
"Na'huyong i taotao siha,"

"Ginen i ha'of-hu,
Fa'tinåsi siha ni langet,
Yan i maolek na månglo',
U masu'on i layak siha,
Ginen i tatalo'-hu,
Fa'tinas i tano' yan i ekso',
Na'huyong i mames na hånom,
I sen mames na hånom,
I hanom Hagå'-ña,"

"Chule' i matå-hu,
Ya u fanmanli'e' i taotao siha,
I atdao gi ha'åni,
Yan i pilan gi pipuengi,
Ya annai monhåyan,
Na'huyong i isa,
Yan a'kalåye' gi langet,
Gi sanhilo' i taotao tåno',
I manaotao tåno',
I manaotao tåsi,"

I manmofo'na na taotao!
I Matao!
Ho!

The Beginning (A Translation)

In the beginning, the beginning,
Within the mind of the Most High,
All things were combined as one,
Infinite and limitless,
Within the mind of the Most High,
Within the mind, within the mind of the Most High,
Hui! Infinite and limitless
Hå!

In the beginning, the beginning,
When there was no land and no water,
All things were combined as one,
Infinite and limitless,
When the Elder spoke, thunder emerged,
And it flooded his thoughts,
Then came rolls of thunder,
Then came rolling thunder,
Then came rolling thunder,

Then Pontan[3] smiled,
And he knew it was good,
Fo'na[4] too was happy,
And she began to sing,
Like the wind, she resounded,

---

3. Pontan, "a ripe coconut which has fallen from the tree," is the name of the male sibling in the indigenous creation story. In the story, he empowers his sister in order to create the world for human beings. In theory, he is the initial discoverer of the archipelago, who ultimately leads his matrilineage in the initial settlement effort, thus securing entitlement as first male paramount leader in the traditional social hierarchy, ultimately achieving mythic status.

4. Fo'na, "to be first," is the name of the female sibling in the indigenous creation story. In the story, she is empowered by her brother to create the world for man. In theory, she is the senior ranking female of her matrilineage, and thus she receives entitlement as the first female paramount leader in the traditional social hierarchy. She too ultimately achieves mythic status.

When she was heard by Pontan,
He began to dream,
He began the dream,
He began the dream,

He saw a place for people,
He saw the rice fields,
There was much sea life,
Plenty of turtles and fish,
And when he awoke,
He called to his sister,
"Come close and listen,
For soon I will die,
For soon I will die,"

"Take the red earth,
And mix it with sand and water,[5]
Make the woman,
The first daughter,
Make the man also,
The first son,
Now bring them together,
And create all of the people,
Create all of the people,"

"From my chest,
Make the sky,
And the good winds,
They will push the sails,
From my back,
Make the land and the hills,
Create the sweet water,
The sweet water,
The water of Hagå'-ña,"[6]

"Take my eyes,
So all the people may see,

---

5. A reference to the ingredients for pottery manufacture, and the implication that females participated in this activity.
6. A reference to the freshwater spring of the paramount village of Hagå'-ña, which translates as "his/her blood." The position of Hagå'-ña in the traditional village hierarchy and the meaning in its name (an additional reference to the matrilineage of Pontan and Fo'na) suggests that the village was the site of initial human settlement in the archipelago.

The sun in the day,
And the moon at night,
And when it is completed,
Create the rainbows,
And suspend them,
Above the people of the land,
The people of the land,
The people of the sea,"

The first people!
The Matao![7]

Hoi'!

---

7. A pre-caste, pre-European contact name for the indigenous inhabitants of the Mariana Archipelago. *Chamoru* is the post-European contact name of both the indigenous people of the Mariana Archipelago and their language.

Fu'una and Pontan

Evelyn Flores (Guåhan)

"Bai matai" ilekña i che'lu-ña,[1]
"I will die," said her brother;

"Ya debi na un fa'tinas nu guao
and you must make of me
nuebo na tiempo.
a new era.

"Chuli i taotao-hu,"
Take my body

Ya un hutu huyong gi i innako-ña i tasi
and spread it out across the length of the ocean.
gi i mås tådodong na lugåt
Here near the deepest part,

Estira-yu huyong gi i maigo entieru-hu
stretch me out in my burial sleep."

"I will do this, che'lu," she said.
"I will do as we have wished."

This she said when he was yet alive,
their wishes predestined

The poem is based on the Chamoru mythos of Guahån's origins through the death of a brother god Puntan (perhaps Pontan, one term for the ripened coconut, the most valued staple of the Pacific islands) and the life-giving force of a sister god, Fu'una (possibly Fu'a or Fo'na). It focuses on the female life-force in creation.

1. *Ilekña i che'lu-ña* – said her brother. Reflective of the ancient Chamoru's egalitarian gender system, the word "che'lu" makes no distinction between brother or sister. The designation is gender-neutral, equivalent to the English word "sibling" but much more a term of endearment. When necessary, one adds onto the word "sibling" the gender of the person to distinguish between brother and sister.

their must-be
of new worlds, galaxies, universes, cosmos
spawned by the breathing of their immortality.
But it was easier said than done.
She was strong as she wrenched
the wind into his death chant,
unerring as she rolled the black, lightning-blasted sky
into the blight of his mourning;
no tears flowed, but she could not see her
way to the edge of the universe and to the ocean;
i patås-ña[2] stumbled over where Africa would be,
i tummo-ña[3] bumped into the future Himalayas,
carrying her brother's limp body
that was a planet's weight
cradled like a baby in her arms
to the deepest part of i tasi.[4]

Tenderly, she laid down his shoulders, broad and brown,
smooth yet muscled, i apagå-ña,[5] with his once-was strength.
As she closed his clear, black eyes
whose light would warm the universe's coldness,
and sang the song of moon and stars, of night and day,
the songs of creation and destruction, of darkness and light,
of earth's hundred ages,
as her chanting voice changed into that of a new era,
a new time that his death ushered in,
the jagged edges of missing him already
swept her body
and into the song of joy tugged surging maelstroms
of her wailing.

Aaaaaaaaaa[6]   aaaaaa

iiiii   eeeeee

eeeeeee

eeeeeeeeeeeeeeee   aaaaaaaaaaaaaaaaaaaa

uhhhhhhhhh

uhhh

---

2. *i patas-ña* – her feet
3. *i tummo-ña* – her knee
4. *i tasi* – the ocean
5. *i apagå-ña* – his shoulders
6. The poem is constructed to be performed; this section indicates the length of the wailing chant.

In answer to that maternal sounding of
the soul of life and death,
a blood roar shook through night
and out of earth's womb
thrashed a subterranean lightning
that shoved until it burst out of dark canals
and spewed geysers of water into the cosmos,
cataracts of earth's longing that
Fu'una rode up past sun, moon, and stars,
her brother's body in her arms roiling into land,
which, as the force of the ocean was spent,
lowered down into settling.

She lived for countless millennia after,
ageless, measuring her life only against the breathing of time
and in the explosions of stars reeled in i fuetsan i che'lu-ña.[7]

And then during the third era before her rebirth,
the pangs of newness returning
and the labor of her birthing swelling within her,
she retraced her footsteps to the deepest part of the ocean
where he had bloomed into
relentless green,
rooted.

The winds of the blinding galaxies roared around her
spread her long, black hair across the sky.
The ocean heaved once more in its desire,
threatening its boundaries.
Its moans called the leviathan Gadao from its lair,

but she would not be moved.
Though the stars fell and the sun went out
and total darkness shrouded the earth,
she stood there, near her brother, unswerving,
until she died,
ripened into eternity.

---

7. *i fuetsan i che'lu-ña* – the strength of her brother

In death as in life, chume'lu i dos,[8]
he the prone, she the upright
he the land, she the spirit
of i taotao-ta,[9]
i tátaotao-ta.[10]

---

8. chume'lu *i dos* – the two remained brother and sister (siblings)
9. *i taotao-ta* – our people
10. *i tátaotao-ta* – the poem juxtaposes the linguistic phenomenon of these two words, one meaning "our people," the other (with the addition of the accented prefix) meaning body, land, people, and identity. The two meanings are locked together through this integration of mythos and language.

Time

Canisius Filibert (Belau)

Long ago my
Ancestors knew time
They counted moons
They watched sunrises
No one needed hours
Nor tiny little seconds
Days were enough
Shadows told time
Time was on our side
We were simple but
We were free brown
People of the blue sea
Simple lives uncomplicated
Then a new dawn came
With the shipwreck
Of a ship from the east
Days of the pale race
My fathers and mothers
And theirs and theirs and theirs
Life changed and time
Time was theirs to control
Now life revolves around
A face with endless
Circling hands and ticks
Tocks became rules
Now moons go unnoticed
Sunrises sunsets unlearned
Hearts beat to a new
Time as was known to
My people of brown
Now unsung and
Never untied

Previously published, *Storyboard: A Journal of Pacific Imagery* 4, 1996.

Uchelel a Tekoi Chuab, Kotel Belau

Isebong Asang (Belau)

It is said—

In the beginning *Uchelianged*, foremost of the heavens,
roamed the earth and the sea amidst the stars, in the age of darkness.

Before giants walked this land,
the stars came down with the wind and the rain
creating the island of *Ngeriab*, and the shoals of *Mekaeb*, from its
   sacredness.

In the shallows of *Mekaeb*,
the light gave birth to a baby clam *Latmikaik*, who grew
until the soft petals that lined her shell, swelled with the life that was to
   crown the sea.

Union with a male god, *Latimikiak*, birthed the life teeming the ocean
   bowels, and
her only begotten girl-child, *Obechad*,
sent to land,
became mother to man,
chad from the sea.

Obechad gave birth to the goddess *Turang*.
Turang gave birth to the goddess *Chuab*,
who grew until her head grazed the thatch that sheltered her from the
   wind and the rain.

The land, the sea, and the sky fed *Chuab*
until only the corms of the taro roots remained,
and so the people starved,
until *Chuab*'s short life ended through the people's pain.

Coconut sheaths the people brought, piled high reaching the top of the
    grassy mound,
Embracing her length from head to toe, and back again, until she was snug
    and tight.
Sensing the heat from the fervor of the people, *Chuab* asked, "*Ngera
    chised e sechelei?*"[1]
Avoiding her gaze, them of the same womb lulled her with dirges into the
    cool of night.
The blaze of the sun and the heat of the flames from the pyre made known
    to *Chuab*
the conundrum the people would not name, for the way is nameless, the
    way is *omelau.*

Chuab thrashed and kicked as she fell into the sea,
the course of the pendulum known,
for, from the ashes, from the felled body of the goddess *Chuab,* an island
    is born—
Belau.[2]

---

1. "What is all the excitement?"
2. Words of cosmology or origin: *Chuab,* the origins of Belau. *Katel* implies the village of one's birth, the village of one's mother, or one's lineage. In line with the cosmological origins of Belau, I have composed this poetic narrative embodying *Chuab* as a woman and a mother from whose ashes emerged the islands of Belau.

Chuab—Belau

Canisius Filibert (Belau)

Belau was born
When the great
Giant Chuab
Fell on the sea

He tripped
And kicked
The Island of
Anguar

Split the
Island in half
Made twins
To the South
His toes came
Apart created
Sonsorol Tobi Fana
Merir Pulo Anna

His toenails
Broke and
Floated to make
Helen's Reef

The felling
So strong his
Head came off
Made Kayangel

Previously published, *Storyboard: A Journal of Pacific Imagery* 3, 1994.

His neck
Ngerchelong
His chest and
Great stomach

Formed Babeldaob
Arms poised for
Support broke
Formed reefs

His torso became
Aimeliik to Koror
Legs crumbled
Made rock islands

Merry Ancestors

Teweiariki Teaero (Kiribati)

Years back
On a night so black
Natiu[1] ran to me
Seeking refuge
In my arms

In the blackness
Our tiny atoll was all shaken
Heaven had burst
Proud palms bent low
Saluting the furious wind
From all corners came
Bellowing rumbling roars
Answered by
Snappy
Bright lights

And so *Natiu* ran to me
For they were scared
On that dark night
I held their hands
So tiny and damp
I heard their hearts
Beat beat beat
In their chests

I whispered now
Low, slow words

Previously published, *On Eitei's Wings*, Pacific Writing Forum, 2000.
1. children

Up there in Matang
The ancestors are partying
That is all they do

Hear thunder
They pound the *bwaoki*
Palms slap the *kabae*

Feel rain
They are sweating
And crying
Wetting the earth

Feel the gale
Grass skirts swing in the *buki*
Raising the angry wind

See the lightning
They are taking pictures
Of them, you and me
With cameras
Made in Japan

Nei Mwanganibuka
The Legendary Fisherwoman

Tereeao Teingiia Ratite (Kiribati)

Nei Mwanganibuka was a legendary fisherwoman whose expertise in fishing was at first unknown to her brothers. Her brothers had pride in their fishing skills and were famous throughout the Kiribati group. When the brothers learned about her fishing expertise, they took her out to the great ocean and left her there.

Nei Mwanganibuka drifted on a piece of log and arrived on the island of Nikunau, where she found a companion. She had three sons whom she taught how to fish. The sons became experts in fishing and competed with their uncles, Nei Mwanganibuka's brothers, who conquered the Kiribati islands by fishing out all the great fishes. Through Nei Mwanganibuka's fishing expertise, her sons defeated their uncles. This brought them fame throughout the seas of Kiribati.

I've always wanted to be like Nei Mwanganibuka
With all her skills
I could survive, conquer the realities of life
Put back the little fishes where they belong

I've always wanted to be like Nei Mwanganibuka
With all her knowledge
I could promote better lives
Put the sickly fishes back where they can be cured

I've always wanted to be like Nei Mwanganibuka
With all her wisdom,
I would help sustain the benefits of tomorrow
Cheer the elderly fishes to continue to be valuable
maintaining kinship

I am like Nei Mwanganibuka now
With her skills, knowledge and wisdom

Previously published, *VASU: Pacific Women of Power*, 2008.

Of fishing
Supporting my dearest kin
Fulfilling each role and responsibility—
Signs of a good fisherwoman

To Swim with Eels

Emelihter Kihleng (Pohnpei)

part of me comes from rodents
a rat surrounded by kemisik
in Saladak, land of lasialap[1]
all my friends are kemisik[2]
while I am only part kitik[3]

I could have been eaten, then
taken to the mouth of the river

the other part of me is empty
with no animals to call family
whiteness mistaken
for nothingness

I swam with lasialap girls
and their ancestors who
lurked behind rocks
and was never afraid although

I could have been eaten, then
taken to the mouth of the river

I have heard of children in Kitti
who swim with sacred eels
in freshwater pools and streams
never to be bit

Previously published, *My Urohs*, Kahuaomānoa Press, 2008.
1. the ruling clan of U; their eni (ancestral spirit) is the kemisik
2. freshwater eels
3. rat

my fingers bled twice from
the mouths of eels who
tried to eat the food off my fingers
a warning

I could have been eaten, then
taken to the mouth of the river

Saladak is theirs eternally
descendants of Lien Madauleng,
their eel ancestress, who came to Pohnpei
on a school of marep
and gave birth to four eel daughters

I am not one of them
Sounpasedo, of chiefly lineage
and kemisik blood, yet
we swam and ate together like sisters
but I must remember

I could have been eaten
by kemisik girls and their mothers
long, slick bodies full,
manaman,[4]
swimming upstream
to give birth to male chiefs

---

4. spiritual power

I Have Seen Sirena Out at Sea/ Gua na hu li'i' si Sirena

Evelyn Flores (Guåhan)

I have seen Sirena out at sea call to
  me,
slender brown arm raised,
half in farewell, half in beckoning.
"Come," she says,
"Leave behind the ha'iguas[1] to those
  ironing;
Leave behind the schoolyard, and
come with me;
they will go on without you—"

I cannot hear her,
but I can read the words
blown back from her lips as she
  arches
through the mouth of the Minondu.[2]

And I have made as if to go,
turned half willingly toward the
  shore,
half toward the door
of my mother's house.

Gua na hu li'i' si Sirena
ha å'agang yu para bai hånao huyong
  para i tasi.
Hu li'i' kannai-ña, kulot i tanu'
ha hahatsa, lamita despidi, lamita
  alof.
"Maila," ilekña.
"Dingu i ha'iguas para i prensa;
Dingu i uriyan i eskuela.
Siempre mankonsisigi ha mo'na sin
  hågu."

Ti siña hu hungok håfa ilelekña
lao hu taitai i fino'-ña
guinaifi tatti nu i manglo
annai numañangu gui
huyong gi pachot i Minondu taiguihi i
  tuninos.

Ya hu bira yu kulan mohon bai dalalaki
  gui
lamita gi ya guåhu para guatu gi tasi;
lamitå yu sinasaggue' nu i pe'tan
i gima Nanå-hu.

Previously published, Brian Millhoff and Evelyn Flores, eds., *Images of Micronesia*, M-m-mauleg
Publishing, 2006.
Chamoru Language Consultant, David De Leon Flores Sr.
1. *ha'iguas* – coconut shells burned like wood to heat up the iron
2. *Minondu* – the mouth of the Hagåtña River where it pours into the ocean

My mother pleading,
my godmother whispering,
"The land, the land, the land,"
and Sirena out to sea,
paused again at the channel's divide
to glance back with knowing eyes
   at me.

Si Nåna sigi ha pågat yu;
i matlina-hu duru ha ñangon yu, put
"i tanu, i tanu, i tanu,"
Ya si Sirena gi halom tåsi,
Pumåra annai måtu gi
umasad i kannat yan i tasi
ya ha atan yu tåtte nu i tadong na
   inatan-ña.

Halom Tano'

Anne Perez Hattori (Guåhan)

we heard the *binadu*[1] bark
deeper than any dog we'd ever heard
loud enough to make the jungle tremble
but we weren't afraid
the deer never scared us
because they were so gentle
more private than people
more protective than parents

the boars didn't scare us either
their babies pranced like puppies
around my father's flagpole
and we fed them,
and gave them names.
and worried when they didn't come to eat

even the *hilitai*[2] didn't scare us
our uncles would catch them
and tie them up
and walk them around
and if something green was on our fiesta table
we'd know where the *hilitai* had gone

years have passed and the jungle's still there
and despite those supposed millions of snakes,
the birds still sing and shit on our clothesline
despite the military's invasion of our land,
the pigs still play and the *binadu* still bark

Previously published, *Storyboard: A Journal of Pacific Imagery* 5, 1998.
tano - jungle
1. deer
2. monitor lizard

and up there in Yigo
far far north
where nine siblings once played
and where new generations now grow
the jungle's still there,
still showering us
with *donne'*[3] and mango and *abas*[4] and all
the jungle's still there,
forever filled with sheltering spirits
forever calling me home.

---

3. wild hot pepper
4. guava

Nareau's Return

Teweiariki Teaero (Kiribati)

Nareau floated in the endless sea of time
In the middle of nothingness, te akea

He was an old man
His silver beard as long as time
His hair a silver crown
Homesick, he decided
To return to his creation
To Tungaru his nation

And so he glided to the atolls below
Almost collided with
Air Tungaru's noisy Trilander
And Telecom's nosy dish
Nareau hovered there a second
Wondering

He flew from karawa
And glided over marawa
Looking for Bakoa
And Teraaka the seafarer of note
But saw on sea only alien baurua
Slashing the Kiribati blue
Bakoa and Teraaka now dead
But alive in mere print
And the back of the I-Kiribati mind

Nareau strolled on the beach
Soothing his aching ageless feet

"Nareau's Return," *On Eitei's Wings*, Pacific Writing Forum, 2000.

In the timeless wet sand
And the frothy kiss of the Pacific
But his feet got tangled
In endless plastic miscellanea
And blue mountains of Fosters cans

The old man strained his eyes
Looking for a place to rest under
Only roofs of blinding kaabwa greeted him
Fierce and ugly in mocking sun

The old man looked for a home
His stomach tight in hunger
None beckoned him kaaraki!
So he trudged wearily on
Stooping lower to the earth he made

He went on the road
Noise shattered his peace to pieces
He saw his people
Held in rusty metal boxes
Going madly everywhere
Yet nowhere

For Nei Tituabine and other anti
The old man now searched
But he saw only
Women in white, with flowing cotton hair
And men in sulu and ties
Carrying strange books

The weary teary old man staggered on
A stranger in his own creation
His grey weary head, he laid on the grey gravel
Bitter tears rolled free, his heart bled
To join the setting sun
In its crimson dying glory

Ode to the Fisherman's Hat/ Te bwara te taraai

Tereeao Teingiia Ratite (Kiribati)

Tungaru is a string
Of white beads on a blue dress
Deep ocean currents
Make her breast ebb and flow

I-Tungaru, the descendants
Of Tabwakea
Sailing the oceans to
Meet Bakoa's siblings

Te bwara te taraai
I-Tungaru fisherman's hat
Guards our heads, sacred,
From hot sun and heavy rain

Te bwara te taraai
Woven of pandanus leaves
Neat in shape
Tied with coconut string
Into triangular transformation

The shape signifies
Wisdom and unity
A link to everyone
Peace, harmony, and prosperity
Te mauri, te raoi te tabomoa
Iaora ni bane.

Previously published, *Mana* 3.2, 2004.

Return to the Sea

Sandra Iseke Okada (Guåhan)

*These islanders are expert underwater divers, because from the time they
are born, they bathe and swim as much under the water as above it...
They are the most skilled fishermen ever to ave [sic] been discovered.*

—*Fray Juan Pobre in the Marianas, 1602.*

*The sport is to go in their boats to catch those flying fish with hooks made of
fishbones. And the form of their boats is painted... Some are black and
white, and others red.... Their sails are of palm leaf sewn together like a
lateen sail to the right of the till... And there is no difference between stern
and the bow in the said boats, which are like dolphins jumping from wave
to wave.*

—*Antonio Pigafetta, describing Guåhan,*
the first island Ferdinand Magellan landed
on in his historic 1521 voyage across the Pacific.

The Invitation

"You need to come with us to Luta."

I couldn't believe what I was hearing from Ron Acfalle, vice president of
Traditions About Seafaring Islands (TASI) and crew leader. The launching ceremony for the *Saina*, Guam's first open-ocean flying proa, or sakman, in nearly
250 years, had just concluded. I could not fathom how or why I, a diluted
Chamoru woman, was being offered this immense honor, and I found myself
totally speechless. Was he serious? Minutes later it would be confirmed: he was
very serious.

In November of 2007, I found myself in the cool shade of a thatched-roof hut,
known as the boathouse, erected on a small patch of sand along the channel of

the Hagåtña Boat Basin. While the sun was setting, Dr. Lawrence Cunningham (historian, TASI co-founder & voyager) and I huddled together in a quiet corner of the hut. I braced my back against one of several large pillars that formed the hut's foundation. As he spoke, his eyes filled with the same passion that had sparked my curiosity more than thirty years earlier. I listened intently. He told me about TASI (*Tasi* in Chamoru translates to "sea" or "ocean") and the task it was undertaking in the boathouse. As a result, I have come to know and deeply respect the efforts of TASI: *Palu* Manny Sikau, master navigator, Dr. Cunningham, Frank Cruz, Ron Acfalle, David Laguana, Ron Laguana, and the many other fervent members, board, and supporters.

Over the course of a year, I watched in awe as TASI members undertook the monumental task of constructing *Saina*. They were guided by a 1742 Anson Expedition diagram; by Manny Sikau, a seventh-generation Carolinian master navigator; and by ancestral spirits.

The flying proa was traditionally made from the log of a large seeded bread-fruit or *dokdok* tree. For this boat, however, TASI was using California redwood logs, delivered from the sea herself. The logs had been part of an open raft that was beached on Guam in 2003; its Russian crew had been on a mission to set a world record and had abandoned the raft when bad weather blew it onto our shores. Some wondered whether its beaching was a force of Mother Nature or the work of ancestral spirits in preparation for the building of *Saina*.

On the first day of construction, *Palu* Sikau cut into the first of the ocean-hardened logs while the group I Fanlalai'an chanted in Chamoru, celebrating the keel ceremony, the beginning of the build. Each stage of the boat's evolution was celebrated with a unique ceremony.

Finally the naming ceremony day arrived. On July 20, 2008, Pa'a Taotao Tano' performers sang *O Saina*; their voices filled the air with the ultimate blessing, a song that came forth from the depths of each performer. The 33-foot sakman, dressed in traditional colors of red, white, and black, was officially blessed and named *Saina*, a term of honor and respect for addressing elders and our ancestors.

On a cloudy Saturday afternoon in late September, hundreds of people sur-rounded the humble boathouse to witness the official launching ceremony of *Saina* in preparation for her maiden voyage. It was to be the same voyage that had been navigated routinely hundreds of years before by our ancestors, one that required crossing the treacherous Luta (Rota) Channel.

It was at the conclusion of this launching ceremony that Ron stepped off *Saina* and said to me, "You need to come with us to Luta." The emotions I felt in that space and moment were so pure and so raw that I was totally speechless, petrified by the thought of participating, feeling immeasurably unworthy of the potential honor. These emotions soon passed replaced by a sense of responsibility to honor my seafaring ancestors and my indigenous identity. In preparation for the voyage, I was subjected to the same sea trials and tests as my male crew members: distance swimming, sailing, self-recovery from sea to canoe. I suc-cessfully passed each test. I was physically prepared.

Saina's maiden voyage was set for Monday morning, September 22, 2008, and I was ready, having set aside all logical reasoning about the risks of this venture. On the voyage to Luta (Rota), I would fulfill the role of mother, a role symbolizing respect, peace and family. I spent the morning stoked on adrenaline, filled with a profound fear of the unknown balanced by faith in my ancestors and my God. Out of respect for my ancestors, but unknown to the rest of the crew, I had prepared, in a small palm-woven basket, offerings of raw grains of rice, *pugua'* (betel nut), *pupulu* (pepper leaves), *åfok* (lime powder), and turtle shell pieces. I was hoping that during our voyage I would have the opportunity to present this small offering as a token of my respect, along with a small prayer to ask for protection and for forgiveness of my ignorance in these matters.

Thoughts of the elements—of the air, the fire, the burn of the sun, the emptiness and vastness of space, and the power of the sea—consumed me as I waited patiently with the crew and supporters in the shade of the boathouse. Together, we watched *Saina* in the water, straining her tether with each wake. I knew the risks were high, but I needed to witness and feel *Saina* fly—her sequestered spirit set free.

The hours went by, and then, as we watched, the sky began to darken ominously and the sea waves began pounding the shoreline. We were not ready, however, to abandon hope. We filled out customs and quarantine forms for arrival in Luta and occasional chuckles filled the hut. "What is our vessel and flight number?" someone asked, to general laughter. We were embarking on an historical voyage, navigating an ancient passage, but this time, proof of our citizenship and U.S. federal forms would be required on our arrival in Luta, Commonwealth of the Northern Mariana Islands (CNMI).

The officer-in-charge of the Guam Police Harbor Patrol brought weather updates to us as we waited for the sky to clear. We were also in constant radio communication with the Office of the Governor, the United States Coast Guard, and Customs and Quarantine agencies. Hopes for departure faded as we listened to the ominous reports coming in. Finally, master navigator Sikau, Cruz, and Ron Acfalle, knowing it was time to make a decision, gathered privately outside the hut. The crew and I waited nervously inside; we all knew that if we did not make an attempt that day, we would not have another opportunity until spring 2009.

Then the fateful moment arrived: TASI's president invited everyone to gather under the thatched-roof hut and made the announcement no one wanted to hear: *Saina* Voyage, No. 001 had to be postponed due to severe weather conditions. Not just one but two storm formations were approaching. Everyone was silent. Ironically, 2008 had been proclaimed by the governor of Guam as *Silabråsion I Ånon I Sakman*, the year celebrating the proa. But things don't always go according to plan. The spirits had spoken, the leaders had listened, and now we had to follow. *Saina* would silently wait for spring.

My fears are still there, of course, but they have been assuaged somewhat by the knowledge that, by the sweat, hands, and hearts of our people and our neighbors, *Saina* was born upon our shores. When our ancestors allow it, she will traverse an ancient passage, symbolizing the passage of our own indigenous identity out of the past and into our future.

The tireless efforts of TASI members will reap the ultimate reward for all: a boundless, borderless, bird-, cloud-, current, and star-navigated voyage that will return the Chamoru spirit to its original life force, setting her *free*—returning to the sea.

Postscript

News Release, Rota, CNMI, 22 May 2009.

The Saina, on her historic maiden voyage, along with her seafarers, successfully arrived on the shores of Rota, CNMI, at sunrise. Saina is a large 33-foot open ocean going sakman (flying proa). The Chamoru sakman was last recorded in history in 1771. . . . The voyage traversed the Rota Channel. Symbolically it hailed the fearless spirit, ingenuity and uniqueness of an ancient seafaring society of the Chamoru people. After nearly three hundred years, the spirit of the Mariana seafaring islands is renewed and reunited through Saina's safe arrival.[1]

I Fanlalai'an, Pa'a Taotao Tano', and TASI are only a few examples of the many organizations that exist on Guam today, each one uniquely different but all unified and purpose-driven to create, sustain, and perpetuate our culture and traditions.

The brave *Saina* crew of eight that completed this historical voyage from Guam to Luta are Palu Manny Sikau, Frank Cruz, David Laguana, Ronald Acfalle, Jose Martinez, Sandra Iseke Okada, Sanry Efin, and Jerry Onopey.

1. Lawrence Cunningham, "Saina Returns to Rota," *Traditions about Seafaring Islands Sailing Society*, news release, May 22, 2009.

Tinaitayon Hinanåo Såkman Saina/Prayer for Safe Journey

Ronald T. Laguana and Rudolph E. Villaverde (Guåhan)

O Asaina,
tayuyuti i hinanåo-ña i sakman
na u hinago' i chi-ña
yan i hinanånao-ña mo'na gi tåsi.
Imbråsia i Saina para i hinanåo-ña guatu
gi tano' Luta yan ta'lo tåtte gi tano'-ta Guåhan.

Na un dirihi nu i anghet-mu
na un adahi i manåotao såkman
gi hinanao-ñiha yan gi chalan-ñiha;
I tinayuyot-mu u sen didok,
yan i mina'ase'-mu u sen annok
gi inatan-mu yan para todu ni' umi'ilåo' siha.

O Asaina,
sen adahi i mambiaheron såkman
gi i hinanåo-ñiha gi tasi.
Na u chinahlåo ni' tinayuyot-mu,
i minesngon-mu ante yan pudent,
na u fansåfu gi hananao-ñiha
gi chalan Sinahi, ya ti u fandåñu.

Esgaihon ham nu i minesngon-mu
para in layåki mo'na ini na sagrådu na såkman.
Nå'i ham ånimu yan minenhalom para hami todu,
na in fanenkatgåo na u såfu
ya in fanmåtto guatu gi hinanåo-måmi.
O Saina

Mina'åse' Asaina ni i fiet na guinaiya-mu nu hami,
na in faninadadahi nu hågu kumu hami i mambiåheron tåsi.
In taitayi para i minaolek tåsi

yan para pinasensia nu hami todu,
na u fåtto i chin-måmi mo'na.
Saina Mina'åse'.[1]

Prayer for Safe Journey

O Father,
We pray for your blessing to guide this Flying Proa
to reach its landfalls over the depths of the sea.

Embrace the Sakman Saina on its maiden voyage
to Luta (Rota), Sa'ipan and its return to Guåhan.

May you direct your spirits
to protect the voyagers
along their seaway;
May your kindness and your mercy shine forth
in your watch care over them for all to see.

O Father,
Shield our mariners
in their flight over water.
Accept our fervent and sincere prayers
that through your great power and unfaltering spirit,
those who travel the Sinahi crescent archipelago
will be secured from danger.

Grant your divine guidance and infinite wisdom
to all who navigate this sacred vessel.
Inspire us with a sense of duty and knowledge that will guide us
who have entrusted ourselves to your care,
to arrive safely at our destination.

O Father,
We thank you, Father, for your gracious mercy and love
and for extending your protection to all seafarers.

We pray for calm seaways, patience for all,
and for our safe journey's end. Amen.

---

1. Ronald Laguana and Rudolph Villaverde, chanters from the island of Guåhan, delivered this chant and their other chant, "Gutos i Finihu: I Hinacha Hinanåo," during the launching and inaugural voyage in the summer of 2009 of the first proa in over 250 years to sail from Guam to Rota, the Sakman *Saina*.

Gutos i Finihu
I Hinacha Hinanåo/Rite of First
Voyage of the Sakman Saina

Ronald T. Laguana and Rudolph E. Villaverde (Guåhan)

Guelo yan Guela Mañaina-ta!
Tånom gi Saina
i pao i tano'
na u magåhet tåtte i chi-na
gi hinanåo-ña.

Ancestor Parents!
Plant within Saina's timber
the spiritual scent of this soil
which this sacred vessel must
    seek on its return voyage.

Annai gaige gi afok yan gi edda'
    tåno',
u gini'ot i pinacha-ña i tano',
na u gini'a i sakman, kumu
    haggan,
tåtte gui' gi mafañagu-ña.

White quicklime soil and earth
    hold the essence of the land to
    guide this vessel,
like the haggan, the turtle, back
    to its place of birth.

I apon i sinenggen påtma,
u annok i finatto-ña tåtte yahåmi,
    taiguihi i manila' guåfi nai
    a'annok.
I chinachak påtma na gaige
i laina'la' i patma
ni' u gina'a tåtte i sakman,
tåtte tano'-ta.
(In palai i etpos gi hilo' i sakman.)

The black charcoal of burnt palm
fires will show us our way home.
The scent of the palm oils from
    the slashed trees will draw the
    sacred vessel once again to
    the place from which it came.
(We cover the proa's skin with
    this crushed palm poultice so
    it can learn the scent of its
    homeland.)

Saina! Hågu i saina,
guatdai yan putåhen i
    manlålayak.
Saina! Tumu adotno!
Hågu ininan tano'-ta Guåhan.

Saina! You are parent, shelter
    and sustenance for your crew.
Saina, adorned with earth.
You are our motherland, Guåhan,
made manifest.

Saina! Sagåyi na gumaige hao gi
  hilo' i tasi yan gi tano' gi
  fi'on-ta
Saina! Ilåo mo'na i tano',
echa ham gi tumaimanu.
Såkman Saina! Tiningo' Ulitåo na
  mansasakman! Akudi!
Saina! Sågui' mo'na i guinaifen
  manglo' yan sufa mo'na ni'
  punta!

Saina! Reveal your spirit moving
  over the ocean and islands
  before us
Saina! Guide us forward to land
  and serve the navigator
  faithfully!
Sakman Saina! Ancient School of
  the Great Spirit of Navigation!
  Lift your spirit!
Saina! Ride the winds forward
  and
Pierce the waves with your bow!

Quipuha's Sin

Joseph Borja (Guåhan)

Because of it
The Archbishop thrives
And Ricky committed suicide
Matapang was disgraced
And San Vitores canonized

Because of it
The poor go to mass
And when the basket comes round
They give everything they have
Paychecks and pennies found on the ground

And when they get home
The water gets disconnected
They pray and pray to God
Only to find that the hope line is also disconnected

When you're poor and Chamoru it's always disconnected

Meanwhile the priests drive around in shiny cars
And offer feasts and treats
To politicians and businessmen
Who give them money to gas their cars

I guess the contents of the soul are reflected in the car

And the poor go to the priests
And beg for salvation
And the priests politely reply
"Sure enough my son,
but you must first make a donation"

A donation for salvation

It's all for salvation

Holy water is expensive these days

Silent Warriors

Innocenta M. Sound-Kikku (Chuuk)

Mama
a silent warrior
a familiar and comforting
voice I often hear
as my mind travels back to a time
when her tales of many
silent warriors
are as vivid as her voice in my head

Silent warriors
speak and whisper names of
mother ancestors
who carry virtues of love,
loyalty, respect and honor

Silent warriors
bravely enduring
birth of a new
generation of nations

Silent warriors
breathing and weaving
core values, beliefs,
cultures, customs and traditions
identities of their race

Silent warriors
heartbeat of a clan
key keepers and holders
of honor in the land

Silent warriors
peace makers and builders

of strong, brave,
honorable champions

Silent warriors
wind blowers of language,
songs and chants that drum
to the beating of the island waves

Silent warriors
storytellers of tales and legends
about ancestors who
demand never to be forgotten

Silent warriors
hope and wisdom of a better community
teach
respectable characters of a tribe

Silent warriors
sacrifice
life for another life

Silent warriors
planters and nurturers of a future
yet to be seen but dreamed of faithfully

Silent warriors
fragrant and aromatic peace
warming the heart of her men

Silent warriors
all (Chuukese) women
young and old
who understand and hold these
roles and responsibilities
wholeheartedly without a doubt
always are
silent warriors

Fino' Finakpo'/Final Words

Leonard Z. Iriarte (Guåhan)

Ho! Uma'adingan yu',
Ayugue', hu li'e' i sagå-hu yan i tano'-hu,
I tano' i mannanå-ta yan i mantatå-ta,
Ayugue', hu li'e' si nanå-hu yan si tatå-hu,
Sumisiha yan i mañaina ni' mofo'naigue siha,
Ayugue', i mina'ok na håga' i taotao-hu,
Taiyinamak ginen i tinituhon,
Mannananggan tai'ine'son siha guihi,
Manggaitinituhon yan manggaifinakpo' gi i sakkan siha,
Gi i finakpo', mamomoddong lokkue' i manmå'gas na håyun hålom tåno',
Ayugue'! Hå!
Ayugue'! Ho!

Final Words

Ho! I speak,
There, I see my home and my land,
The land of our mothers and our fathers,
There, I see my mother and my father,
With the elders who came before them,
There, is the enduring line of my people,
Unbroken since the beginning,
There they wait patiently (for me),
Every season has its beginning and its end,
In the end, even the great trees of the interior of the land fall as well,
There! Hå!
There! Ho!

Language consultants, Mark A. Santos and Jeremy N. C. Cepeda

Manotohge Hit/We Stand

Leonard Z. Iriarte (Guåhan)

Manotohge hit gi sanhilo' i manåmko' na to'lang siha,
Ya in tina i Manmatao, i manmofo'na na taotao,
Ni' manmåtto gi mamfine'nana na sakman siha,
In tina i mañainan-måmi,
Ya in tina i manåmko' na to'lang siha.

We Stand

We stand over all of the old bones,
And we praise the Matao,[1] the first people,
Who arrived on the first sailing canoes,
We praise our ancestors,
And we praise all of the old bones.

Language consultants, Mark A. Santos and Jeremy N. C. Cepeda
1. The use of the term *Matao* in a recitation makes reference to pre–European contact ancestors. *Chamoru* is the post–European contact name for both the indigenous people of the Mariana Archipelago and their language.

RESISTANCE

Forefathers

Anne Perez Hattori (Guåhan)

Our forefathers
  not foremothers
  not foreparents
but forefathers
With their white-wigged hair
and exquisite accents
With their delusive diplomacy
And   quieted   conquistadorial   cruelty
these men,
these forefathers
are our historical superHEroes
or so we've been educated,
again and again.

Our forefathers,
like Washington and Jefferson and Franklin and Lincoln
who are these gentlemen anyway
whose faces flatter bulletin boards
and whose manifestos are memorized
by school children islandwide
but did they sweat sweet tropical perspiration
did they plant *suni*[1] and pick *lemmai*[2]
and beseech the blessing of *guela yan guelo*[3]
under the sweltering sun of latitude 14?

So why do We
yes, We
teach that They

---

1. taro
2. breadfruit
3. female and male elders; in this reference, female and male ancestral spirits

are everything
or something
or even anything
to us,
Chamorro natives
who work the soil,
ride the sea,
inhale our exhalations,
and inherit the land
immortally.

Lbolb/Wolf

Canisius Filibert (Belau)

Bo le biusech	Be alert
A medam er a	Eyes be keen
Rechedam	To the countrymen
E le lbolb a	For the wolf
Mla mei	Has come
El becheleleu	White is
A bsechel	Its fur
E becheleleleu	White are
A ungelel	Its teeth
E diak el	Not
Chutem a	Brown are
Chelsul a	Pupils of its
Medal el	Eyes
Mekemangel	Long are
A ungelel e	Its teeth
Meklou a	Big are
Dingal	Its ears
Bo merikle	Be bold
E bom	And be
Bekeu e le	Brave because
Biskelengem a	Your spear is
Ngar er	In your
A chimam	Hand
Msisichii a	Strengthen your
Rengum e	Heart and
Berchii a	Spear the
Lbolb el	Wolf who
Mla me	Has come
Tuab era	To visit at the
Kotel a	Heel of
Ochim	Your foot

Previously published, *Storyboard: A Journal of Pacific Imagery* 4, 1996.

The Lord's Prayer

John Mangafel (Yap)

Our Fathers, who art in Washington,
Hallowed be thy funds;
Thy authorizations come;
Thy appropriations be done,
In Saipan as they are in the President's budget office.

Give us this day our quarterly allotment,
And forgive us our over-runs,
As we forgive our deficits.

And lead us not into dependence,
But deliver us from inflation,
So ours will be the territory, and the power,
And the fiscal authority forever.

There are many versions of Mangafel's 1975 "Lord's Prayer." This version is from the August 1975 edition of *The Pacific Islands Monthly,* published out of Sydney, Australia, by Pacific Publications (p. 23).

What Am I

Frederick B. Quinene (Guåhan)

My great and dearest Uncle Sam,
This letter is addressed to you,
For I do not know what I am,
I want to know, I really do.

Forget that you ruled Guam,
from 1899 to 1941,
And then began your rule again,
After WWII was won.

In August of 1950,
The Organic Act came to Guam,
This Act made me your citizen,
But I still don't know what I am.

Thirty-six long years have gone by,
Many years of I know not what,
I still do not know what I am
Where am I going, nor where I'm at.

In your hallowed halls of Congress
Am I really represented?
And I know that in the Senate
I have never been Consented.

Uncle, when it suits your fancy,
I am a citizen of yours,
And, when it does not suit you
I am no citizen of course.

You say you do not colonize,
Yet I feel Guam is a colony.
You say I am your citizen,
Then why is it I don't feel free?

You promised me a lot of things,
One is self-determination.
Yet I cannot get even this,
Without your inclination.

Yes, you pour all kinds of goods
Into my lovely little land,
But then you hit me on my knee
When I would try to stand.

Even when you're clothing me,
I still feel stripped of dignity.
Which makes me ask you, What am I?
Please Uncle Sam will you tell me.

It is true you educate me,
But for what and then for why,
For even with all that I have learned,
I still ask, What am I?

You say you are the champion
Of all men who are oppressed,
So if I am a part of you,
Why do I still feel depressed?

I beg of you to recognize,
If nothing else, I am a man,
I want my self-determination,
Please grant it for I know you can.

I do believe my Uncle Sam,
That I am mature enough right now,
That I can decide my destiny,
For you yourself have shown me how.

Please allow me, Uncle Sam,
This little shred of dignity,
I am not asking for much more,
Than that which you have promised me.

Let me take this cobweb off,
My deeply troubled mind,
I really want to know what I am,
This treasure I would like to find.

Grant me the right to reach for goals,
No matter if the goal is high,
Allow me to expand myself
And let me find the answer to What am I?

Excerpt from "Freedom"

Hermana Ramarui (Belau)

America,
A giantman
Is fishing
In a U.S.-made
Fish pond
Called Micronesia.

A school of fish is
In that pond.
America has thrown
Its fish hooks
The silver hooks
And caught the fish
By the mouth.

Micronesia
Is hooked
By a tiny bait
On a silver hook.

It
Bit the hook
And bit the bait
With open mouth.
It
Swallowed the hook
And swallowed the bait
With open heart
Because it was greedy

Previously published, Hermana Ramarui, *The Palauan Perspectives* (self-pub., 1984).

And it was blind
And it was weak.

Now hooked Micro is
Fighting to be loose,
But doesn't know
How to unhook
Its own mouth
And remove
The tiny hook
Held by the strong,
Giant fisherman.

Perhaps the fisherman
Is the only one
Who knows how
To loosen the hook
And set free
The hooked fish.

Micronesia
Who is hooked
And placed in the pond,
The aquarium in the Pacific,
Looks now
With mistrusting eyes
At the generous giantman,
Looks with envious eyes
At sister fish
In the surrounding
Pacific Water
Eating meager food
They earn
By the sweat
Of their brow
But
Swimming free.

Giantman
With limited eyes
And
Limited mind,
You are aware of only
One Micronesia,
The Micronesia

Of your making,
The creation
Of your hands,
Of so-called
Civilized man.

You hooked me
By the mouth and
No matter how hard
I struggle
I cannot be free,
For the hook rips me
As I struggle.

America
The beautiful
The powerful
The great,
Unhook me.

Let me live in living Sea
And not in the Aquarium.

Liberate me.
To a new dawn
Where reincarnated
I can greet you
Not as hooked fish
But as freed
Micronesia—
GOOD MORNING
AMERICA!

To Belau

Hermana Ramarui (Belau)

Come, Belau.
Come to your sense.
Vote no, Belau.
And use your common sense.
Can't you see, Belau?
Unity is nonsense.
Because, as for Belau,
Unity makes no sense.
It does not free Belau.
It binds Belau in a real sense.
Don't vote yes, Belau!
Yes means colony in a real sense.

Self-governing is the general aim.
Self-reliance is a sign of growth.
Belau, young nation is your name.
Self-reliance is a height of your growth.
Self-governing is the ultimate game
Everyone plays at their full growth.
To opt for unity will be a great shame.
Micro unity stagnates Belau's growth.
Vote no and play the game of fame,
Fame of carrying your own load.
And use your energy to the full flame.
Vote no and lead Belau to healthy growth.

Previously published, Hermana Ramarui, *The Palauan Perspectives* (self-pub., 1984).

Belau Be Brave

Cita Morei (Belau)

Belau be brave . . .
Thy nobleman's creed is in the grave,
Decaying by greed,
Their loyal deeds, once engraved
At Ulong in Wilson's log,
Are gone, lost in history books,
Dusty, buried in Leeboo's grave.

Why do people rave? Why do I feel rage?

We were never wanderers; We've been Adventurers.
We were never drifters; We are Navigators.
We were never beggars; We are Providers.
We were never without a Home.
We never lived without Hope.

Disasters, diseases and deaths,
Come and gone; we were not alone:
Family and friends bound us as one.
We survived.

Beachcombers, traders and foreigners
Came and claimed . . .
They exclaimed, "What beautiful real estate!
Best they be barriers for our disasters,
Maybe forward bases for carriers . . ."

Previously published, Marjorie Crocombe, Ron Crocombe, Kauraka Kauraka, and Makiuti Tongia, eds., *Te Rau Maire: Poems and Stories of the Pacific*, Ministry of Cultural Development and University of the South Pacific, 1992.

For goodness' sake, is not Bikini enough?
Mururoa? Hiroshima? Nagasaki?
Is Three Mile Island still without life?

Belau be brave, our lives at stake.
Never sell your seas, your soul
For everlasting food stamps.

Belau be brave . . .
Your dignity, your pride
Will take in its stride
Your sons and daughters yet to come.
We must survive.

Nauru in 2001

Ruby Dediya (Nauru)

"Wake up, girl, and see where you were born," said my father.

"Do I have to? Why the rush?"

"Yes, you have to," he said. "This island is changing so much and so fast that you might miss out."

I got up on my wobbly legs and peeped over the edge of my home of straw. I saw Nauru, the island of my birth, for the first time. This was 1989. At first, I thought I was in the cemetery amongst all kinds of tombstones of various shades of grey. In fact, my parents had chosen to make our home in the safety of the pinnacles of the mined-out lands of Nauru. My parents had fed and nurtured me until I developed into the prettiest noddy on the island. They taught me how to fly so I could get a better view of my island home. I mastered the art of flying in no time. I was the proudest noddy of them all.

On my first flight I decided to record all the incidents that happened each time I went out. I recorded a most unusual incident that occurred in October 1990. As I flew over the Aiwo Primary School and the Civic Centre region, I saw people gathering at one particular building, so I flew down and perched on one of the branches of a nearby tree. The people coming out of a building were carrying bundles of colored notes. One of them came too close for comfort so I flew off for the safety of my home. There, I told my parents what I had seen. They told me that this was the payout of the Nauruan Ronwan Interest—the riches gained by the people of Nauru from what their island was famous for: phosphate.

"You should be a proud noddy," they said. "Our ancestors were very much involved in the formation of these riches."

After teaching me a bit more of our history, they then told me that they wanted to leave the island. "It has become too hot," they said. "There must be some truth in the talk about the greenhouse effect. Soon some of the islands of the Pacific will be covered by the ocean as it rises higher and higher. We are getting out," they said. "Come with us."

Previously published, Marjorie Crocombe, Ron Crocombe, Kauraka Kauraka, and Makiuti Tongia, eds., *Te Rau Maire: Poems and Stories of the Pacific*, Ministry of Cultural Development and University of the South Pacific, 1992.

"I want to stay here," I replied. I kissed them goodbye and they flew off. But I don't know where they went, for I never saw them again.

I was very lonely at first, but I soon got over it. I had learned to fend for myself. I had mastered the art of avoiding the bird catchers who cleverly tried to imitate our mating calls. They caught some of us when they shone their special aluminum cans into our faces and blinded us.

As the years went by, trees were replaced by buildings and electric poles with high-voltage wires that were dangerous for us. I had to stop flying at night, as it was no longer safe to be out. Large planes belonging to Air Nauru were also a menace to us. More and more people were clogging up the place. Some were employed, but some seemed to waste their lives away. Some appeared to be walking in a dream. Others seemed to be high on some sort of drug. I saw more and more people queuing up for food.

One day as I flew slowly past, I overheard a lot of complaints because there was not enough food and the prices were exorbitant. This made me wonder how these people governed themselves and who was attending to their needs.

One day I took a special flight called "House Hopping." I was surprised and saddened by what I saw. There was overcrowding in most of the buildings I saw; many were dilapidated and falling apart. Drains were blocked, and an obnoxious odour rose from them, making it very hard for me to fly properly.

Most ominous of all, there was no more shoreline. It was completely covered with piles and piles of litter that even the sea could not remove. Nauru had become an island of debris. I couldn't help crying at what I saw. "What has become of my country?" I asked myself. I got no answer. No one could give it.

Even the people themselves had undergone changes. Their skins had become pale, and their eyes protruded because they only came out at night to scrounge for food. It was too hot to be outside in the daytime. They had formed themselves into bands of hunters who went out after dark, hunting for something to eat. And I was one of the most wanted of all. Every single living thing wanted to kill me for their meal. They had forgotten that I and my ancestors had helped build up what they called their "natural resource."

It is not my fault that this natural resource, phosphate, had been used up and that there was nothing else for them to exploit to keep them alive. It was because of their own carelessness and arrogance that they had allowed foreigners to take every bit of our resources.

I am very thankful that my fossilized grandparents, so visible in the rock that is used for the presidential doorstop, will never see what has become of the country they helped to enrich. In this year 1990, I thank God I won't be here to witness what happens to Nauru in the year 2001.

Tampering with Bible Translation in Yap

Dolores Yilibuw (Yap)

> *The discovery of the book is . . . a moment of originality and authority, as*
> *well as a process of displacement that, paradoxically, makes the presence of*
> *the book wondrous to the extent to which it is repeated, translated,*
> *misread, displaced . . . —"signs taken for wonders"—an insignia of colonial*
> *authority and a signifier of colonial desire and discipline . . . .*
>
> —Homi Bhabha 163

> *I have neither been chosen to speak, nor do I claim to speak, on behalf of all*
> *Yapese women, or any women for that matter. But if you are a woman and*
> *the scriptures—be they Christian, Muslim, or Jewish—directly or indirectly*
> *affect your life, and your context is anything like mine—a "third world" island*
> *or continental nation enmeshed in both capitalism and patriarchy—my voice*
> *could be an echo of yours, or perhaps our voices are intersecting.*
>
> —Dolores Yilibuw

I am not writing from a "disinterested" position, nor is this essay a mere intellectual exercise; rather, I want to articulate the cause for the liberation of Yapese women in the Yap Evangelical Church (YEC) and Yap State at large. By liberation I mean decolonization of the Yap male-dominated ecclesiastical and societal structures.

"Decolonization" here refers to a Yapese woman's goal to forge an in(ter)dependence of genders as opposed to a polarity, where women are subservient to and dependent on the whims of men. Such a goal is not easy to accomplish, given the multifaceted factors that promote and enhance the duality of the female/inferior and male/superior dynamic.

Previously published, *Semeia 76: Race, Class, and the Politics of Biblical Translation*, 1996.

For instance, Yap has a matrilineal clan and a patrilineal clan and may appear egalitarian. But within the culture, power and prestige lie in the land that is passed from the patriclan. The matriclan functions as a safety net of the society. A person in crisis can count on her/his matriline for material and moral support. The Yapese proverb "ba' tafen u laniay," literally "a woman's land/home is in her feet," implies that a woman's land/home is with her husband. Basically, a woman is born and dies playing only a supportive role in both the home and the community, because the cultural system is set up so that a woman's wealth and honor are moored to her husband. In case of a divorce, the woman not only loses her land but also risks losing her children. A woman's authority over her husband's land increases only as she grows old in the marriage. Thus, wives endure abusive treatment because they want their children to be materially secure. This is an act that also requires women's complicity in their own oppression.

But the fact that, like many other women, we Yapese women are involuntary accomplices to these oppressive systems does not mean that I/we cannot theorize strategically for the alleviation of gender, race, and/or class/caste oppression as well as for the promotion of their in(ter)dependence. These objectives can be accomplished when alternative means for the conscious and active participation of the colonized are created and nurtured, in order for them to have some control over the way in which their own cultures and lives are shaped. It is in this spirit that I propose an alternative theory and praxis of Bible translation.

In the Beginning and at the End

In the beginning, Bible translation was a blatant criminal act of the colonial "gods" to destroy the Other's myths, memories, and histories, by replacing them with an imperial culture. But the attempt has not succeeded as intended and planned. For as cultures and/or texts clash, they resist and appropriate each other, a process wherein existing myths and cultures are transformed while hybrid ones are created.

Tejaswini Niranjana equates hybridity with living in translation (46). Translation, like hybridity, is an open-ended process of affecting and being affected by multidimensional changes, a praxis where ambiguity and multiplicity of "meanings" are the rules rather than the exception. Hence the Yap hybrid culture is a culture in translation through an open-ended process of cultural displacement for both Yapese and missionaries (Bhabha, 173–174). Within this influx of culture there are intended consequences: missionaries aim to "civilize" the Yapese culture and to "tame" native females. However, a woman should take advantage of the "unintended" consequences (Massey, 266) in the hybrid to effect agency. For instance, YEC women (and men) need to subvert their given roles as translators and reviewers to produce a translation that is conducive to their liberation. I contend that men and women need to come together and negotiate ways of dealing with issues of race, caste/class, and gender in Bible translation simultaneously and coextensively in Yap for the good of the society at large.

Men's Monopoly and Women's Multiple Jeopardy: The Discursive Process of Bible Translation in Yap

Yapese is an oral language and culture, in which there are multiple versions to one story with no desire to "canonize." This is because myths (and legends) are preserved not only in storytelling but in other forms (e.g., dances). In an oral culture, the "origins" and "authenticity" of a story are not as important as the relevance, application, moral, lesson and/or purpose, and implication of the story to the present context. As stories become part of people's lives, they (i.e., the stories) live on. When they cease to be part of people's lives, stories die and others are invented.

An oral syntax is fluid and moldable, while a written syntax is more rigid. Thus, making Yapese a written language led to the colonizer's syntax creating and reinforcing the subjugation of certain folks. Knowledge became hierarchical and limited to the few who could read. When the Yapese language was put into written form as the "word of God," it became a powerful tool for a few to validate their beliefs. As the only major piece of literature in Yapese, aside from government documents, the Yapese Bible still plays an important role in the culture today.

The aim of the United Bible Societies (UBS) and its missionaries in Bible translation is a "civilizing" mission. The written word serves to legitimize that mission as original, creating a "measure of mimesis and a mode of civil authority and order" (Bhabha, 168). For example, converts to Evangelicalism literally try to replace Yapese culture and values with the "godly" culture and values of the "book" in its translated form without realizing that the content of the "book" is the Western cultures and values from a particular period in history. Some of these converts (men and women) stopped participating in Yapese dances and other customs because the racist missionaries and the Bible itself taught them that these aspects of Yapese culture contradict true Christian virtues.

In the Protestant church, authority is in the scripture. Thus, it was strategic for the missionaries to translate the Bible, the locus of authority, in order to legitimize their mission as "original" and "authoritative," justifying the intentional process of cultural displacement (Bhabha, 163–165). In the case of Yapese women, Bible translation was strategic to contain and control the Yapese women in order to construct them as a brute and exotic Other that needed to be dominated and appropriated (Niranjana, 34) in the image of the missionary's wife or the "chaste" single missionary woman.

Bible translation in Yap was started by the Liebenzell Mission (LM) in collaboration with the UBS, and continues to be under the supervision of the latter's consultants based in America.[1] The translation policy of the UBS in the

---

1. Ferdinand Magellan's arrival on Guam in 1521 was the beginning of Western colonization of Micronesia. As a result of Spanish influence, Yap is predominantly Roman Catholic. In 1947, when Micronesia was placed under the U.S. administration by the United Nations, Yap became the playground for various Euro-American missions. In 1959 the Liebenzell Mission, from the Reformed Lutheran Church in Germany, officially established a branch in Yap.

so-called "field," where many translators do not know biblical languages, is to follow the Revised Standard Version (RSV) as the closest in form to the Hebrew and Greek, while using the Today's English Version (TEV) as an example of a dynamic equivalence translation.

Without the knowledge of biblical languages, a subversive Bible translation is more difficult, as the translator continues in the uncritical tradition of reinforcing multi-layers of ideologies in the process. By not training translators in biblical languages, the UBS reinstates colonial control.

Sister Hilde Thiem, a Liebenzell Mission missionary from a sisterhood in Germany, who studied New Testament Greek at Liebenzell Theological Seminary, came to Yap purposely to translate the Bible into Yapese. When she arrived, she spent several years learning Yapese. In 1965 she started translating the New Testament (NT). Her assistant was a dentist, my father, Yilibuw Wa'ath, whose passion for reading and curiosity about the content of the Bible drew him into the process.

Sister Thiem and Yilibuw Wa'ath began translating the Shorter Old Testament (SOT) soon after completing the NT in 1973. The SOT is a selected forty percent of the Hebrew scriptures that is privileged by the UBS as "directly" related to the NT. Sister Thiem did not study Hebrew, so she relied on various translations (German, Spanish, French, Dutch, and English) as source texts.

Sister Thiem retired and returned to Germany in 1981. She turned the remaining sixty percent of the Hebrew scriptures yet to be translated into Yapese over to Sister Doris Eberhardt (also from a sisterhood in Germany), who translated several portions. She, in turn, left in 1983 for another mission post before finishing the translation. Ruth Baamer, a YEC Yapese woman who was on the previous review committee, kept alive the process of translating the sixty percent.

Bible Translation as Feminine

After earning a Master of Divinity degree in 1988 in the Philippines, I requested ministerial ordination within the YEC. My request was met with resistance from both male and female white missionaries and many Yapese men and women in the YEC. The YEC board decided that I could not be ordained because I was a woman and single, culturally unacceptable to the YEC's lead men.

In the eyes of Yapese men, Bible translation is a "feminine" role, because it requires hours in solitude rather than in public, and because it involves technical and tedious paperwork. Like a secretary, the translator reads, rereads, thinks, rethinks, writes, rewrites, types, and retypes. The translator, who is also the coordinator of the project, is paid by the UBS based on her degree of achievement (ranging from a high school diploma to a master's degree).

Thus, rather than being ordained as a minister, I was given the more "feminine" job of continuing the translation of the sixty percent of the Hebrew scriptures that Sister Eberhardt had started.

I had completed this sixty percent when I left Micronesia in 1991.[2] But review of this newly translated portion did not start until 1993, when the UBS, with the approval of the YEC, hired Anna Gorongpin, a member of the YEC and a graduate of the Liebenzell Mission high school in Belau, to coordinate a review committee composed of Catholics and Protestants.

The Culture in the Process

When the Bible was printed in Yapese, some illiterate older women began to use the Yapese Bible as a tool to learn to read Yapese; due to domestic obligations, they had missed out on the mandatory primary education imposed by the Yap government in the 1960s. The Yapese language is read phonetically and, therefore, for those who already speak it, it is not difficult to learn to read it. Lydia, an older female member of the YEC, taught herself to read in this manner. Ever since then, she has been reading and expounding the "book" to others on a daily basis. Because of her ability to read the Bible, Lydia no longer relies solely on her memory in retelling the "holy" stories. Now she has her own personal reference from which she can always retrieve information.

Lydia seems to wield some power in explaining the "meaning" of the biblical text, just as the missionaries do, even though she can never fully mimic the missionaries because of her difference as a Yapese woman (Bhabha, 169). Lydia's testimony that God enabled her to read also reinforces the "authoritative" sign system attached to the "holy" book without questioning its undergirding ideologies of race, gender, class, and/or caste.

The irony is that while the Bible unlocks the door to literacy for illiterate women, when they step inside the world of literacy, they become "hostages" to another male-dominated culture, presented as divine, authoritative, and not to be questioned or doubted.

The epigraph by Homi Bhabha accurately expresses this phenomenon, and I would go a step further and argue that the Bible is a signifier of *engendering* gendered colonial desire and discipline. For instance, it is common for missionary wives to use the scriptures as the text for teaching a few Yapese women how to be good Christian housewives, and they in turn instruct other "native" females.

Women's subservient roles in the Yapese culture are reinforced and reinscribed when both men and women read verses like 1 Pet 3:1–2 (as well as Col 3:18 and 1 Cor 14:34–35) admonishing wives to accept their husbands' authority. Reading such verses in the Yapese tongue encourages traditionalists to perpetuate misogynistic behaviors and attitudes, now sanctioned through divine imperatives brought by the missionaries. Here we see an alliance of Bible translation and indigenous Yapese culture colluding against Yapese women. Resistance to such biblical understanding and Yapese cultural beliefs is equated to heresy and sacrilege. Some unsuspecting Yapese women have fallen victim

---

2. In Yap, I am the only Yapese person involved with Bible translation who knows the biblical languages.

to this scheme and have internalized such oppression to the extent that they seem to articulate it better than men.

Hybridity: Living in Translation

In translation, the voices of both brown and white men assert and dominate conditions, while the voices of brown women are doubly silenced (Spivak 1988, 307). For example, in a tradition where repetitions are taken to mean importance, weight is given to any subject that occurs more than once in the Bible. A translation that contains many reinscriptions about women's inferiority, such as 1 Pet 3:1–2, Col 3:18, and 1 Cor 14:34–35, therefore justifies gender oppression in the Yapese culture.

And yet, whenever the biblical readings contradict a major Yapese tradition like the caste system, most Yapese simply ignore that text.[3] In spite of scriptures like Gal 3:28, where there is a call for people's equality in the Lord, including equality between slave and free, men and women, both missionaries and Yapese ignore the liberation motif of such verses. Therefore, members from high- and low-caste villages worship together, but intermarriage between the two is still unacceptable, because "it goes against the honor and interest of higher caste men."

In the Catholic and Protestant churches, missionaries collude with Yapese men in creating a hierarchy of power where the Yapese women, especially those from low-caste villages, are relegated to the bottom of the power structure. The Bible and the Yapese culture coalesce to engender asymmetrical ethical standards for Yapese men and women. For instance, biblical teachings on fornication (e.g., 1 Cor 6:18) validate the stigma and condescension that single mothers receive in the church and society at large, while men are pardoned based on biological impregnability. The Yapese woman's body and actions are controlled, channeled, and appropriated as symbols, consumers, workers, and comforters for the benefit of white and brown men in positions of power.

Received traditional Yapese Bible translation reinscribes oppression in the lives of Yapese women inside and outside the church, and such oppression has far-reaching implications in religious and non-religious realms of life. Thus, there is the need for a Bible translation that foregrounds transformation.

A transformative translation will take place when Bible translators and interpreters cease masking ideologies of sexism, racism, and classism in the Bible, as it continues to engender colonization of women in particular. While tampering with translation, we need simultaneously to unmask ideologies. It is frightening

---

3. Yap has a stratified caste system moored to villages. A person is born into the caste village of his/her father. But the introduction of a cash economy has displaced this caste system to a certain degree. Many so-called low-caste folks have used retail businesses as a means of subverting the domination of their high-caste villages and chiefs. A low-caste person with money can travel off-island and become whatever he/she wants to be without having to live in an inherited subservient position. Traditionally, caste and class were one and the same. However, today the Yapese society still largely discriminates against a low-caste person regardless of his/ her class status.

to hear some YEC women (e.g., Lydia) argue that the Bible is "tradition-free" because it is from God. These women, like the missionaries, want to give weight, authority, and originality to their own biblical exposition. We need to recognize that the Bible is taken as the standard of life by folks who accept it as a religious book, thus affecting and altering their way of life in a manner that an ordinary autobiography or a novel could not. Therefore, tampering with the text becomes necessary for liberation to be palpable.

In our Yapese hybrid cultural discourse, where orality rules, the spoken word impacts the written word and vice versa. In our prominently oral culture, a story is shaped and reshaped according to the imagination of the storyteller. A transformative Bible translation should allow the individual Yapese female reader to shape and reshape her own reading. I agree with Renita Weems that the "meanings" African American women derive from the Bible depend not only on the text but also on reading strategies determined by the reader's context (64, 67). But translators need to take a step further and construct a "woman-friendly" atmosphere in the text by tampering with translation in order to enhance gender, race, and class/caste in(ter)dependence and political relations. For this to happen, gender, race, and class bias in the Yapese translation has to be loosened, leaving some creation of "meaning" to the imagination of the Yapese woman reader.

Grounds for Tampering

Bible translation can easily be exploited for domination or liberation for two reasons. First, the translator is dealing with an archaic language and culture from one major (Qumran and ancient Near Eastern texts being minor) source, the Bible. Since there are no extant ancient news media, translators improvise for "missing" information. Second, the translator's signifier never fully captures the signified in both worlds. Therefore, YEC translators, both female and male, need to take advantage of this slippage to exploit the biblical Hebrew, Aramaic, and Greek languages in creating their own words and meanings. Male (and co-opted female) translators have been doing this for many centuries under the guise of "objectivity" to produce translations that dominate women.

The following are classic examples of how Euro-American translators have generated asymmetrical gendered signifiers based on their dualistic worldview in order to subdue the female body and its actions. Prov 31:10a contains the Hebrew phrase 'ešet-hayil, which the New Revised Standard Version (NRSV), supposedly the most inclusive in terms of language, renders as "a capable wife," while the RSV has "a good wife." The Hebrew word 'ešet, a construct of 'iššah, can mean either "woman" or "wife," while the Hebrew word hayi can mean "strength," "valor," "might," "power," "virility," "wealth," "ability," and so on.

In fact, in the Hebrew scriptures the signifier hayil is used interchangeably to describe a woman, a man, and God. But, in the English translations generally the signifier hayil is gendered in its usage. For instance, it is readily translated when describing God or man as "strength," "valor," "might," "power," "wealth," and "virility," and so on (e.g., 1 Sam 14:48 and Prov 31:3). But it is translated as "capable," "noble character," "virtuous," "good," and the like in reference to a woman (e.g., Prov 31:10, 12:14 and Ruth 3:11). Embedded in the English translations is the Euro-American male assumption that when the ancient Israelite male used *hayil* to describe a female, it was not in the same capacity as it was used for a male or Yahweh. This assumption may well be true. However, a translation for transforming gender boundaries cannot afford to reinscribe these views without problematizing them.

The female subject *'iššah* (woman or wife) has multiple meanings in Hebrew; in English it has only one (wife). Hence, the English rendition limits its representation of *'iššah* to one category of women: the wives. To further divide and conquer female bodies and symbols in the English versions, this group of women (the wives) are described with the adjectives "capable" and "good" rather than "mighty" or "valiant." This kind of Bible translation writes gender lines in a grossly subservient manner, allowing no chance for a multivalent reading. Furthermore, it securely reinscribes the image of women as having no merit in their own rights except in relation to their husbands as the "complementary" Other.

Sister Thiem and Yilibuw Wa'ath both had no command of Hebrew. They consulted various translations and rendered Prov 31:10a, "a good wife" in the RSV, in Yapese as *be' ni ppin nib yal'uw ma ke mabgol*, "a righteous and married woman," *'ešet-hayil* in Hebrew. By using the adjectives "righteous" and "married" to describe the woman, this translation not only reinstates gender dependence but splits the female body into images of wild/bad and domestic/good. It "racializes" the brown woman's body in the sense that the image of the white missionary wife becomes an original to be mirrored by the Christian Yapese wife, writing the single and sexually active Yapese woman as the "original" island "savage" needing to be "tamed." This kind of translation serves to secure further the cooperation of women in their own oppression. In order to transform racial and gender boundaries, this kind of translation needs to be changed.

The Hebrew phrase *'ešet-hayil* in Prov 31:10a occurs two other times in the Hebrew scriptures, namely in Prov 12:4 and Ruth 3:11. (Due to lack of space, Ruth 3:11 will not be discussed in this essay.) Prov 12:4 is where the *'ešet-hayil* is contrasted with her opposite other, the *mebišah*. Literally, the verbal ending *ah* is feminine. This phrase is conventionally translated as *"she who brings/causes shame."* The whole proverb (in Prov 12:14) in the NRSV is

a *good wife* is the crown of *her husband*
but *she who brings shame* is
like rottenness in *his* bones.

First of all, the *'ešet-hayil* is again given as "a good wife." Second, the Hebrew *ba'elah* (a construct of *ba'al* for lord, master, husband, owner, or the god Baal) with the feminine ending (*ah*) is translated "her husband" here. Third, the active participle with a feminine ending, *mebišah*, is rendered "she who brings shame." This rendition not only emphasizes a male and female relationship, but also further categorizes it as that of a husband and wife. The NRSV amends the text asymmetrically to bind a woman's worth to a man. This translation reinforces the husband's power over his wife while polarizing further the "good" and "bad" images of the woman for the purpose of reinforcing the negative socio-religious stigmas on the "bad woman." Such a process reinstates colonial norms set by the colonizers. (This verse, Prov 12:14, is not in the Yapese SOT. See my translation of it below in the discussion of an alternative.)

There are several reasons YEC women (including myself) have continued to engender the subjugation of women in their translations. First, we are merely utilizing the Euro-American, male "dynamic equivalence" theory; hence, we continue to preserve in our society the oppression inscribed in the scriptures. Second, as translators we seem to have bought into the missionary-constructed image of us as exotic wild beasts of paradise to be captured and tamed, by continuing to produce a translation that binds women's worth to men and polarizes women's images into the "domesticated" (i.e., the obedient Christian wife or the "chaste" single woman) and the "wild" (i.e., the opposite of "domesticated woman"). Third, we are also awed by the aura of authority of the Bible; therefore, in translation we hesitate to be creative and imaginative. These factors have hindered us from producing a more liberating Bible. They serve as pointers that it is time for change.

An Alternative

The alternative translation theory and praxis that I am negotiating is one that is committed to the liberation of the colonized. Thus, it requires that the translator foreground the need of the receptor's community while translating. Drucilla Cornell argues the necessity of a "double gesture" in legal interpretation for the transformation of moral and legal practices (114). In other words, the purpose of interpreting the law, and in this case, the Bible, should not be solely the preservation of the law but, most urgently, for the transformation of society.

Translators can no longer afford to be insensitive to and uncritical of issues of gender, race, and class within the biblical text and their own culture and tradition. When we take into account the fact that Bible translation does not end in the actual choosing and writing of words on paper, we realize that it is an open-ended discursive process that continually affects the lives of persons and communities, nations, and the world. In Bible translation it is imperative that the translators render words and construct syntaxes that make for multiplicity of meanings and images for the purpose of blurring gender, racial, and/ or class/caste lines. Done in this way, Bible translation becomes an art of social transformation.

For example, going back to Prov 31:10, I would render in English the Hebrew phrase 'ešet-hayil as "a woman of valor" instead of "capable wife," and in Yapese I would translate be' ni ppin nib mdangdang literally, as "a woman of mdangdang." The word mdangdang is (un)translatable because, depending on the context, it can simultaneously or separately mean the following: strength, industriousness, fearlessness, or independence, and may connote sexual aggression. The adjective madangdang is more transformative and liberative because it describes women in the same capacity that it characterizes men. There exists in this translation a potential to explode gender roles.

For the proverb in Prov 12:4, a decolonizing Yapese translation would be *"be' ni ppin nib mdangdang e te'liyaw rok e en tolang rok. ma en ma k'aring e tamra' e bod e t'ay nga fithik i yilen e en tolang rok,* literally "a woman of *mdangdang* is the crown of her *tolang* but the *one* causing shame is like rottenness to the bones of his/her *tolang."* This translation decolonizes in several ways: first, it renders the Hebrew *ba'al* as *tolang,* a generic word for a position of authority and power, rather than *figirngin,* "husband." Unlike the NRSV, my translation does not directly reinforce husbands' control of their wives. Second, the Hebrew participial phrase *mebisah* is rendered as *en ma k'aring e tamra',* "one causing shame" rather than *"she* who brings shame," as in the NRSV. My version has more potential to liberate because it does not capitalize on the gender of the person who brings shame. Thus, it allows the female reader to participate in reshaping the story by using her imagination in an emancipating way when filling in gender "blanks."

From a gender perspective, the long-term effect of a transformative translation would be a more egalitarian Yapese society where men and women would not hesitate to exchange roles for the sake of mutual partnership in building a more wholesome life and community. From the perspective of race and class, people of color and the poor will suffer less discrimination legitimized by the racist, classist, and sexist ideologies in the Bible.

The Story Continues

Since the original publication of this article, much has happened in Bible translation. Anna Gorongpin's career in Bible translation was brief. Re'tin, a single, bright woman from the YEC, and Mutnguy, a married, educated woman from the Yap Catholic Church, resumed translation responsibilities. They were assisted by the late Yapese Jesuit priest Apolo Thal, who not only had a Ph.D. in psychology but was also steeped in the Yapese language and culture, and Annie del Corro, a UBS consultant from the Philippines who has an understanding of both biblical Greek and Hebrew. They eventually completed the translation project. The Yapese Canon came off the press in the Philippines in December 2007, and it was celebrated by both the YEC and the Catholic Church in Yap. I subsequently received a copy, which I kept as a reminder that translation of the text goes on with or without intentional tampering for the liberation of women in churches in Yap. The Yapese Canon shall now live and be lived in translation of the Yapese culture and society, for better or for worse, and for all in the interstices of the now and eternity.

Conclusion

I want to conclude by stating that in the Yapese hybrid culture, there is neither space for a "pure" Bible nor the possibility of retrieving it. As it exists today, Bible translation serves as an instrument of power for those who control and define language. It demeans the dispossessed, in this case Yapese women. The aim of an empowering translation is to produce a referent that is more liberating, in order that avid Yapese women readers like Lydia would be more likely to perpetuate emancipating views of women in Yap rather than merely reinforcing their own colonization.

In order to effect in(ter)dependence of gender, race, and class/caste and to diminish stereotypes and myths about certain groups of people, the YEC translators (males and females) need to (in)vent beyond the binarism of the present social order. In the Yapese hybrid culture, as in other societies, an open-ended Bible translation process is not an exception but a rule. It takes place all the time. Hence, Yapese women Bible translators are called upon to get used to redefining themselves as they are constantly being defined by language (Minh-ha, 44). In this case, redefining oneself in translation is accomplished through problematizing ideological and social constructs in both the text and the translator, as it is a necessity to translate for the benefit of the disempowered.

Virginia Woolf, in *Three Guineas*, writes that as a woman she has no country. I want to appropriate her words by substituting "biblical scholar" for "woman" and "Bible" for "country" to say, "As a woman and a biblical scholar, I have no Bible. As a woman and a biblical scholar I want no Bible. As a woman and a biblical scholar my Bible is the whole world"[4] (166).

Bibliography

Anzaldúa, Gloria. "How to Tame a Wild Tongue." In *Out There: Marginalization and Contemporary Cultures*. Eds. Russell Ferguson, Martha Gever, Trinh Minh-ha, and Cornel West. Cambridge: MIT Press, 1990, 203–211. Print.

Bhabha, Homi. "Signs Taken for Wonders: Questions of Ambivalence and Authority under a Tree Outside Delhi, May 1817." In *Writing and Difference*. Eds. Henry Louis Gates Jr. Chicago: University of Chicago Press, 1985, 163–184. Print.

Cornell, Drucilla. *The Philosophy of the Limit*. New York: Routledge, 1992. Print.

Massey, Doreen. *Space, Place, and Gender*. Minneapolis: University of Minnesota Press, 1994. Print.

Minh-ha, Trinh T. *Woman, Native, Other*. Bloomington: Indiana University Press, 1989. Print.

Mohanty, Chandra Talpade. "Under Western Eyes: Feminist Scholarship and Colonial Discourse." In *Third World Women and The Politics of Feminism*. Eds. Chandra Talpade Mohanty, Ann Russo, and Lourdes Torres. Bloomington: Indiana University Press, 1991. 51–80. Print.

Niranjana, Tejaswini. *Siting Translation: History, Post-Structuralism, and the Colonial Context*. Berkeley: University of California Press, 1992. Print.

Spivak, Gayatri Chakravorty. *In Other Worlds: Essays in Cultural Politics*. New York: Routledge, 1987. Print.

——. "Can the Subaltern Speak?" *Marxism and the Interpretation of Culture*. Eds. Cary Nelson and Lawrence Grossberg. Urbana: University of Illinois Press, 1988. 271–313. Print.

Weems, Renita J. "Reading Her Way through the Struggle: African American Women and the Bible." In *Stony the Road We Trod*. Ed. Cain Hope Felder. Minneapolis: Fortress, 1991. 57–77. Print.

Woolf, Virginia. *Three Guineas*. New York: Harcourt Brace, 1963. Print.

---

4. I am grateful to AbdenNebi Ben Beya, a colleague and friend, for this idea.

"Local"

Jan Furukawa (Guåhan)

Call me Navy brat,
born at the military hospital,
treated by baby-faced pediatricians,
raised on Nimitz Hill (named for the captain),
dependent of stateside-hired sansei carpenter
employed by the Public Works Center.
Kindergarten at Naval Station's Monkey Tree,
shopping at the ship store, commissary, base exchange,
furniture, automotive, outdoor and hobby shops,
and bookstore and toy store.

Took in the latest out of Hollywood at NAS amphitheater,
took out pins at any of the base bowling alleys,
took special occasion suppers at the Fiddler's Green.
Took Military Airlift Command flights out of Andersen
to visit family in Hawai'i, into the college years,
still "dependents."

Dad retired with 38 years of dedicated service, and
three years after seeing my *nobiu* off to training,
I married into the Navy,
my enlisted husband on sea duty at NAS.
At time for the baby, we sped right up to—where?
The same hospital in which I had been born.

Baby girl then growing up whole—
beautiful, sharp, compassionate young lady.
But imagine: "Holiday shopping" one Liberation Day
turned away at Big Navy front gate,
base inaccessible without a sponsor.
(Divorced from her father, I could not be it.)
Policy adopted that very morning
by the base CO. Admin clerk asked,

Shouldn't you be at the parade, anyway?
As if that were where we ought to have been.

The last chapter of our dependent history
Has been written, and is sealed
By not-our-multibillion-dollar buildup plan.
No More Dependence, we pray.
Independence preferred,
we work patiently, faithfully,
acting to "reverse injustice, restore hope."
We are now relics of a naval experience on Guam—
brat, wife, and finally, ex- or widow.
We are "local."

Inside Out

C. T. Perez (Guåhan)

Thirty years ago, I sat as a young girl in the back seat of my mother's car. With my face pressed to the window, I squinted and focused my gaze on the car that sped alongside us on a parallel road. We were separated by only a seemingly endless fence, which I could blur to nothing if I held my eyelids just so.

Across the fence lay another world. It was another world on the same land, a world we called N-A-S. Naval Air Station was one of the several U.S. military force bases on Guam.

I was never able to follow the fence long enough to see what it encompassed, but I quickly learned the lingo and the feeling of exclusion it created. We needed an I.D., a military identification card, to go "inside." They didn't need anything to come "outside."

"Inside" lay spectacular cliff-line views and expansive, well-manicured fields. "Outside," so I was repeatedly told, held nothing more than a distasteful quagmire of pothole-ridden, mud-lined roadways, undecipherable landmarks, nameless streets rampant with loose dogs and other remnants of what some described as an uncivilized world.

I knew that we were "outside" the luxuries of what was contained "inside" the fence. I had visions of the houses I could never see from "outside." Theirs was an orderly world of tidy streets and neatly kept lawns, showcasing houses straight out of the home section of a Sears catalogue. We lived "outside," in a rented Quonset hut, marked by an inclined gravel roadway and a proliferation of *tåke biha.*[1]

"Inside," I had heard, kids were paid to do household chores that we did as a matter of course. I used to want what they had, or what I thought they had. I mimicked their style of dress and remember wanting a pair of faded blue jeans more than anything. I was ecstatic when, after my relentless nagging, my mom

Previously published, Rachael Kamel and Deborah Wei, eds., *Resistance in Paradise: Rethinking 100 Years of U.S. Involvement in the Caribbean and the Pacific,* American Friends Service Committee and Office of Curriculum Support, School District of Philadelphia, 1998.

1. Medicinal plant

agreed that I could buy one pair of jeans. Her only prerequisite was that they be bought on sale at Town House, the Old Town House.[2]

I learned quickly that my success in life would be measured by how well I could emulate "inside" attributes and suppress "outside" characteristics.

The acquisition of the jeans was soon followed by the purchase of a jacket that would have kept me warm in the tundra but should have been illegal in this tropical climate. These things could only be followed by my newfound desire for a Brady-inspired family room and a separate laundry room and dining room.[3] It was a tall order for my single-parent mom to fill with our typhoon-proof, compact, yet functional Kaiser home and a teacher's modest salary.[4]

I'm sad to say that my mother died long before I learned to value my life "outside." I grew to my adult years accumulating the material wealth I associated with being from the "inside." I've long since surpassed the Sears catalogue ideal with a blend of *Architectural Digest* and *This Old House*.[5] A house, a condo, and some acquired land later, I've had my fill of trying to mirror the "inside." I have everything they had and more—and still I find myself on the "outside."

Now, three decades later, I pass the same stretch of road. The fence still stands, although they say the base has been phased out and the land has been returned. I manipulate my gaze to send that fence into oblivion once more, but when my eyes tire, the fence still stands.

When I first heard N-A-S would be closed, I dreamt of how the fence would come down. I thought we could make a day of it. We would assign sections of the fence to different families to take down, accompanied by roadside barbecues and a freedom parade. Then I remembered the fuel line. Upon realizing that the fence was still needed to protect the pipeline, I altered my vision.

On the day of the closure, I thought we should have a million and one Guam flags tied to the fence. That would be a sight to behold. There could even be a kite-flying picnic on that huge field by the main entrance, or a caravan of cars through the grounds.

Then we heard. They weren't giving the land back.

The gates would still be maintained, softened only by a color changing of guards.

As time passed, they put even more fences on their side. These fences marked where they had dirtied our lands in perpetuity. They'll give the land back, they say, after sufficient time passes to prove we are competent caretakers of the land.

---

2. One of Guam's oldest department stores. There are actually three "Town Houses," three buildings of the same store. There is a "New Town House," an "Old Town House," and the "Old, Old Town House."

3. "Brady" refers to the television family depicted in *The Brady Bunch*. They represented the ideal mainstream American families of the seventies.

4. Name of the first major subdivision housing development on Guam.

5. *Architectural Digest* is a high-gloss magazine featuring fine homes. *This Old House* was a public broadcasting television program featuring renovation of fine homes.

Where the fence once made me feel wanting for the treasures I thought it contained, it now makes me feel anger for the stolen treasures it retains. I flash back to the man who scaled that fence in protest of the land being taken. He was apprehended and shackled by the military police. While others criticized his actions, I could only see him as brave. Restrained though he was by human force and metal handcuffs, he was free. He had freed himself in that moment from the mental bondage of our colonial existence. In retaliation, he spit on his captor.

At first, though, I had shuddered in disgust. "What low had this cultural hero sunken to?" I thought. After much reflection, my judgment changed. He had shown bravery. What else could he do?

Now, the landscape is changing. Whether you call it Tuyan or Tiyan, N-A-S is gone forever.[6] As formerly military homes are remade into GovGuam offices,[7] as the struggle continues between local government and private landowners, as the land tries to purge itself of negligent dumping, as motorists try to reclaim passage, as confusion reigns, the landscape is changing.

I've kept the blue jeans, worn in a style and meaning all my own. I've long since discarded the jacket, having found no ornamental or functional use for it. I've given up trying to turn myself "inside" out. Now, 30 years later, I can stand on either side of the fence. There is no "outside." There is no "inside." There is only what I allow to persist. The land is one. Today, the air smells sweeter and the sun shines brighter. The landscape is changing.

6. In the renaming of N-A-S, traditional place names were suggested. These were the two names used.

7. Government of Guam. Territorial Government.

My Mother's Bamboo Bracelets
A Handful of Lessons on Saving the World

Julian Aguon (Guåhan)

Dear Classmates,

Thank you. It is an honor to be able to share some of my thoughts with you on this beautiful evening.

I have thought of you so often in the last several weeks, as I have meandered the landscapes of my mind to figure out what I could possibly say that could be of use to you. You have no idea how much I've agonized over constructing my talk away from my usual bullets: human rights, self-determination, demilitarization. You'll be impressed. I have, for the most part, succeeded. But, as a writer, I know that nothing of worth can be written that is not culled from the light of my own life. So bear with this writer-activist from Guam, as I relay twelve minutes' worth of what I have come to know of the world. Hopefully, you can take something of what is imparted with you in the new morning. If not, feel free to throw it out a high window.

Despite what we've been told, the world is not ours for the taking. Indeed, the world we have inherited comes to us bruised, a tender shard of her former self, having passed clumsily through the well-intentioned hands of our mothers and fathers, seeking, seeking a generation it can trust enough, and long enough, to drop its shoulders.

Of the belief that love can save the world, I have a story to tell: In the old days in the land now known as Guam, when the people lost their connection to their way, when the rains would not come and the people grew wild with hunger, a giant grouper fish determined to destroy Guam began to eat the island widthwise, one giant chunk after another. Day after day, the men of Guam tried to stop it. They pursued it with spears, tried in vain to trap it, to catch it with nets they had made. They called upon the ancestors to aid in the capture. Every day, the women of Guam offered to help catch the giant fish, and every day the men,

This speech was given at the commencement exercises of the William S. Richardson School of Law, Honolulu, Hawai'i, on May 17, 2009.

forgetting the strength of women, rejected them. One night, while the women were weaving the pandanus leaves, the answer came to the *maga'håga*, the elder and leader among them. The women would weave a giant net from their long black hair.

One by one, the women, old and young, came forward, knelt on the black stone, and parted with their beauty. Then they got to work, weaving and chanting through the night. By first light, they finished the net and set the trap. Though the giant fish convulsed violently, it could not break it. Imbued with the women's intention, the net had been woven with deep spiritual affection and was therefore unbreakable. However, the women could not haul the giant fish ashore alone. When the men heard what was happening, they rushed to help the women and, together, they hauled the fish ashore. Its meat was shared with everyone.

They say it was our women's offering of beauty that saved Guam.

It has taken me many years to understand what this story is about, and why it is still passed down so many millennia later. I am convinced that its lessons, which have served my own people well, may be of some use to us today, as we look out at a world whose contours give us pause and make us feel at times as if whatever we do, whatever we are, will not be enough.

But, and here's the first lesson, no offering is too small, no stone unneeded. All of us, whether we choose to become human rights attorneys or corporate counsel, or choose never to practice law at all but instead become professors or entrepreneurs, or disappear, anonymous, among the poor, or stay at home and raise bright, delicious children—all of us, without exception, are qualified to participate in the rescue of the world.

But this is a quiet truth, and quiet truths are hard to hear when the cynics are outside howling.

Like the women who wove their hair into a magic net, we would also do well to remember that saving the world requires all of our *hands*. As a group that has largely chosen the life of the mind, this will be especially important to remember. It would be a great folly to think that our ideas, no matter how good, would be enough to reverse the dangerous, downward trajectory of our planet. As an activist on the ground, I have often suspected that it is harder for people to rush to the rescue of a world whose magic they have not encountered for themselves, have not seen, felt, touched, turned over in their own hands. I for one can say without pause that a large part of my own devotion to the cause of justice is that I have hiked up my pants and stood in other peoples' rivers. Moved to their music. Carried their babies. Watched them come back from burying their dead.

Our next lesson is that any people who profess to love freedom permit others room. Room to grow, to change their mind, to mess up, to leave, to come back in. In our story, the women did not reject the men who had done this to them. They accepted their help, welcomed it. True, they could not haul in the fish alone: they needed the men. But perhaps that is the whole unromantic, utterly useful point: the part, no matter how pure its intention, cannot save the whole.

And I think this should not so much make us tentative, as it should anchor us in the reality of our collective vulnerability, in the immediacy of our connection.

So anchored, another truth becomes plain: it is strength, not power, that must be the object of our affection.

Finally, a word about beauty:

I have been thinking about beauty so much lately. About folks being robbed of it, folks fading for want of it, folks rushing to embrace only ghosts of it.

There have been periods in my own life when my grief felt more real to me than my hope, moments when my rage, sitting up, threatened to swallow my softness forever. It is here, in these moments, in these fields where older versions of myself come to die, that I am forced again to clarify what exactly it is that I believe. For example, though so much of my energy of late has been in the service of opposing the largest military buildup in recent history, which is now underway in my home, Guam, I don't really believe that I am—that we are—going to stop the U.S. Defense Department from doing what it will. So what is it that I—that we—believe, really?

In law school, we are taught early on the importance of tight argumentation. We learn to revere the elegance of restraint. We become tailors who sew beautiful clothes of our reason. Somewhere along the way, we pick up a reflex. An intuitive feeling that we should fight only the fights we can win, lawyer only inside the narrowest possible nook.

But this is not *our* way. As lawyers fashioned in the William S. Richardson School of Law tradition, sharp analytical skills are not the only tools in our toolkit.

In our hands, we hold a *precious* version, passed carefully to us by our teachers, of what it means to be a lawyer, of how it looks to begin cool from the premise that the law is not neutral, and then thoughtfully, strategically, politically go about using it in the service of justice.

This is what I love most about Richardson. If we have paid attention, even to the silences, we leave here knowing that it is not good enough just to go out and fight the fights we can win. Rather, Richardson nurtures in us a respect for possibilities and, when we are ready, gently says to us, even without saying, "Go out and fight the fights that need fighting."

In the relay, something else, something so quiet it can barely be heard, is also transmitted. Let us look at it in the light.

Each of us who decides to engage in social change lawyering must find our own way to build an inner life against the possibility, and a certain measure of inevitability, of failure. Indeed, part of our work as people who pattern our lives around this belief—this deep, daring belief—that what we love we can save, is to prepare our wills to withstand some losing, so that we may lose and still set out again, anyhow.

I for one, especially of late, feel like I'm at a funeral when I go home. I see her: Guam as a fishbowl for so many different kinds of dying. As many of you know, while here with you at law school, I have always been there, too. My focus, always split. Three years later, I can tell you: the pipes of everything I've wanted desperately to stop are being fitted and laid. Despite how wide our movement has grown, and how fiercely articulate is the generation rising to challenge the changing tide, we are losing.

But then, if I am quiet enough, I hear them, trooping in: the women who taught me how to go about this business of keeping on keeping on. I hear them, all the sounds that saved my life: my mother's bamboo bracelets, back and forth on the kitchen counter, as she, after hours on her feet, gets dinner ready; the hooks on the bottom of my grandmother's net, dragging on the floor as she comes back fishless from the sea; the steady hooves of Cec's horse, as she rides into the evening on the back of the only god she has left.

The Mango Trees Already Know

Julian Aguon (Guåhan)

Last night I dreamt of tangerines and
my father, smiling.
Jumping, full of life, out of our
pick-up truck
on a drive to the
family ranch
to pick tangerines
from that tree
still green
still thick
in my mind.
My dad, before cancer, was
like those fruit:
bright and
delicious.

The smell of his skin
left me years ago
though it stayed
for years
with my sister.

But those afternoons feel
so far away,
as if part of
another life. In Guam
today
so much feels so far,

Previously published, Michael Bevacqua, Victoria-Lola Leon Guerrero, and Craig Santos
Perez, eds., *Chamoru Childhood*, Achiote Press, 2006.

so strange.
Violent distress grips
the ancients,
and the rocks themselves
tremble.
They know that the
outsiders are coming to shatter
what's left
of our
grandmothers' mirrors
so that, when it is
done,
we will not recognize
ourselves or
the ocean
or the rhythm of
either.

How I fear for the kids
now growing up
that they will not know
how it feels to wake up to
roosters and laze long
mornings
away in
outside kitchens
with coffee and *biscocho*,
or love the sun
down
at the ranch, smelling of
fresh-cut grass and hard
work, letting
J.D. Crutch and the rain
falling on wood and tin
break their heart.

How badly I wish
we could
still be saved
by afternoons.

But the mango trees
already know
better
and all this pretending

is putting us in graves
before our time.

The truth is
we have fallen asleep
in a prison of soft bed
and can't, not even for our children, roll over,
can't even reach
to shake our lovers
and tell them:
"I smell smoke."

I say
let the fire take it all.
the ash after
will smell better
than all this balm.

I pray hard these days
for a typhoon, for
something to blow down
these straw houses
of our illusion.

The truth is
even
tangerines,
those proud
trumpeters
of elation,
look languished
in the
morning
light.

Juan Malo & the Tip of America's Spear

(a malologue)

Craig Santos Perez (Guåhan)

Guam has been a sleepy supply depot for decades, but it is now christened the tip of America's military spear in Asia. Our long coastal passages stand poised to receive the "tip" of U.S. force projection, a slice of America in a strategic location. Of course *we* have to sharpen the edge out here as the tip of the spear thrusts. With the familiar tan of the Guam people, we maintain the tip of spear readiness: a genital sadistic fantasy—isn't Guam as much a part of America as Hawai'i? For those of us who spent part of our lives at the tip of the spear, we love our "tip of the spear" look. There's nothing like a Full Moon Drunken Platoon that "beats their spears into plows" (this incident was later downgraded to a *bent spear*).

But the story of the 212-square-mile island, affectionately called the "tip of the spear," begs a bit more history. In the beginning, dark brown–skinned Aborigines, wearing loincloths to cover up the tips of their spears, were no match for America's Holy Tip. What's really fucked up is that despite all our efforts and money and land, we ended up as the "tip of the spear," rather than, well, the shaft. I didn't have my heart set on Guam becoming American anyway! The "tip of the spear" image, carried over from the Vietnam war, is overrated: Marines won't change, regardless of whether they are in Australia, Guam, or Okinawa. There's something very foreign about seeing armed American military patrolling The End of The Spear and asking every native they see, "Hey, Brother, can you spear a dime?"

After effectively acquiring one-third of the entire island, the American military ceased performing ancestral and bachelor cults, thereby breaking their spears. Instead, they made a kooky film called *The Spear of Destiny*. In terms of military tactics, the new weapon, a short stabbing spear, is called a "Guam."

My grandfather used to tell me that throwing a spear through the air could change the weather. Now, the unchanging weather is only the tip of the spear.

Juan Malo & Where America's Day Begins

(a malologue)

Craig Santos Perez (Guåhan)

Guam is truly where "America's Day Begins." Yes, Guam is a part of the United States. Located 2500 miles west of the International Date Line, Guam is 20 hours ahead of Hawai'i and one day ahead of the United States. At sunrise, we hear army personnel singing in the English sections while children on Guam wave Old Glory, shout "U-S-A," and sing patriotic American songs. But Guam is also where injustice, waste, and abuse begin. A bumper sticker I hate so much bears that deadly slogan "Guam: Where America's Day Begins."

Guam is the westernmost frontier of the United States and 15 hours ahead of the Eastern Seaboard time zone. So Guam is also, geographically, where America's Dream ends. Guam is literally the first American community to greet each new day, a privilege manifest in one nonvoting congressman and the idea that we "Practice Democracy in Paradise." Guam's tourist bureau promotes the Pacific island as "where America's day begins," a big draw for Japanese tourists (1 million annually), which helps preserve our culture.

I'm from Guam and we are a day ahead of the mainland, so we actually got our PS3s while ya'll were still sleeping or something. Guam is truly "Where America's Products begin." Language is not a problem—everyone speaks English, mostly with an American accent of sorts. Too many people still think of Guam only as a bleak outpost for the US military. Just in case you are confused, Guam is where America's day begins. We are 15 hours ahead of New York! BUT if the house of your culture was burning down, then you'd have to look beyond the whole "Where America's Day Begins" propaganda. That's why they say, "Here today, Guam tomorrow."

SO, me and the rest of the Chamorros are ahead of y'all. Sorry if I threw everybody's timing off.

The Storm

Joseph Borja (Guåhan)

A typhoon is coming
8,000 soldiers in diameter
An eye as big as an atom bomb
Powered by B-2 jet engines
And supersonic F-22 Raptors
The Weatherman says it's coming fast
Touchdown 2014
Bringing gusts up to 42,000 dependents per hour
Nana says we should prepare
Stock up on
Heart-food
Mind-water
Soul-batteries
And beer
Better board up the windows
And tie down the roof
This one could blow our minds away
Literally
But not to worry says Mr. Governor
12 million bucks
Courtesy of the American military
Will save us
It'll boost the economy
Improve the infrastructure
And overall make our lives much better
It all sounds fine and dandy
But I wonder if that money will buy us out
Of the oppressive winds that the typhoon will bring
Sounds like Mr. Governor
Is putting all his money on the storm
Praying it'll hit
The faster the better
But Nana knows better

Typhoons are unpredictable
You can never predict the behavior of the storm
How the wind will change the landscape
And what the rain water will forever wash away
A typhoon is coming
8,000 soldiers in diameter
An eye as big as an atom bomb
Powered by B-2 jet engines
And supersonic F-22 Raptors
With room to grow
The Weatherman says it's coming fast
Touchdown 2012
Bringing gusts up to 24,000 dependents per hour
Better board up your soul
Tie down your mind
And stock up your heart
With hope supplies to last a lifetime
Cause the Suruhanu says
That what the storm destroys
Can never be replaced
No matter how much money FEMA gives.

Dance

Arielle Taitano Lowe (Guåhan)

D a n c e s perpetuate our culture.
Our body movements tell our history,
but 400 years of colonization
paralyzed our native form of storytelling.

Today, I am one of many

hollywood-Polynesian show girls
who sell lies in the form of body language.

My smile is the w e l c o m e m a t
to an exotic paradise.

As dancers we take the Chamoru greeting, "Håfa Adai,"
and sell it with our voices:

    "Haa-faa adayyyy!"

We represent Guåhan's women
in a dance show that's only 12% indigenous,
but the tourists *don't know that.*

The audience listens to Polynesian melodies
with Chamoru lyrics w o v e n into them.

Our bodies are covered
with foreign *te manu* feathers
while the leaves of our local coconut trees,
our *trongkon niyok,*
silently watch from their branches.

We e n t i c e with the hands of hula
and tease with the hips of Tahiti—
and like birds, we scream****, to make our show exciting,

as if our native tongues
weren't breathtaking enough.

The tourists perceive this as genuine,
and we perpetuate the lie.

This once sacred village, *Tomhom*,
now called pleasure island,
is a graveyard of indigenous traditions.

But the tourists c h e e r f o r u s—
for the m o v i n g postcards
that stage imitations of culture.

The crowd's applause drowns the truth.
This is not Pacific custom . . .
            This is a *show*,
s p o n s o r e d b y: the suits
who tied traditions to profit.
Businessmen
traded traditional Chamoru dances
for their fake versions of
Auwana, Poi, and Otea.

We're twirling and
        swaying and dipping
                and shaking and dying
to try and find an escape from our debt
as if we could dance our way into a better economy.

The spirituality of our culture falls as dollar bills
r i s e like new hotels over buried villages.

Our dances have become
more profitable than meaningful.
These businessmen have turned worship
into entertainment.

It's a shame that we
e x p l o i t Pacific culture,
when indigenous dance
should e n r i c h the livelihood of
the natives they belong to—

Not the pockets of businessmen,
who monopolize the ancient

practices of Pacific people
and control them
like cheap commodities.

Representation belongs in native hands,
so our stories can be told beyond promise of income,
our bodies become vessels of truth,
and our dances become b r i d g e s to our ancestors.

They are called our *Saina*,
and by respecting them we learn
to respect our island.

The leaves of our *trongkon niyok*
should no longer watch from their branches.
They should find a home a r o u n d our women's hips
so the c l a p s of our p a l m s against our skirts
could beat like the pulse of our culture.

It may be almost impossible
to revive authentic Chamoru dance,
But we are the p i e c e s that breathe life into it.

Te Manu feathers can s o a r
a w a y from Chamoru skin
and once again nest on the curves of
their Polynesian women.

The calls of Tahiti can find refuge
curled in the tongues of their people,
while Chamoru chants d a n c e in our mouths.

Our women can hold seashells
in their palms, so the flames of Aotearoa can
burn bright within the hearts of their rightful homeland.

Our dances are as beautiful as our people.
There is so little of our culture left,
that the importance of salvaging it, has far greater wealth
than any business or tourist attraction.

Owning a business—
gives you no right
to own our culture.

More than Just a Blue Passport

Selina Neirok Leem (Marshall Islands)

Looking out my window
There sits my grandparents' and my mama's grave
White rectangle they are closeted in
It's inside
Gray and still
My backyard is
A four-meter history
of waves crashing and breaking
sea-walls built with uncles', brothers', and grandpa's sweat
that one great wall
two meters high
my family's only protection from the water
made a mockery
as the water has risen
level with the land
and spilled over human debris weaving
a remnant
a reminder
of human being's greediness

To the developed countries
To the advanced nations
You think you know us
But you know NOTHING—NOTHING
at all

Should I tell you what is happening in my backyard?
What is that?
You think you already know?
You think you know better?

No, no
You have no say

You have had yours
When the man from the military said
Testing nuclear bombs
67 of them
on tiny strips of land
with many parts
barely a meter above sea level
is "For the good of mankind
and to end all world wars"

How many wars have ended now due to nuclear weapons?
How many?
How many innocent lives killed?
Remember March 1, 1954
When they dropped the Bravo bomb on Bikini?
Bravo! Bravo!
Ever-famous for leaving their mark behind

Like the mark
on my home
The Marshall Islands
is now a weary mother of
A dome filled with radioactive waste,
all from the bombing, "For the good of mankind"
With a sign that said, "Do not return for 25,000 years"
It has been seventy years
We have 24,930 years left
Until we can go back home to Runit
The land, the island this dome burdens
But now the waters have washed it away
Eroding parts of this dome away
Cracking it
Leaking harmful radiation out into the open
So foreign men who have visited the dome to study it say
the outside is even more contaminated than the inside
and they leave again
with numbers and calculations
No solutions
Not a thought for us

Foreign men, do you think
Do you think about the waters rising?
My island ain't got no time for 24,930 years
Scientists have predicted by 2050
We are NO MORE

NO MORE

2016 I am here
My island's got 34 years left
34
But in 24,390 years, we will be able to live on Runit.
How far do you think she will be underwater?

Looking out into horizons of waves angry
hungry for redemption
A bubu sits on her plywood
10-inch-high bed
She looks at me
Confusion and sadness in her eyes
"What is wrong with our islands?
I don't ever remember it being like this."
It hits me
She does not know
She does not know what is happening in our islands
Not knowing these waves pounding her shore
are human-induced
but I swear
I will fight for this grandma
I will fight for my family
I will fight for my country's survival

For bigger countries mock us
after they have violated the earth's virginity
with their carbon-filled aphrodisiac
Digging and pumping out fossil fuel
from our mother's womb
Relentlessly
Constantly

Mocking us
At 1.5 degrees
At us
At the risk of my people becoming climate refugees
Becoming stateless
Becoming landless
Becoming just a blue passport
The only identity of this grandmother and me
Will the first three pages of Marshallese stamps
Be the last stamps I get from home?
Will this blue passport be the last one I will ever have from home?

My backyard
is not like your backyard
My backyard is trees, crippled
It is broken bones unearthed from graves
It is nuclear-radiation rich
It is tides with white fangs
It is houses broken down, no more occupants within
It is the land getting smaller
and smaller
My backyard is my bubu, jimma, and mama lying in their graves
It is my grandpa telling me while in pain
"Jibu, I cannot wait to go
I will soon be resting
resting from all this world's chaos
I will now sleep
Peacefully."
My backyard is a promise
a promise to let them sleep peacefully
It is we, Marshallese, saying
1.5 is all we got
Mock, be skeptical
1.5—pffft. Impossible. Unattainable.
Again
It is all we got.

My Island Is One Big American Footnote

Michael Lujan Bevacqua (Guåhan)

Guam, Where America's Day Begins!!![1, 2, 3]

---

1. Life in the colonies, the borderlands, the territories sucks.
Sucks like nationally strategic words and verbs used to keep my ethnicity selfishly un-determined
It sucks like cluster/mustard bombs buried in your land or landing on your head.
It sucks like carefully crafted, beautifully bound footnotes that no one bothers to read or quote.

My island is one big American footnote,
Sitting black/brown as day on the bottom of every red whitewashed and blue page
Through textual treaties or wars these narrow margins are our new, now, old or eternal homes.
Whether we liked it or not (Wanted it or not) our bloods were mixed with colonially supplied inks and our lives recast, set typed and dyed woven into tyrannical threads of foreign flags that call us to war with familiar terms of friendliness, unity, warmth, love of life, yet that same textual flag will blind a budget, or an international summit to our superfluous "footnoted" needs.

Footnotes? Small islands of text really,
Off the margins, somewhere between margins of national importance we sit there, ideologically spaced/almost erased like far-flung chick-peas etched/embossed on these pages of strategic seas by a constitutional, conscious and colonial disease,
Colonial *dis-ease.*
We cannot be incorporated for insane and inconsistent reasons
A hundred years ago it was because our skins were different.
Then it became because we spoke different languages
Or our lack of rights and liberties was integral to military strategy,
Now it is because we would receive too much power if we became a fair and equal part of the union.
We are the territorial thoughts that are too precious to let go, but not precious enough to bring into the fold.

Not critical enough to really think on, and not real enough to think critically about.
Welcome to the footnotes, like the foothills of some forever inferior land.
Because when you look up upon the wealth of words, verbs, periods, commas and paragraphs of the text, their completeness of thought, their unlimited potential, their self-referential existence (while yours seems so conditional, contextual, so dependent on the text) their ability to endlessly reference their "glory"
You realize that in this world, In This text
It is not hard to believe there is something inferior about inhabiting this tiny footnote.
And thus we exist always trying to live up to the sprawling, overwhelming example of the text.
Its structure, its syntax, its semantics are all implanted in our tiny notes.

Alas, we are nothing but footnotes. Barely quotes.
We are the crap between America's political toes that no one knows or care about.
The exceptions and imperfections are excesses that don't really belong in this "glorious" document of democracy and freedom.
In the case of Guam
Our existence uncontroversially and uncontrollably questions established "truths" about the espoused equality of the text's democracy, its unfreeing military strategy of freedom, and its supposed support for human rights.

2. **See, a footnote always poses a question, or supplies an answer**
Is an excess or an extra thought,
Always articulates something that just doesn't fit into the regular text
So what does my footnote do?
Among other things it calls for American people to reconcile their proud to be not colonial not imperial existence with the fact that what they keep off their margins of layouts/maps/discourse proves blatantly that they are.
My island footnote is an uncontroversial example, but other milityrannical tramplings around other texts, in dozens of languages all make the same point.
American style democracy is really just American sovereignty
Anywhere on the page and anyplace in this world.
The discourse on domination, on control, on sociopolitical subjugation local, foreign and domestic is coded into each line of text just as much as liberty, equality and justice seem to be.

Why can't the this "great text" see that with their very apathy, with their disinterest, their notorious anti-human patriotism, they allow their text to create genocide, allow their text to abuse human rights, to deny human rights?
For me to hear people believe in the pieties of American benevolence or grandeur is like watching snow fall slowly back up into the sky, or bombs being dropped up, sliding and imploding back into the planes that birthed them.
It is supposed to be unbelievable, but how then can so many people believe it?

3. **But back to my footnotes that don't and I quote "fit in" with the flow of the text.**
Since we don't fit, since there isn't room for us on the flag, or in the Capitol, let us go I say!
Release us to flutter beyond these American borders and margins!
Leave us to determine self-fully! A text of our own!

But no, that would never do the Congressional chorus calls back

And they are right, as national (in) securities will always intercede and strategic reasoning will sweep us politely to the bottom of any flag/budget/page, but push us unknowingly to the forefront of any imperial activities.

Speaking of which, should the son or daughter of a footnote die on a field of battle, distant or far, and the eulogy can be politically profitable—the flag is stripped from its perpetual half-mast posture on the book's spine and placed, draped into patriotic pose over the footnote's footsoldier's fallen casket.

But a soldier, fallen out of a footnote, absorbed into the field of the text at the last second is an unknown soldier nonetheless.

With no voice, no space other than silent cries to flag stained states of the textual union, the makeshifting of this patriot only obscures where in the hell he came from.

But I'll tell you where he came from. He came from my tiny island, and he went to war without a vote! Without a voice! Without so much as a space or place in that big book of apple pie American wonderfulness! But now after his passing words will be shed of how his death and sacrifice were not in vain, but what could be more full of uselessness than words of regret that have no effect? All the words sacrificed or laid before the altar of freedom, equality and justice mean nothing if they do not produce, protect or pursue freedom, equality or justice.

Such is the fate of those unfairly placed in the fringes

And it is that cruelly formalized fate that guides my frustrated fingers daily into silent and dissident prayer.

That God please help the footnotes

Because if the book whose constitution is supposed to be built upon freedom, liberty, democracy won't liberate, elevate or make equal its own footnotes, then who will?

The Revolution Will Not Be Haolified

Michael Lujan Bevacqua (Guåhan)

You will not be able to ignore it che'lu
This time you will not be able to blame it all on Anghet
You will not be able to change channels
And watch Fear Factor, Rev TV or Salamat Po Guam because
The Revolution will not be televised

The revolution will not be televised, nor will it be advertised
It will not be sponsored by the Good Guys at Moylan's or the better guys
   at AK.
It will not be something easily explained by radio callers
Whether they be Positively Local, Definitively Settler, or Surprisingly
   Coconut
It will not be cornered by the Calvos and explained by Sabrina Salas
   Matanane
After the story about the incoming B-52s or 1000s of Marines careening
   towards Guam, and how we should be economically energized and not
   terrorized.
Jon Anderson will have no TT anecdotes about it
and Chris Barnett won't malafunkshun it because the revolution will not
   be televised

The revolution will not be televised or editorialized
It will not be something cannibalized with two inches here two inches
   there
Dubious headlines everywhere
Lee Webber will not edit it
Joe Murphy will not put it in his pipe and smoke it
Nor dream about it, or tell others the wonders and blunders of it.

There will be no letters to the editor quoting scriptures or denying its
constitutionality
And there will be no American flag inserts saying these three colors just
don't run
As the revolution will not be editorialized

The revolution will not be televised or politicized
It will not play the same old gàyu games
And promise you that same old talonan things.
The revolution will not wave at you as you drive by on Marine Drive
And seduce you with its hardworking eyes.
It will not be territorial or popular, and not encourage you with maolek
blue.
The revolution will not put maraming salamat po after its speeches to get
more Filipino votes in the next election because the revolution will not
be politicized

The revolution will not be televised, not be theorized
It will not be something GCC or UOG friendly.
There will be no books at Bestseller offering to help you lose something in
90 days
Or Rachael Ray helping you cook the revolution of your way.
Ron McNinch will not survey it
and will not poll people about their revolution of choice.
There will be no WASC review report demanding accountability
demanding autonomy
And no beachcombing carpetbaggers will proclaim their own terminal
authority
Over the histories, the laws, the thinking of those for whom they see
nothing but corrupt and corrupting inferiority
The revolution will not be colonized

The revolution will not be televised, not be supersized.
The revolution will not be something you can buy at Ross, or get at blue
light cost
It is not just red rice, kelaguan uhang, or popcorn with Tabasco sauce.
It doesn't come with Coke and it doesn't fit on a fiesta plate.
The revolution will not make you gof sinexy, cure your jafjaf, or make
fragrant your fa'fa'
The revolution will not force you to be where America's empire begins
Or where Japan's golf courses and Jerry Yingling's credit card debt ends.
You won't need a credit card, or be charged for the tin foil to cover your
balutan
As the revolution will not be economized

The revolution will not be televised, blownback or militarized
There will be no more physical ordnance buried in people's lands
And no more patronizing propaganda buried in people's minds
The revolution will not get you cheaper cases of chicken or increased
    commissary privileges.
It will not make freedomless flags feel more comfortable in your hands
Or make uniforms fit more snugly around your mind.
The revolution will not deny racism or exploitation
And not create histories about landfalls of destiny
But instead publicize the racism and evils of American hegemony.
The revolution will not be subsidized by construction contracts or the
    race of Senator Inouye or Congressman Burton
It will not be laid waste to by daisy cut budgets or Medicare spending
    limits
Instead it will be sustained by deep memories that refuse to die
The revolution will not be televised.

The revolution will not be televised and will not polarize based on blood
    or color
It will not make your skin lighter
It will not make your skin darker
It will not test your blood the way Hitler or Uncle Sam would have done
It will not hate some and love others based on their time of naturalization
Or incept date of their compacts of free association.
But the revolution will help some find comfort, find strength, find power
In their connections to the land and to each other
Allow some to discover the sovereignty that can be found in solidarity
The revolution will take and remake this consciousness that doesn't need
    to be televised
But does need to be revolutionized
The revolution will not be haolified
The revolution will not be haolified

Cha-mu pumupuni este che'lu

Sa' i revolution ti pau mahaolify

REMEMBERING

From *The Constitution of the Federated States of Micronesia,* 1975

Preamble

WE, THE PEOPLE OF MICRONESIA, exercising our inherent sovereignty, do hereby establish this Constitution of the Federated States of Micronesia.

With this Constitution, we affirm our common wish to live together in peace and harmony, to preserve the heritage of the past, and to protect the promise of the future.

To make one nation of many islands, we respect the diversity of our cultures. Our differences enrich us. The seas bring us together, they do not separate us. Our islands sustain us, our island nation enlarges us and makes us stronger.

Our ancestors, who made their homes on these islands, displaced no other people. We, who remain, wish no other home than this. Having known war, we hope for peace. Having been divided, we wish unity. Having been ruled, we seek freedom.

Micronesia began in the days when man explored seas in rafts and canoes. The Micronesian nation is born in an age when men voyage among stars; our world itself is an island. We extend to all nations what we seek from each: peace, friendship, cooperation, and love in our common humanity. With this Constitution we, who have been the wards of other nations, become the proud guardian of our own islands, now and forever.

History Project

Kathy Jetñil-Kijiner (Marshall Islands)

at fifteen i decide
to do a history project on nuclear testing in the Marshall Islands
time to learn my own history

i weave through book after article after website
all on how the US military used my island home for nuclear testing after
    World War II
i sift through political jargon
tables of nuclear weapons
names like Operation Bravo
Crossroads
and Ivy
quotes from generals like
            9,000 people are out there. Who   *cares?*

i'm not mad at all
i already knew all of this

i'm quiet
as i glance at a photograph
a boy peeled skin legs arms suspended
a puppet next to a lab coat
lost in his clipboard

i'm calm
as i read firsthand accounts of what
we call jelly babies
tiny beings with no bones
skin red tomatoes

Previously published, *Iep Jāltok: Poems from a Marshallese Daughter,* University of Arizona
Press, 2017.

the miscarriages unspoken
the broken translations
    i never told my husband.
    i thought it was my fault.
    i thought
        there must be something   wrong
    inside me.

i'm fine

as i glance through snapshots
of American marines and nurses branded white with bloated grins
tossing beachballs sucking beers
along our shores
and my islander ancestors
cross-legged before a general
listening to his fairy tale
bout how it's
    for the good of mankind
to hand over our islands
let them blast radioactive energy
into our lazy limbed coconut trees
our sagging breadfruit trees
our busy fishes that sparkle like new sun
into the coral reef
brilliant as technicolor splashes of paint
into our steady
loving islands
    God will thank you they told us
yea
as if god himself ordained
those powdered flakes
to drift onto our skin our hair our eyes
to seep into our bones
we mistook radioactive fallout
for snow
    God will thank you they told us
like god's just been
waiting
for my people
to vomit
    vomit
        vomit
all humanity's sins
onto impeccable white shores

gleaming like the cross
burned into our open scarred palms

this
is not new information

i knew all this already
my father my mother
spoon fed me these stories
whispered it bitter into my open mouth
and patted my back
when anger hiccupped
from my burning throat

so i'm not so mad
really

but then
but then
i stumble
on a photograph
of goats tied to American ships
bored and munching on tubs of grass
At the bottom a caption read
> Goats and pigs were left on naval ships as test subjects.
> Thousands
> of letters flew in from America
> protesting

> animal abuse.

So how bout we
photocopy this onto billboards shall we parade with a bullhorn scream
ANIMAL ABUSE?
ARE YOU SERIOUS?
cuz this
is the last straw
i wanna rip apart this history pierce it through those generals' potbellies
so give me fire give me tnt megatons
a fancy degree give me everything i could ever need
to mold a bomb like the ones you
catapulted into my home so i can
catapult assaults into your picket fenced white house dome
send ripples of death
that gnaws your father's bones

your daughter's marrow
so you can see
what i watched happen
to my grandfather
and my cousin
so you can stand over their bed
watching life drip across a black screen
knots of knuckles tied to a steel table
cold with their dying breath
then you'll see what i've seen
give me destruction ordained
by your god
give me blood smeared crosses and
your money all of the money
all of the thousands of dollars
funneled across the pacific
exploding like a second sun
and sprinkling over us in the form of
cans of spam, ramen, and diabetes
how you stuffed it
into the mouths of my people
till we grew so hungry
we faded into shadows
into murmurs of a people a home
the world has forgotten and ignored

so i finished the project
glued typed stapled my rage across
a poster board i bought from office max
and entered it in a school district
competition called History Day
with a spray-painted title that said
FOR THE GOOD OF MANKIND
in bold stenciled yellow
my parents were quietly proud
so was my history teacher
and when the judges finally came around
to my project
one of them said
    yea
    but it wasn't really
    for the good of mankind, though
    was it?
and i lost

Thieves

Anne Perez Hattori (Guåhan)

Thieves, they called us.
Religious converts, they made us.
Said we were sinful,
naked, savage, primitive
Playmates of Satan,
native souls blackened and corrupted
by immoral appetites

Exterminated, they called us.
Half-castes, they branded us.
Said we were impure,
racially—culturally—spiritually
Casualties of inauthenticity,
native blood contaminated and polluted
by casual miscegenation

Infantile, they called us.
Wards of the state, they made us.
Said we were immature,
UNeducated, UNdeveloped, UNcivilized
Victims of illiteracy,
native intelligence retarded and muted
by indifferent laziness

Now they tell us
we are simply, sadly, contemptibly
OVER-developed
OVER-modernized
OVER-theologized
OVER-Americanized

UNDER-Chamoricized

Previously published, Deborah Lee and Antonio Salas, eds., *Unfaithing U.S. Colonialism*, PACTS and Dharma Cloud Publishers, 1999.

Guåhan

Lehua M. Taitano (Guåhan)

The Beginning. Before Time

There is a crack in the ocean. Deep beneath the flake of reef, beneath the darting parrotfish and unicornfish and slippery eel, the earth gapes, an open mouth. Deeper still, past the lips of the trench, the black throat of the earth lies empty, a hollowness where no light can reach. Yet thirty-six thousand feet above, a glinting string of islands—and in the middle, Guåhan floats in the sun.

How was it made? Atti made it with her brother, Puntan. Brother and sister existed in the void, the nothingness of nothing. They played and fought as siblings do. They were neither bored nor idle, because they had each other.

Atti pulled on Puntan's long, black hair. Puntan pinched the underside of Atti's strong arm, and then ran away, smirking. They kicked at each other with bare, round toes and wrestled and laughed.

One day, Puntan grew tired, and a strangeness came over him. He closed his eyes and became quiet and still. In the nothingness of the void, even the sound of his breath was swallowed, so he listened in the silence for the small sound coming from within.

His soul spoke to him in a whisper. From a round space deep inside him, the void of his own body, his soul formed lips and a throat and spoke to Puntan and told him he would soon die. Puntan heard this from his soul and did not deny it.

When he told the news of his coming death to Atti, she was beside herself with anguish and worry. Without her brother, she would be alone. Without her brother, the nothingness would surely close in around her, and even her own soul would not keep her company.

"Do not worry, sister," Puntan said. "You will not be alone. You will make a world of my body. You will live in this world, and you will never be without me."

Atti understood, as she was equal to her brother in knowledge, wisdom, and strength. In the quiet of the void, they sat together, hand in hand, and Puntan spoke the words of his soul. Atti remembered the words and promised to do as Puntan asked.

When her brother at last drew his final breath, Atti collected his body in her arms and chanted even as she cried.

—*The skies from your last breath, sweet brother,* she sang, and drew the air from his lungs and created the clouds.

—*A sun and moon from your eyes.* She plucked each of Puntan's bright eyes from his head and cast them beyond the clouds, high into the void.

—*Rainbows to color the skies, my brother.* Atti pulled free his eyebrows and placed them among the clouds.

—*The earth below, ridged with mountains, dimpled with valleys.* She laid her brother's back gently at the bottom of the void and created the land.

—*A deep ocean swelling, dear Puntan, as vast as the void.* She gathered his black tresses and created the depths of the swirling sea.

And the land and the sea remembered Puntan's breath and the beating of his heart, and night and day patterned themselves to the rhythm.

Atti surveyed what she had created and entered the sea. She walked to a string of small islands that she had placed under the shining sun of Puntan's eye.

From the sea around the most beautiful of these islands sprang ocean grasses and algae, fanfish and sea cucumbers, whales and white sharks. Up from the island's soil sprang crooked-limbed yoga and arching pandanus, flowering starfruit and ifit trees. Ghost crabs scuttled across the sand, and singing reed warblers and swooping flying fox took flight through the canopy.

Seeing the paradise that she had created from her brother's body, Atti smiled and sat at the edge of the surf, letting the ocean spill over her feet. In the rhythm of the surf, she heard her brother's breath, and this made her happy. But there was no one to share her happiness with.

She understood, then, what she must do. She stood, lifted her head to the shining sun, and walked into the ocean from the southern tip of the island. She crouched slowly, tucking her chin to her chest, and turned herself to stone.

The churning sea crashed over the rock formed from Atti's body, and pieces of stone that broke away and were carried to shore became the people of Guåhan, the Chamorro, all of whom contained Atti's spirit. *Guåhan. We have.*

Contact. 1670

Someone had to put it on a map, so Magellan was no big surprise. He had a boat; that was *his* thing. Of course, it depends on whose history you want to hear. I find it best to trust the brown historians on this one. They have less reason to lie. Better yet, trust the brown women, who have nothing left to lose.

Magellan landed on the shores of Guåhan, stinking of scurvy and sawdust and Europe, brandishing a steel sword and a white, homesick penis.

"What a Paraíso!" he thought, just before ordering the decapitation of seven Chamorro men and burning down their homes. "Now where's the pigs and women?"

Guåhan has no pigs.

I am being unfair. Old Magellan probably asked, quite politely, if he might re-supply his three ships. The natives granted his request, and he honored the beautiful string of islands in which Guåhan happily sits with the name *Las Islas de las Velas Latinas*, after the sails of Guåhan's swiftest boats. Then the Chamorro men boarded his ships, taking what they could find. Magellan had refused to pay for his supplies. He renamed the lovely string *Las Islas de los*

Ladrones. Island of Lateen Sails? Island of Thieves? Magellan wouldn't stay long either way, so it didn't matter much. But he had made contact. His heavy boot-prints were all over the place, and soon, others followed.

Here's how it happened.

Diego Luis de San Vitores came to save the Chamorros, first with gifts of iron and clothing (given to Chief Quipuha), then with Bibles, crosses, and a new name. He was a pious man. A basilica was built, Chief Quipuha was converted, and the lovely string of islands became *Islas Marianas*. (Oh, little string, like shimmering pearls, how easily you slide into the velvet pocket of a Spanish queen.)

Catholicism was a stealthy thing that crept over the island, appearing here and there like suggestions, small hints of salvation whispered into Chamorro ears, until it felt at home. Once it crossed the threshold of thatched houses set upon latte stones, it denounced ancient traditions and elbowed its way beyond the front door—into kitchens, bedrooms, and graveyards.

For the ancients, there is no heaven or hell. Puntan and Atti were no gods, just a man and woman with power, caring for each other as brother and sister. This is why Chamorros keep their dead near. The *maranan uchan*, the skulls of our loved ones, are kept in baskets and placed among the rafters, for protection and good will. Respects are paid.

Vitores buried Quipuha near the basilica. What did he think would happen? There are no lovely words to describe it.

So here is Atti now. Fifteen years old, the daughter of Dahi and Man'oga, whose own head is lost among the waves and will never find its way to our basket. The women are becoming all of what is left. Our village of Yigu sighs with a woman's breath. This is no time to be in love.

Mama tells me that it is not love, anyway, and that I should not say such things. She tells me I am confused, traumatized, growing up. What would my father think? We have no word for this kind of love on our island, and Mama says, simply, it is "sisterly." She is careful to watch us, though, when Tasi and I are shredding coconuts on the back steps or making spondylus shell necklaces. She peers through her weaving or chopping and pokes her head out the window, asking questions she already has answers to.

Tasi is not my sister, though we have always been friends. Her fingers are slender and delicate. She can carve the roundest of holes in the center of her shells, chewing her lips with the effort. When she is done and holds one up to test its symmetry, it is me she sees through that perfect space.

I cannot forget that our island is at war, but when I press my own fingers to the center of the dangling shell against my chest, I am reminded of the sea and the tide that always takes away what it has first brought to shore. At night, I walk into the jungle and ask the ancestors, the Taotaomo'na, to rid the island of Spaniards. So far, they have not answered, but I will continue my chanting, even when the soldiers come to our village and tell us that our families are to take surnames, in the Christian way.

Our people have only ever needed one name to identify ourselves. Dahi, *friend*. Man'oga, *one who is snared*. Atti, *one who plays tricks*. Tasi, *the sea*.

I tell my mother that if we are forced, we should be known as Taitano, *without land.*

America, Japan, America. 1944

My nanan biha is dying. We sit on overturned buckets outside the concrete house, watching the sun bleed into the treeline. Her legs are swollen and blotchy. She squints at me with cataract eyes, resting her thick arms on her knees. The concrete house is shaded in a copse of breadfruit trees and will be turned over to the lenders soon enough. She signed the reverse mortgage years ago. Doctor bills. She knows I will leave for the mainland when she is gone.

When she speaks in English, her accent is warm and rhythmic, yet punctured, like the sound of a quick pumping heart that has a slow, pinprick leak.

"Soon it is happening," she says, nodding.

I listen. If I listen long enough, she will find a length of thread and tug on its end with a round thumb and forefinger, teasing it until it runs out. If I am silent and follow it to its end, I will see how it unravels. Later, I will remember its way, and imitate it.

"The doctors, they tell me, Maria you don't eat so much, it will kill you, these diabetes. I say but I love it, I love it, the *kelaguin binadu*, the *eskabeche*, the *kadon monnok*. If they kill me, let me die with a full stomach."

Her breath is heavy. Her earlobes are plump and brown. She smiles.

"Ai' adai, I don't know. You know, when I go, Atti, I want you to make sure they don't take these flowers. Some of the bougainvillea I started from tiny sprouts."

She shows me with a measurement of her thumb and pinky.

"These hibiscus, oh, you know they are so much to be caring for them. You have to be careful and not put too much fertilizer, a'ha, that's how they get small, you know. Because, you know, 'cause they are usually big, like the dinner plates. Your mama used to love the hibiscus in her hair. Oh, I tell her she is vain, for the boys. Every day before school, I am packing her, plus your aunties, titiyas for lunch, you know. That's all we had, the titiyas, and I call for her. I say Catalina, don't be forgetting your titiyas! And you know where she is? Your mama is in my garden picking the small hibiscus for her hair, and I tell her I pinch her if she keeps doing it because how will they be growing, you know, big like plates if she is always picking them?"

She pauses and squints out beyond the white buckets filled with potted flowers, so many they have overtaken the yard. She used to sell them at the market, lifting these heavy buckets that spill over with red hibiscus onto a two-wheeled cart. She begins to sing in the old language, and I listen, though I don't understand.

"Atti? You don't understand?" she says. "Ai' adai, for heaven's gracious. It's from your living on the mainland. Your father just is wanting you to speak the English, only the English. When you go back, you tell him he did a good job. No one knows you are Chamorro when you go back. Just here we are knowing. I don't know. Is it cold there in North Carolina? It's cold there. Well, I tell you something before you go back, Atti. I show you how to sing the Tsamorita, the old Chamorro songs. You need to know how it's done, the rhyming. My mama and aunties and sisters and me, we would sit around while we are doing the cooking or, you know, the washing. We sing the Tsamorita—also it's called Kantan Chamorita—which is, you have to be smart to sing it because you make it up, you know, and it's like this. Four lines, dos e trés lines, two and three lines, they are rhyming, at the end. Okay, so last line is finished. You take the last word, the finished line, and it is the rhyming word for next one, two and three lines. I think, Atti, this is how. It's hard to remember."

She sings. She sings and sings and I listen, unknowing, hearing only the punctured rhythm, quick but warm.

I do not have her words, but I have words. Words to tell my biha's story. My story.

When we count, it is not in our way.
Whose tongue then, give numbers their shape?
Which Spanish man, his breath on the nape
Of my mother's mother's mother's frame?

Uno, dos, trés, cuatro, cinco, seis.
In English, we are taught words for the same.
Thank Henry Glass, Confederate by name,
For saving us, again, from our own kind.

Guåhan, *we have*, Guåhan, we have not.
Stars and stripes form Guam from the rind.
Lovely little string, a fortunate find
Impressed with the States, United, in bold.

So we call it Guam—flat, America's wealth.
Capital, a shell, to be bought and sold.
Its traded worth, ten thousand-fold.
The number of Chamorros shrinks to none.

Then the claim of the Japanese
December ten, nineteen forty-one.
Call Guåhan Omiya Jima of the Rising Sun.
A cluster of bombs bloom red on the sand.

Chamorros with white ribbons
Cinched by Japan's Imperial hand
Now slave to the rice paddy, our land
Taken, our tongues taken, left with dust.

Spotted dogs creep from the jungle edge,
Tongues wet with roadside lust,

And feed upon Chamorro livers, thighs, while blood's rust
Bakes beneath equatorial sun.

In Manengon, ten thousand Chamorros
Shit in the Ylig River, waiting to be undone
By bayonet, grenade, katana sword, machine gun,
Errant blooming bomb of America's liberation.

If a prayer escapes my lips,
Let it be for mercy of amputation.
The long arm of America's occupation
Would as easily smother as liberate you.

America, America, America. 2008

In North Carolina, I make jewelry, display pieces not meant to be worn—necklaces and bracelets that dangle medallions, shells, lead weights, chunks of pipe, artillery casings, bones. I string them with braided wire cable, lengths of steel chain, rope dipped in caked silt and mud. They are meant for a giant's neck, for monstrous wrists and ankles. Weight is what I'm after. Weight and mass. Adornments that take up so much space they cannot be ignored.

My father will die having never seen them. He does not understand the transition of my life into such things. To him, I have changed into something I am not. What happened to young Atti? What happened to the young teacher of children?

I think, "I was displaced from my home." Home is Guam, and this is what I remember: the bend of coconut trees over the bay, the spindly fingers of the medicine man mixing a poultice for a wound, the shadow of sea squirts in a shimmering pool, my grandmother's face. When people ask me *Have you been back?* it is this short list that comes to mind, all that I remember. I am eight thousand miles away. I have not been back.

It pains my father to speak to me. When I saw him last, he distracted himself with memories. Living in the past, he can see me as he wishes. A good girl. A good American English teacher, with a good head on her shoulders. Lovely daughter with the exotic look but lacking any accent. Atti Smith.

"So you've found a place?" he said.

"Near the beach," I said.

"You always did like the beach. Used to run around half naked; couldn't force you to put a shirt on. We had to catch you just to get some underwear up over your little brown bottom." He reached to adjust his glasses. His hands were pale, sun-spotted, older than I remembered.

"So you remember Racquel? She's an artist, too," I said. "Sculptor."

"When we moved to the States, you didn't change a bit. Still shirtless when it was fifty degrees out. Liked to worry your mother to death."

"Guam is part of the States, Dad," I said.

"Territory. A territory, my dear."

When he met my mother, he was a pilot, stationed in Yigo.

Racquel and I met at the high school where I taught. She was a visiting artist giving a lecture during senior convocation. Things happened in the usual way. Eyes, smiles, numbers exchanged.

It caused a stir. My father vowed to disown me. *No daughter of his,* etc., etc. He's getting old, though, so he has no choice but to let me come creeping back in. Who will take care of him if he doesn't? My mother left him long ago, moved to the next state over.

Their meeting was military related, of course. (Right after they ask *Where're you from?* what comes next is *Father in the military?* Air Force. *Thought so. He's white, then?*) My mother's from Hagåtña. They call it Agana now, the *a*'s flat as dollar bills.

Once, at the car dealership near my father's house, the salesman looked at me while going over the papers I was to sign and said, *Hawaiian?* When I raised an eyebrow, he said, *Just looks like you got a little somethin' in you, is all I meant.* I wished Racquel were there. She is never shamed into silence.

The flag of Guam, U.S.A., boasts as its emblem the shape of a slingstone, an ancient weapon. Racquel has become interested in carving them out of limestone.

"How much do you think they should weigh?" she said.

"More than a fist," I said. "Less than a coconut."

When she is done, they will sit in a gallery window somewhere, or on a pedestal. The transparent label nearby will read, *Chamorro Slingstones.* Someone will buy them, put them on a fireplace mantel, and point them out to guests at a dinner party.

My father does not want me to move. It is out of love, I say, but he won't hear it. What do I know of love, he asks.

I love Racquel more than is necessary. Enough is sufficient, but I know I have given myself up to her. Mornings, we sit across a tiny card table and drink coffee with too much cream and talk about who we are.

"Artista types," Racquel is fond of saying.

"We're just girls who make stuff," I say.

We laugh and reheat our half-filled cups in the microwave. Racquel has a way of saying, *Uh huh* with her hips. Side to side, *Uh huh.* My father met her once, under the pretense of *friend.* He gets it. He just doesn't get that I get it, too.

"Remember taking those standardized tests?" I say, our coffee steaming again.

"Uh huh," says Racquel.

"Were you an 'Other'?"

I remember exactly how it looked. Faint green print, the color of bleached seaweed, the paper stained pink and brown with cheap eraser.

Caucasian? No.

Black? No.

Hispanic? No.

Asian?

. . .

Asian?

. . .

No.

American Indian? No.

Other? A heavy, dark mark.

"I always lied," she says. "Tell them what they want to believe. White."

After administering the last round of end-of-grade tests, I was "let go" from the high school where I taught. Technically, I resigned, but there was pressure. My relationship with Racquel. Racquel reminded me this is North Carolina, not California. One out of three trucks here boast rebel flag bumper stickers, or in some cases, actual rebel flags. I reminded her that it doesn't matter where we are. We will never be what we are not. At least at the beach, there's the constancy of the waves.

I wanted to stand up on that last day, in front of my students, to tell them the reason I was leaving. In the end, I could not form the words. I am guilty of that, I know. Making jewelry is my penance. If I make enough, it will fill a gap, plug up that void created out of shame.

In our small apartment at the beach, Racquel and I collect postcards. Most of them are reprints of works of art—sculptures, paintings, photographs. We find them in gift shops and galleries and tack them to the ceiling above our bed. I like to write on the backs of the ones I buy, short little notes to Racquel that she will find someday when we move again.

My favorite is the one I found in a random craft store down by the Inter-coastal. The caption in the upper left corner on the back reads: *Michael Heizer's Double Negative. This notable earthwork is a sculpture created on the eastern edge of the Mormon Mesa, northwest of Overton, Nevada, 1969.*

On the front is an aerial photograph of the work, which spans a quarter of a mile. From above, a framed patch of red mesa. The mesa is a face—her open mouth a deep, gaping hole created by landslide and erosion, her lower jaw missing. It has been this way for thousands of years. What is new is the trench, carved in a continuous line across one side of her remaining upper lip to the other, spanning the gulf of her mouth, the work of bulldozers and heavy machinery.

It is shocking and violent. It is beautiful, too. Simple and absurd. I turn the postcard over and scrawl my message, in runny, blue ink. *Racquel. We are trenches, speaking to each other across this gap.*

Who digs trenches in a desert? Who takes away what is there and calls the nothingness *something*?

In Racquel's studio, a perfect slingstone sits amid a small pile of chiseled debris. It fits perfectly in the cupped palm of my hand. I will string them on a giant coconut-fiber necklace when Racquel is done. It will take thirty, maybe forty of them to inscribe the history of Guåhan I will write into their polished skin. I will start from the beginning, before time.

From *I Dos Amantes*

Baltazar Aguon (Guåhan)

Editors' note: In I Dos Amantes, *Baltazar Aguon develops one of the best known of Guåhan's legends, that of Puntan Dos Amantes (Two Lovers Point). The original legend characteristically has few details about the actors, their motives, or the times they lived in. Aguon imagines these details in as he conjures the forces that might have driven each of the actors to their tragic end.*

They sat at the long ifit-wood table, Sirena on the left and Isa on the right of Antonio. Breaking the silence, Antonio cleared his throat, smiled, then spoke.

"I spoke with Captain Quiroga today. He is very taken with you, Isa." Antonio grinned, growing giddy with the thought of the financial well-being of his family and the secured future of the daughter he loved.

"He has asked for your hand in marriage. He says he will take good care of you." He finished chewing his food, threw his napkin on the table, and then grinned. "In Spain," he said. "The marriage will take place in Madrid upon your arrival."

Isa's heart sank; her face contorted in anguish.

Although outwardly calm—something she had acquired in their marriage—Sirena's heart raced with anger. She could not believe he would act so quickly without first asking Isa. What was wrong with him?

"You told him yes?"

"Of course!" he said, surprised. "There is no finer man around! And I thought this would make you happy too, Sirena." He looked at her hard face and frowned. "Quiroga is an honorable man. This union will bring prestige to our family. Think of it. Isa will live in Spain, learn the ways of our people, and be among the best of families!"

He took in Sirena's twisted face and Isa's blank stare, and then sighed.

"I gave him my blessing," he said decidedly. "Tomorrow, Isa, you will be on your way to Spain to marry the esteemed Captain Quiroga."

Isa began to tremble, and sweat began to bead on her forehead. She sat silent, lost in a vertigo of emotion and growing despair. She felt as if she were

Previously published, Baltazar Aguon, *I Dos Amantes* (self-pub., 2005).

being sucked into darkness, with no hope of ever again seeing light. All her strength left her as her mind became numb with horror. Tears began to well in her eyes.

"No, never . . ." Isa whispered, slowly shaking her head. "You can't make me go."

Antonio grabbed his daughter's delicate hands, thinking of the happiness she would find in Spain. "You will thank me for this later, Isa. It's for your own good. The Captain is from a noble family in Galicia. Every privilege will be afforded to you, my daughter. There are so many marvels beyond these isles, Isa! A new world awaits you!" He took a deep breath to calm himself and refocus his thoughts. "Most important, you will be loved and committed to an honorable man, a respected captain in the service of the king. You will be happy, my daughter."

Isa looked at her mother and began to cry, and with every intake of breath her anger and despair grew until no words could come. She wanted to scream and call the captain a murderer. How could her father give her to the man who spills the blood of Guåhan's people!

Sirena's anger grew until rage overtook her. "I cannot let this happen," she said to herself, her body trembling as her blood rushed wildly to her head. She could no longer contain herself, and for the first time, she let her anger take its course. She stood and pounded her fists on the table.

"This all for *your* good," she yelled. "You think only of yourself!"

Surprised, her husband rose and tried to strike her, but swiftly, adrenaline coursing through her veins, she shoved him back into his chair with an unnatural force. He sank, stunned, onto the hardwood chair, his face contorted in anger, his pride trampled and his machismo threatened.

"For too long," she continued, "I have said nothing. And for too long, I have tolerated your arrogant belittling of my people. But I will never let you do this to Isa! I will not let you give her to a stranger she does not love! That is what my father did to me."

She looked deeper into his eyes. "There is no union if there is no love. Only bondage."

A stunned silence crept into the room. Antonio stared at his wife, numb with disbelief that she would defy him this way, that she could stand over him like he was a little child in need of scolding! It dawned on him that she held no love for him whatsoever. Despite all he did for her and their daughter, his wife believed that he was the enemy!

Antonio snapped, and a blind rage took over. He did not hear his daughter crying, or see the mother of his child standing before him. He jumped to his feet yelling, grabbed Sirena by her hair, and threw her hard against the wall.

A momentary dizziness overtook her, and she swayed a little, but did not fall. With the hope of her daughter's happiness urging her on, and the years of misery and bitterness fueling the fire, she charged and tackled Antonio onto the dining table, knocking the white dishes and beautiful hand-blown glasses to the floor.

Isa screamed hysterically, begging them to stop. She came between them, but Antonio easily shoved her aside and the fight continued. He swung wildly at his wife, not caring where he hit, as long as he hit some part of her. Sirena, on the other hand, dodged many of his punches and landed solid blows of her own with heavy, clenched fists.

On Antonio's last attempt to injure her, he fell exhausted to the floor, gasping for air. He thought he saw that being of light he had seen earlier, wavering before his eyes, grinning. He fiercely blinked the image away.

Breathing heavily, her face set in grim determination, Sirena towered over him and spoke defiantly: "Isa stays."

He looked up at her, and she turned away to begin cleaning the food off the floor, furniture, and walls. Isa sat huddled in a corner, covering her face with her hands, rocking and crying softly. Sirena started towards her, her heart filled with sadness that her child had had to witness such hostility between the two people who had brought her into this world.

She saw Isa look up and scream.

Antonio slammed the solid wood chair against the back of Sirena's head. She reeled to the floor and saw only darkness.

From *An Ocean in a Cup*

Stephen Tenorio Jr. (Guåhan)

Editors' note: The novel, set in Spanish-controlled Guåhan during the late 1800s, follows Tomas, a young Chamorro, as he travels across the island with his cart and carabao to deliver his cart of goods to the capitol. A mysterious darkness plagues him as do elusive memories as he makes his way across the island's landscape. The story explores life as it might have been for the Chamorro living in Guahan at the turn of the century, including the shifting beliefs and world views precipitated by colonialism, voyages and voyagers, and increasing international exchanges.

Chapter 2

Wearily getting up from the ground, Tomas exited the boonies and continued onward to deliver the contents in his cart. While transporting the supply of salted, dried venison and fish, Tomas noticed a limp figure in the distance.

The blurry figure seemed to be staggering along the bottom of the cliff that merged into an area not too far from the road he had chosen. Tomas found it eerie and was uncertain whether the moving figure was human. As he got closer, he saw that the thin shadow was a *bihu*[1] in distress at the bottom of the cliff.

Grabbing the rings lodged into the nose of the *karabao*, Tomas led the beast down and brought him to a complete halt. In a snap, Tomas sprinted across the low felt of grass that dissipated into sand. He tossed his sandals and charged into the damp areas along the cliff base.

Twice, Tomas slipped on the rocks and the sharpness of the earth tore into his ankles. Pain seared as blood seeped out, but adrenaline pushed him forward. Cursing, he bit his lip as the tide washed across his feet and body, trying to drag him out to the big open.

When Tomas slipped the third time and a small rock scathed his elbow, he decided to just jump in. As he dove into the shallow blue waters, the frigidity of

---

Previously published, Stephen Tenorio, *An Ocean in a Cup* (self-pub., 2011).

1. elderly man

the water clutched him tightly and, as he broke for air, he yelled, shocked by the intensity of the cold water. Tomas was silenced again as the salty blue dragged him out.

The big open muffled any attempt Tomas made to call out for help or to communicate with the staggering *bihu*. Relentlessly, it pressed Tomas with its massiveness, wrangling and pinning him to the floor.

Towed back underneath, Tomas held fast to a coral to keep himself from being dragged out to the deep. Quickly, Tomas came up for air as the next wave passed over him and then immediately dove back down and held on to a groove in the seafloor.

Tomas moved beneath the water surface by moving from rock to rock, and with each pull he could feel the force of the tide as it tried to drag him out. His body had grown numb in the cold water but still, he made his way through the big open.

Bringing his head slightly above the water and with his foot hooked onto a piece of driftwood wedged into the reef, Tomas's eyes were burning in their sockets. The saltwater was proving too much for him as he tried to keep his eyes open each time he dove underwater. Still, Tomas looked for the old man. Finally spotting him not too far off, he dove underwater and crawled across the cold bed like an octopus.

Rising from the water again, Tomas gasped for breath and tried to determine what to do next. The *bihu* was oblivious to Tomas's presence.

"Can you hear me?" Tomas yelled in Chamorro, his native tongue, then Spanish, but the *bihu* did not respond. Tomas tried calling out to him in Filipino and broken German. Still, no response. The *bihu* remained unmoved, grasping the rocks.

Now soaked and acclimated to the water, Tomas submerged part of his body to escape the frigid air. As the sun rose, a crevice along the cliff, near the *bihu*, became visible. Not far from the opening of the crevice, the *bihu* stared out over the big open, oblivious to the crevice into which he could safely crawl.

Tomas threw a small rock to get his attention. His aim was precise but still, after hitting the *bihu* on the arm, the response was the same—none. Sitting in the calmer part of the water behind a large rock, Tomas started wondering why the *bihu* did not go into the crevice to seek its sanctuary.

The young man watched the big open like a large cat reach with its waves and scratch wildly against the earth. From his safe place, Tomas gazed upon the true titan, the unimaginable force of the blue waters that stretched out to countries unseen, unknown. And, at the bottom of the cliff, it purred at the old man. Then, it became apparent. The *bihu* was paralyzed with deathly fear.

Ai bihu, I cannot speak the language of fear, Tomas thought.

As the sky brightened, the treacherous sea started to withdraw. A calm seeped into the tempest and the Pacific was gradually pacified.

Tomas moved toward the crevice and with the naked light coming off the horizon, he could feel its warmth on his shoulders and neck. Looking at his fingers, he noticed how they had pruned and the salt from his eyelids dropped onto his tongue.

Then, the rain fell. Tomas stopped for a moment, opened his mouth toward the sky to quench his thirst for purer water, and moved to the weather-beaten man. Tomas felt sympathetic toward the *bihu*, this poor soul suffering the consequence of angering nature. For people like Tomas, on a Catholicized island where ancient beliefs and Western religion coexisted, the big open and God were one, so angering God would eventually awaken the wrath of the big open.

For a short while, Tomas sat quietly trying to dislodge a small shell that had cut into his foot. He examined his other cuts and noticed the bleeding had stopped but the cuts were lined with bright red flesh. Tomas drank what little drops fell from the sky, licking his salty lip, and brushing the hair from his face as it soaked up the warmer waters falling.

The *bihu* watched Tomas awkwardly. Tomas stared back unmoved; instead, he shook his head, drank more rain, waited for his nerves to settle, and spat on the ground. Then, he summoned what energy he had left and walked toward the *bihu*.

Beaten, the old man lay a few feet from Tomas. He was flattened on the ground, with his fingers locked into the cracks of the limestone as though the world might fall away.

When Tomas grabbed him by the wrist, the *bihu* resisted his aid. The sudden wailing from the *bihu* surprised Tomas, forcing him backward and causing him to trip. Without thought, Tomas recovered, stepped forward, and landed a closed fist on the bridge of the *bihu's* nose.

Unconscious, the old man went limp and Tomas hoisted him onto his shoulder like a dead *binadu*.[2] He faltered under the weight but rose quickly and carried the terrified, wrinkled man into the crevice.

Chapter 3

"*Gua—I—*Juan," the *bihu* struggled to introduce himself when he came to.

"Juan," Tomas repeated.

Juan continued to shudder with fear as Tomas sat against the opening of the crevice, listening to the ill-fated story of how the old man had come to befall the tragedy he endured.

The old man described how he was fishing with a friend along the reef when they were attacked by a monstrous creature that moved with the stealth and speed of a shark. His voice trembled while he tried to recount the events; then, the storyteller was lost in memory.

"Too much blood," Juan cried, trailing off. The old man tried to explain the attack that killed his fishing partner. He had accompanied him the night prior

---

2. Philippine deer, introduced by the Spanish sometime in the late 1700s

and they were setting up the *chenchulu*[3] in the waist-deep water. As he continued, Tomas learned that Juan's fishing partner was also engaged to wed his only daughter. He started crying about the death of his friend and it was difficult for Tomas to follow what had happened through the sobs that shook Juan uncontrollably.

In Juan's memory, the colors remained vivid. He talked about a pool of blood circled by a thin film of purplish bubbles. In the haze of his fright, the blood was dark red until the blue waters swallowed it all up along with the body and the creature that had attacked them. All sense of hope had vanished with the dissipating blood, spread out across the water's surface, thinning into the mystery of the big open.

"When I saw more blood, the less hope I had he was still alive," Juan said.

"It was inside the reef by the land?" Tomas asked in Chamorro, not realizing that Juan was speaking in broken Spanish.

"Yes," the old man responded in Chamorro. "I thought you were a Spaniard."

"There is Chamorro here," Tomas replied, patting the left side of his face, "and a little Spanish here," exposing the scar on his right cheek as he patted it just the same.

"*Mestisu?*"[4] the *bihu* asked.

"As mixed as everyone else on the island," Tomas replied.

"Oh, you are Tomas. The gifted one," Juan said after examining Tomas's face. "I know your grandfather and grandmother. I'm from the south, like your grandparents."

Tomas struggled to make sense of the man's story and, ignoring his remark, asked, "Are you sure it is in the beach water?" He reasoned that it must have come in during high tide with the typhoon several days ago and was too large to get back out over the reef. Eventually, the high tide would allow it a chance to swim over the reef. For now, it seemed, to Tomas, the reef was the barrier preventing the monster from swimming back out to the deeper parts of the big open.

It must be very big, Tomas thought, but fishermen were known to exaggerate so Tomas was skeptical of Juan's assessment of the size of this creature.

"Yes," Juan wept again quietly.

"The tide is getting low. You should tell people. It's probably trapped in the beach water," Tomas said as he readied to leave Juan to his courage and wits in the crevice. "This is not good," he told Juan before leaving and the old man agreed.

Before Tomas left, he reassured the old man that the tide was subsiding and that walking out of the cave and onto the shore would be as easy as walking on dry land.

As Tomas walked away, he saw a long scar that followed along the old man's hip and curved around his waist. The outline of the scar reminded Tomas of a design he had seen on the edge of a doublet.

---

3. long fishing net
4. mixed heritage

He had been assisting a foreign delegation of Chinese merchants that made their way through the remote islands of the Pacific and was charged with cleaning a ported ship. The doublet he had seen was a gift to the last Spanish governor of the island from an Asian delegate who found it in a collection of European items in Southeast Asia. When the Chinese delegate arrived on the *Maria del Rosario*, a mailing ship sailing from the Philippines, Tomas was ordered to guard the doublet and other treasures as they sat on deck, waiting to be transported off the ship.

Tomas was fascinated with the stitching and craftsmanship of the doublet. For two days while he guarded the garment and the other boxes of intrigue, Tomas studied the sophisticated labor that must have gone into such fine and detailed tailoring. He guessed it was worn for battle or for places where it was colder than the islands. Tomas never found out what value Europeans placed on doublets, but having never seen one, he found it to be a beautiful piece of work, the edges outlined with thin sheets of shiny metal, etched with silver ocean waves and creatures with horse heads with fish bodies.

The image of the doublet left a lasting impression on Tomas's memory. He had never seen anything done with such intricacy and his appreciation of the workmanship made him realize just how little he knew about the world and the capabilities of man. When he saw Juan's scar, the doublet was immediately called to mind because of the familiar outline. Juan's scar looked eerily similar to the silver plated waves that came sharply down the doublet's edges.

Juan noticed Tomas studying him and, with failing strength, pulled his trousers higher to shield the scar that circled his waist. Tomas looked at Juan as he left and felt the old man's embarrassment, like a young woman caught partially undressed.

An Ode to Our Unsung Heroes

Frederick B. Quinene (Guåhan)

Our peaceful island, this dear land,
was greatly shattered from her calm.
December eight of forty-one
Japan that date dropped bombs on Guam.

One hundred twenty men was all
That were recruited for the fight.
The Guards didn't flinch;
Though hardly trained,
The gallant Guards, they did unite.

It is right that we remember,
After all these many years,
That for two days they stood ready,
To give Guam their blood, sweat and tears.

All they had were three machine guns,
And other guns that were so old,
But our Guam Insular Force Guards—
They were so brave, and oh so bold.

From Aporguan they did come,
The Japanese who came to war.
They came in hundreds, and much more,
Sometime after the midnight star.

With hundreds of the enemies,
The Guards acted with great valor.
Against great odds they'd stayed to fight.
Though ordinary and untrained,
They grew immortal on that night.

The defenders, with their old guns,
Fired at the hundreds; they didn't run.

They didn't stop though death hung heavy,
Until each Guard jammed his gun.

By then, Governor McMillin
Told the Guards they must fall back,
For there were just too many of the foe,
And good weapons they sorely lacked.

So even though the fight was short,
And it ended in surrender,
We all must praise, and show the world,
Our Guards' greatness and their splendor.

For love of country and our land,
Our Guards were willing to shed their blood.
It's time we thank our living heroes,
And those who've gone to our God.

Who would run over them roughshod?
Guam's own Guards, brave of heart,
Stood to fight and shed their blood.

From *An Island in Agony*

Tony Palomo (Guåhan)

Editors' note: An Island in Agony *documents the events of World War II through the eyes of those Chamorro who survived. Palomo brings his own experiences to bear on the telling, but the force of his book comes from the other stories he tells as well. The narratives begin with the invasion of Guåhan by the Japanese on the same day that Pearl Harbor was bombed. It recounts the harrowing experiences of survivors from various locations on the island as they engage in survival and tactical activities attempting to raise food for their families, hiding radios and American servicemen, or escaping capture and surviving execution.*

"Monday Ladies"

As early as a month after capturing Guam, the Japanese brought in women of "ill-fame" for the troops. Five homes were selected to house the women: three in Agana; one in Anigua, about a mile west of the center of the city; and one in Sasa, a farming area near Piti. Forty-five women were brought from Japan, most of them Koreans, generally known as Chosens. About 15 local "Monday ladies" were recruited—most of them by Shinohara. The Korean and Chamorro women serviced the troops; the more refined Japanese geishas served the military and civilian officers and were housed in Anigua. The local girls were housed in Sasa, on the upper floor of a two-story building owned by Pedro Martinez.

The "Monday ladies" were hired from a list of known prostitutes kept by the local police. Why Monday ladies? Because these women were required by American medical authorities to undergo physical examinations every Monday.

The houses of ill-fame were so well organized that a soldier entering such a place was immediately confronted with a large board nailed to a wall in which full instructions were given, including the mandatory use of prophylactics (usually manufactured from rubber obtained from Indonesia—better for its strength) and a time limit (not more than 15 minutes). Each young lady was expected to service from ten to fifteen men per day.

Previously published, Tony Palomo (self-pub., 1984).

When an elderly local woman heard about the "evil" system, she complained to a high Japanese official, who explained, "You are being a hypocrite, my dear woman. Would you rather that our soldiers rape your women, or for us to bring our own women?"

When Bishop Olano heard about the women, he was heard to say, "Only God can determine what shall be."

Fray Jesus was less compromising: "God must have left Guam. In His place are the Japanese."

Shinohara had suggested that local women be recruited for domestic service, but Captain-Governor Hayashi vetoed the idea, explaining that the Japanese had their own women.

By the middle of 1942, a number of local women were living with Japanese officers, including the governor and the chief of police. These were generally the same women who hobnobbed with American officials before the outbreak of the war.

When the wife of an American prisoner of war complained that a certain woman was lowering herself by living with a *taicho* (Japanese officer) and was thus no better than a prostitute, the accused responded, "Why is it that when a woman has an affair with a Japanese, she is lowering herself, but when she has an affair with a Chamorro or an American, she isn't? When God proclaimed the Ten Commandments and demanded that 'Thou shalt not commit adultery,' He did not say that any adultery would be sinful only if one of the parties is a Japanese."

She pointed out that several Chamorro women had married Japanese men prior to the war and no one felt their status was lessened. "The Japanese are winning the war," the woman pointed out. "So, how can you say they are lower than other men?" She added that she had had affairs with Americans before the conflict, and should the Americans return, she'd again have affairs with them. "How do you define a prostitute during wartime, anyway?" she asked.

Hidden Radios

Shortly after the Japanese captured the island, they ordered all radios turned in to their Agana headquarters. If any radios were found after a certain deadline, their owners would be severely punished. When, finally, all radios throughout the villages had presumably been turned in and things had settled down, word got around among a few Guamanians that Joe Gutierrez of Agana Heights was looking for a radio. It happened that young Joe Pangelinan Cruz had retained his radio and hidden it in the bush. So one day, Cruz and a friend, Jose Artero, arranged a meeting with Gutierrez. They told Gutierrez they had hidden the radio under a church sanctuary in Agana Heights, across from Mrs. Ignacio Butler's store. Mrs. Butler was the wife of an American civilian internee. Cruz told Gutierrez that if he wanted the radio, he would have to pick it up himself.

So at about seven o'clock one evening, while the area was deserted, Gutierrez and his brother Agusto picked up the radio and hid it in the bushes near a golf course in Apugan.

When Joe Gutierrez's wife, Florence, heard about these goings-on she became worried and tried to persuade her husband not to touch the radio. But

Gutierrez explained to her that his morale would break if he lost contact with the outside world. Now that the radio was his, he could not abandon it.

Together with Gutierrez in this venture were his brother Agusto, Frank T. Flores, and Atanacio Blas. Pete Peredo was also a member of the radio group during the first few weeks but later left the group when his family moved to their ranch in Toto, some five miles away. It was Peredo who found an outlet for the radio at the aerological station at Fort Apugan, near the cliff overlooking Agana. It was an electric radio, a Silvertone, which meant it had to be plugged into a power outlet. And since power was not turned on until five o'clock every evening, the radio could only be operated after sunset.

During the first month, while the four men crouched over the radio at Fort Apugan, Peredo stood guard high in a coconut tree.

The men tuned in regularly each evening to a news broadcast from the Fairmont Hotel Studio in San Francisco. William Winters was the commentator. They kept that radio going on throughout most of the war until the American bombardment of Saipan, at which point they knew that liberation was coming. Some of their friends came occasionally to listen to the news. They included Adolfo Sgambelluri, Mrs. Butler, Ralph Pellicani, Carlos Bordallo, John Roberto, Agueda Roberto, Mrs. G. Brunton, Manuel F. L. Guerrero, James Butler, Joe Torres, and Herbert Johnston. Some came frequently, while others just once or twice at the start of the Japanese occupation.

But there was always a problem with radio parts. The Japanese had ordered that all radios and parts of radios be confiscated. And before the invaders seized radio parts from Mrs. Butler's store, Joe Gutierrez and Frank Flores purchased parts for the Silvertone, including a tube tester.

Hidden among the damp bushes at Fort Apugan, the radio clinked out. Rats, attracted to the warmth generated inside the Silvertone cabinet, set up house and built themselves a nest. It happened, however, that Joe Damian, who had been imprisoned by the Japanese on suspicion of operating a radio, had just been released. Damian was a jack-of-all-trades. So Gutierrez carried the silent radio in a gunny sack to Damian's house. But first, for persuasive power, Gutierrez bought him a jigger of aggie—fermented tuba. Damian was working at the Island Industrial Store. He was naturally reluctant to have anything more to do with radios. One month in jail was nothing to forget in a hurry. Gutierrez offered him a second jigger of aggie and then, when the world seemed a little rosier, Damian forgot his fears and agreed to repair the old Silvertone.

Constant patrols and search parties began to render Fort Apugan a risky place to operate a radio. So, after a few weeks, they moved it to a location near Mrs. Brunton's house, about 300 yards away from the cliff area. They plugged a long extension cord to the top of a telephone pole and hid the Silvertone in the bushes. On several occasions, they operated the radio underneath Mrs. Brunton's house, and on one of these occasions, a Japanese named Morita came to visit Mrs. Brunton, who also was the wife of an American internee. Some of the news enthusiasts in the basement ran for cover. The others simply lowered the volume and placed their ears closer to the speaker.

From time to time, the radio had to be moved to new locations. Once, when it broke down, the men carried the radio into Juan Roberto's kitchen nearby to be repaired. It just so happened that a grass fire had been burning in the nearby hills. Japanese officials were making house-to-house calls, demanding to know who had started the fire. Joe Gutierrez, Flores, and Blas were in the kitchen working on the radio when Agusto Gutierrez rushed in and warned them that a group of Japanese investigators were approaching the house. Joe Gutierrez and Flores hurried outside into the yard, sat on a bank, and pretended to be busy knotting cattle ropes.

Blas, in the midst of heating the soldering iron, and with bits and pieces of the Silvertone strewn all around him, placed his hand on a .45-caliber pistol and did some quick thinking. It was too late to hide the dismembered radio. He quickly left the kitchen and confronted the Japanese visitors in the yard. There he kept them talking. Satisfied that all was well, the Japanese party finally left, and Blas returned to his job of repairing the radio.

Juan Santos and his family lived next door to the Robertos. One day, his eight-year-old son discovered the Silvertone hidden under a large dogdog tree, a member of the breadfruit family. The young boy ran and reported his find to his father. Santos, who had not known the goings-on next door, told his son not to touch the radio and not to tell a soul because everybody, including himself, might be punished. Santos then confronted Gutierrez and Flores and protested their hiding the radio on his property. So, once again, the old Silvertone had to be removed to another area.

As time went on, things got a little too hot, and it seemed that the Japanese were on their trail. Gutierrez then decided to take the radio to a new hiding place at Fonte Valley, about two miles further inland. Adolfo Sgambelluri, a police officer, had kept in close touch with Gutierrez and had passed on information about where the investigating party would hit next. In the event that Gutierrez might one day be accused of operating a radio, he had established a neatly planned alibi. At the time that radios were first confiscated, he had smashed an old one and buried it in a coral pit. If the Japanese accused him of not having surrendered his radio, he would take them to the coral pit and show them the remains, which would appear to have been buried for many months.

Once, when Gutierrez was transporting the radio along a sidewalk leading to Mrs. Brunton's house, he was stopped on the street by a Japanese police officer. The Japanese looked curiously at Joe's load of goods. A small crate he was carrying contained a mixture of vegetables, bananas, live chickens, and, of course, the radio. After a brief and casual inspection, the Japanese took some bananas and walked on.

There were other times when even Gutierrez's instincts warned him to leave the radio alone. Once, when he realized that a search party was approaching the Roberto house, he hastily suspended the radio on a wire above the cesspool—just in time.

Throughout the war, Atanacio Blas carried with him, folded in his pocket, a tiny map of the Pacific islands taken from a Pacific Islands Yearbook. The men would spread the map before them as they followed the news. This way they were able to follow in detail the progress the Americans made from island to island across the Pacific. They were able to follow each major historical event of the war. They listened to commentaries on the Battle of the Coral Sea, the Bismarck Archipelago, and Guadalcanal. They followed the battles in Africa, Algiers, and Tunisia. They heard the broadcast of President Roosevelt from Casablanca, the conference in Honolulu in 1943, and the Yalta Conference.

They were overjoyed to hear that the USS *Guam*, a heavy cruiser, was christened by the wife of Governor McMillin. They learned about the American submarine that, while maneuvering off Japan, sneaked into Yokohama and sank a ship that had just been launched from the dockyards.

To Frank D. Perez, a young businessman-farmer, listening to the weekly news roundup through his Philco and Hallicrafter radio sets was a daring and lonely activity. And he eventually paid dearly for operating the radio receivers under the noses of the Japanese. The Perezes' two-story home was located in the district of Padre Palomo, directly across the street from Padre Palomo Elementary school, where young local children were taught by Japanese instructors.

The 26-year-old Perez hid the radio sets in a small opening above the ceiling in the living room. About once a week, the business-farmer would pull out one of the sets and operate it in the living room. After listening to the progress of the war, as reported by Bob Goodman and Merrill Phillips of station KGEI in San Francisco, Frank would write his own Dare-Devil News and surreptitiously distribute copies to a few close friends, including Pedro M. Ada, Father Duenas, and E. T. Calvo. Ada was a Saipanese-born businessman and Calvo was a businessman and a member of the prewar House of Assembly.

Perez initially permitted Calvo and Father Duenas to listen to the news—usually at about sundown—but because they were too nervous, Perez decided to listen alone and report the news later to his comrades.

To avoid suspicion, whenever he was ready to operate the radio, Perez would make certain the windows and doors of the house were left open. But he also made certain that the gate chain leading to the front door was locked. To enter the Perezes' living room, a person had to open the gate and then walk up two flights of stairs.

From time to time, the Japanese school principal (*senshi*) would walk across the street and visit Frank, who, in turn, was always prepared for these visits. Invariably, Perez would greet the Japanese, offering him a glass of Canadian Club whiskey, obtained from Mrs. Dejima through Tommy Tanaka for five dollars' worth of gold. There usually was a hot meal waiting for the senshi. And, by the time the Japanese left the Perez home, he would be in a good mood, ignorant of the fact that within the confines of the living room were two sets of active radio receivers.

On occasions when Perez had to hide a radio set quickly, he would simply dump the set in a box under a table in the living room, and if there were copies of the Dare-Devil News around, he would slide them into the pages of a thick geography book.

Eventually, someone informed on Perez and the Japanese went after him, but not before he hid the radio sets amidst a basket full of fruits and vegetables and biked his way to the Perez ranch at Oka, about three miles east of Agana.

Perez was forewarned by Adolfo Sgambelluri, who told him that Japanese investigators, accompanied by Saipanese assistants, would seek him out and demand surrender of the radios.

Upon reaching his ranch, Perez boiled salted water in a large cauldron and then dumped the radio sets into the boiling liquid. After a few hours, Perez pulled the two sets and placed them at the bottom of a 50-gallon drum. By this time, the radio sets had the appearance of having been destroyed a long time ago.

When the Japanese arrived at the ranch, Martin Borja, a Saipanese, pulled out a pistol, stuck it against Perez's forehead, and demanded to know the whereabouts of the radio sets. Frank took them to the drum.

When asked why he had not turned in the radio sets immediately after orders were issued for all persons possessing radio sets to surrender them, Perez told them the radio sets were inoperable and he had felt it was unnecessary to turn them in. He explained further that he had planned to repair them when the Japanese conquered the United States.

Perez was taken to Agana, where he was placed in closed confinement at the Agana jail. He was brutalized several times, including the flushing of water into his nose and mouth.

When Frank's mother came to the jailhouse to give him a floor mat, she was met by Henry Pangelinan, another Saipanese interpreter, who told her, "Never come back again. If you do, we'll put you in jail, too."

Before this incident, Pangelinan was a frequent visitor to the Perez home, and was always treated to a warm meal.

As a young man, Perez wanted to become an engineer. Upon graduation from the local high school in 1933, he applied to and was accepted by the University of California at Davis. Through sheer hard work, both at the Bureau of Yards and Docks and at the family farm, young Frank was able to save about $5,000, and had, in fact, paid in advance his college expenses for five years at $328 per year.

A complete college wardrobe had already been purchased for Frank by Commander Carl C. Seabury from the officer's own tailor in Shanghai.

Frank's hopes for an engineering career, however, were dashed when his mother, who was then expecting to give birth, objected to his leaving the island. The infant, a boy, died soon after birth.

Commander Seabury, Frank's boss at the Bureau of Yards and Docks, wanted Perez to succeed in life, but preferably as a Navy yeoman under his command. The officer went so far as to have Frank undergo a complete medical examination and made a promise to Perez that he would not be relegated to the lowly role of mess attendant.

With the chance to obtain a college education denied him, Perez decided to resign from his government job and devote all his time to farming. Within a few years he was exporting extra-large eggs to Wake, Midway, and Canton islands and avocadoes to the Philippines.

When war broke out, Perez had 79,000 hills of sweet potatoes and 150 acres of corn at Tijan, Barrigada, among the best agricultural areas in the island. While he loved America dearly—he called it an earthly paradise—Perez was critical of some of the naval personnel and their attitude towards the Chamorros. "One naval chaplain maintained that the local people did not need an education. As long as they [knew] how to say yes or no and sign their names, [that was] enough," Perez recalled. "The schools were segregated and the American school in Agana had a six-foot fence around it. Any time an American attempted to socialize with the local people, he was ostracized," Perez added.

Another group of daring men and women were operating still another radio at another part of Agana, in the district of Togue, about 200 yards southwest of the Governor's Palace, along the base of the cliff separating the city from Apugan.

The radio, a Sky Champion Hallicrafter, was owned by Jose (Ping) Ada, who was born in Saipan but came to Guam with his family as a young man. Among original listeners were Bishop Olano, Fray Jesus, Father Duenas, Juan Cruz, Ben Palomo, and Chong Torres, whose second-floor quarters in Togue were the radio receiving center for war news.

As time went on, however, the Japanese intensified their search for unreported radio sets and the group had to move the radio from place to place. For a while, the radio was operated from the home of Pedro M. Ada, who was commissioner of San Antonio during the Japanese occupation, and eventually, the radio was lodged inside a wall compartment on the second floor of the residence and store of Luis P. Untalan in San Antonio.

From time to time, the radio would be taken from the wall compartment and brought to the first-floor kitchen, where Ping, his brother, Herman, and Adolfo Sgambelluri would listen to the news emanating from San Francisco. After Herman Ada finished taking notes, the radio would be returned to the wall compartment.

And to avoid suspicion, Sgambelluri would invite his Saipanese colleagues at the police department for drinks at the Untalan home. Among the Saipanese investigators were Juan (Buko) Castro and Jose Villagomez, the highest ranked among about fifty Saipanese investigators and interpreters sent to Guam by the Japanese.

Just prior to the end of 1943, the Japanese got hold of an alleged news report, and Sgambelluri and the Adas had to work fast to get rid of the radio. It was then decided to dismantle the set and bury the parts in the backyard of Herman Ada's home in Agana, after immersing the parts in salted water.

When Jose Villagomez confronted Ping Ada with a list of persons who were suspected of operating a radio and threatened to smash his head with a baseball bat, Ping took the Saipanese to Herman's backyard and pointed to the area where the radio parts were buried. The bits and pieces were by then already rusty.

"You and your friends are lucky that Chamorros were assigned to handle this case," Villagomez told Ada. "Had we been Japanese investigators, you all would be executed."

A New Invasion

Clarissa Mendiola (Guåhan)

They call me Monday
Lady,[1] all rosewater
And red lipstick.

Contrast
of that
hue lathered thick
on brown skin!

Red, that
Red I love.

Come to me, call out
"Comfort Woman!"
or perhaps *"Comfort,*
woman!"

25 ¥ and I will be
an imperial
conquest. Your
small victory—

Tiny,
contained,

explosion.

---

1. A prewar term used to refer to prostitutes who worked for the few clubs on Guam before WWII. They gained the name "Monday Ladies" because of the Naval requirement that they get a physical examination every Monday at the local clinic.

Pin falling bedside,
apparatus
between us.

Refracted light off
ruby lipped curve

25 ¥ or
American $

equivalent,
please—

reconcile
the balance
of things.

From *Mariquita: A Tragedy of Guam*

Chris Perez Howard (Guåhan)

Editors' note: *The novel is set in Guåhan during the 1930s and 40s, before and during WWII. Its plot revolves around a bright young Chamorro woman who dreams of moving beyond the traditional roles in education held by her parents, pursuing a career in office administration, and entering the world of the emerging merchant class on Guåhan. Along the way, she meets a young sailor; they fall in love and marry. Then Guåhan is invaded. The romance ends and the tragedy begins. The story is made even more poignant as one realizes that Mariquita is the mother whom the author never knew.*

Chapter 9

Uneasy Peace

It was March 1944 and a year had passed since Mariquita had written her letter to Eddie; it was more than two years since she had last seen him on that unhappy day of his departure. Although she did not know if he was still alive, in her heart she felt he was, and as she sat on the riverbank in the jungle, where she had taken Chris and Helen to bathe and wash clothes, she prayed for him.

At first it had been advantageous for the Perez family to be living in Agana. Although most of the people had moved out, it was important as a trading center and a place to obtain information. But as time passed, the Japanese became more domineering, and when the war was not going in their favor, they became oppressive. The Perez family became fearful.

During that time, Joseph had been slapped and struck with a stick by his teacher a number of times for "misbehaving." After the latest incident, he had run out of the school building and thrown rocks at the windows. This had brought Japanese soldiers to the house to reprimand Mama Pai.

There were other incidents involving the children that weighed heavily on Mama Pai's mind. The worst was when Johnny was taken to the police station and beaten for being out after curfew. They kicked, whipped, and beat him. He explained to Mama Pai later that one of the men who took him and his friends to the police station was jealous because he liked one of the girls who had been with them. When Johnny took off his shirt and Mama Pai saw the extent of his beating, she nearly collapsed. A couple of the men who had beaten him were interpreters from Saipan and Rota. Being a headstrong young man, Johnny set about getting even. Finding out the whereabouts of the men, he gained his revenge in the dark of the night: he gave them both a sound beating.

Many of the Chamorro Saipanese and Rotanese who came to the island to work for the Japanese were helpful and sympathetic to their Guamanian brothers and sisters. Others delighted in their authoritative role, and they would be long remembered for their evil deeds.

With Chris sitting watchfully besides her, Mariquita was almost asleep when Felix called from the distance. When he arrived, he helped her gather up the clothes and soon the four of them were headed home. The jungle trail they walked led to the main road that traversed the central part of the island from Agana to Pago Bay. When they had crossed the road and reached the entrance to the ranch, several dogs met and accompanied them to the house.

When they arrived, Auntie Da had already started the wood fire in the open kitchen attached to the house and was preparing to cook the evening meal. Papa was feeding the pigs softened breadfruit and taro, and Mama Pai, who had faith in the powers of herbal medicine, was sitting on the front steps applying leaves to a cut on Joseph's knee.

The ranch house was small, not having been built as a family home. It stood on a slope on posts, three feet high on one end and six feet high on the other, in a large clearing dominated by a huge mango tree and surrounded by tall fruit trees and the dense jungle. The roof of the wooden house was made of tin, and ladder-like steps led to its entrance. At the edge of the surrounding jungle were a small outhouse, some animal pens, and vegetable gardens.

❦ ❦ ❦

From within the house, Mariquita could hear the laughter of her children. She placed the laundry on a table near one of the open windows, and as she folded the clothing she also watched her children at play.

One day we will all go to America and stay with Mama and Papa Howard on their farm in Indiana, she thought. And Eddie told me he would buy me a fur coat to wear in the winter when it snows. If it is as cold as he told me, I will need one.

Mariquita's hopes had been lifted by the air strike on Orote Point, and she often thought about Eddie's return and their little family going to America. She knew in her heart he was alive—and she would wait for him.

The older boys arrived around six o'clock. They talked about the recent air raid alarms and how hard it was getting, trying to please their Japanese bosses. It was becoming so bad at the worksites that they often showed bruises where they had been hit. Besides their own stories, they also told of worse that they had heard about.

The evening passed quickly. After dinner, a smudge fire using coconut husks was started under the house to ward off mosquitoes, and the boys bathed using water from the rain barrels and homemade soap. They were careful in using the water because it had not rained for some time; when the barrels reached a certain low level, they would have to refill them by going to the water pump in Ordot. When everyone was ready for bed, the family said their prayers, extinguished the coconut oil lamps, and retired early.

The following morning, shortly after the boys had left for the main road where they were picked up and transported to their worksites, Mariquita heard the dogs barking up the hill. Fearful that Japanese soldiers were coming to the house, she cautioned everyone to go inside. Papa, who was already at work gardening, was also alerted by the barking dogs and soon was at Mariquita's side.

They heard a few muffled shouts and abruptly the barking ceased. Frankie came into view along with the area's *soncho*, a Guamanian appointed to serve as a minor official and messenger for the Japanese authorities.

Humbly, the *soncho* informed Papa that the Japanese had ordered higher weekly quotas of vegetables, eggs, and other farm products and would need more from him to help fill the quotas. He also said that since all able-bodied Guamanian males had been ordered to work on defense projects, Papa would have to go, and that Joseph would have to go to the agricultural camp in Tai with Frankie, who was already assigned there.

Alarmed that ten-year-old Joseph would have to work for the Japanese and be subjected to their mistreatment, Mariquita pleaded to take his place. The *soncho*, whose orders were only to have a certain number of people report for work at Tai, accepted the exchange.

Mariquita was afraid, but she was sure that she could fare better than her little brother. She knew of the conditions to which she would have to adjust, having been told by her brothers and others who had been at various labor sites. Up to this time, Mariquita had been fortunate in that she had not had to fill one of the worker quotas. A close friend and neighbor in Agana, Maria Cruz Perez, a sweet and lovely Chamorro girl with whom Mariquita had walked many miles on bartering trips, had been doing fieldwork for some time. When Mariquita had last seen her, she had hardly recognized her and had felt sorry for her. Now she was going to join her.

Mama Pai would now be worrying about the safety of her husband and oldest daughter as well as her older boys.

Chapter 10

Impending Doom

Together with the returning Japanese Army had come the Kaikontai, an agricultural unit whose job was to feed the military. In their desperation to meet their objectives, they were merciless. For many Guamanians this was the beginning of an ordeal that would ultimately change their lives, and for some, it would be the beginning of their end.

As more Japanese troops arrived in anticipation of an American attack, more food was needed and soon everyone considered old enough was forced to work. Only those who were too young or too old or who had escaped detection were saved from this misery.

By June 1944 there were some 19,000 Japanese soldiers, many Koreans, and approximately 24,000 Guamanians on the island. Besides working on defense projects, such as leveling airfields with their bare hands, the Guamanians were forced to feed everyone, and they were the last to be considered.

With almost everyone working on fortifications and food production for the Japanese, very few Guamanians were left to do subsistence farming on their ranches, and everything that was produced, as well as any livestock the farmers had, was often taken by foraging troops. Many went hungry.

During this time everyone suffered, but the ones most affected were those who daily suffered the injustice of forced labor under the scrutiny of the Japanese, who treated them as dispensable animals.

On the Perez ranch only Mama Pai, Da, Carmen, and Joseph were left to work there. Papa and the others helped when they were able to return home in the evening, but since the Americans had begun bombing in the middle of June, they rarely returned home.

When Mariquita had first gone to Tai in March, she was assigned to help prepare food to be cooked and trucked to the various campsites. Later, she was assigned to a labor gang to do agricultural fieldwork near Manenggon, a farming area to the south. There she toiled in the hot sun from sunrise to sunset with very little rest and a meager ration of food. While there, she often witnessed the mistreatment of her helpless co-laborers and was herself an occasional victim. But now she had a new assignment, and it would be the final test of her strength.

Tai was the headquarters of the Kaikontai, and when several high-ranking officers arrived there at the end of June, girls considered desirable were selected, and Mariquita was forced to return to Tai. It was her beauty that would ultimately lead to her death.

The main camp of the Kaikontai consisted of three makeshift dwellings for the officers. In the center of the camp was a large mango tree, its shading limbs sometimes providing a brief respite for the twelve young women who had been ordered to work there.

For those modest young women, whose backgrounds had never prepared them for such servitude, it was a horrifying experience from which they would never recover.

Besides cooking, laundering, and the general cleaning of the officers' quarters, they were compelled to serve their masters, including bathing and massaging them. If they refused, they were beaten. Their servitude extended to the cutting of the officers' toenails, and, under the threat of death, some were forced to submit to the officers' desires.

From the first day she worked for the Japanese officers, Mariquita had difficulty concealing her resentment, but she controlled her feelings with silence and did the work expected of her. She suspected, however, that there would come a time when one of the officers would try to force her to sleep with him, and she decided that if the situation arose, she would die rather than disgrace her husband and lose her dignity.

The girls at Tai were isolated from the other Guamanians who worked at the camp and were not allowed to converse with one another. And if for any reason one of the officers was displeased, all the girls were punished. This rule was made evident the first morning when the girls were lined up for inspection. One of their requirements was to be neat and clean, but that day one of the girls wore a soiled dress. All the girls were slapped, the offender was harshly struck with a stick, and those who made any noise or cried were likewise hit.

Mariquita felt sorry for some of the other girls, some whom she knew, especially those younger than herself who had never before left their family. She was frightened, but outwardly she tried to set an example of courage. In days to come she often volunteered to bathe and massage an officer herself to spare a young girl from being humiliated. These compassionate gestures helped to single her out from the other girls, as did her appearance, and she came to the attention of the commanding officer, the head *taicho*.

The first two weeks had tested Mariquita's determination to bear the unpleasantness of the situation. At least she had been able to return home several times, sometimes in the comforting presence of Frankie, carrying food she had stolen from the camp, food she made sure was not part of the dogs she had seen butchered and skinned.

Upon her return she would laugh and play with her children and smother them with her love, and at night she had her mother to whom she whispered her fears.

On her last visit, she told her mother of her decision that she would rather die than disgrace her husband by sleeping with the Japanese. Alarmed, Mama Pai had responded, "Tita, I want you alive, not dead. You have to do what you must to stay alive. You have no choice! I will take responsibility, and I will be the one to answer to Eddie. Tita, he will understand. Do not do anything foolish, my dear daughter."

"Mama, I can never do that," Mariquita had said. "Eddie is the only one who will ever touch me."

"And Chris and Helen, what of them? Have you thought of them?"

"If I could not respect myself, I could never face my children, Mama."

"You do not realize the seriousness of what you are saying," Mama Pai said firmly. "Tita, I am older and wiser than you—maybe not in all things, but I am in life. I know that time will heal your wounds. You are only talking this way because of the cruel things that are happening to you, and because you are confused. Do what you must to stay alive—if not for me, then for Eddie and the children. And know, Tita, that I will always be with you."

Mama Pai continued her argument. She knew that Mariquita was listening, but she was also aware that her daughter had already made up her mind. She pleaded with Mariquita, she cried; they both cried, and they prayed, but in the end their positions remained unchanged.

After that visit everything seemed to be happening at once. The Americans started bombing again; Uncle Pepe was suspected of aiding an American serviceman still in hiding and was savagely beaten; family members were scattered; and there were reports of many atrocities being committed by the frantic Japanese.

As the bombings intensified, Mariquita was confined to the camp. Under increasingly difficult conditions, she did what she was told and to the best of her ability. At night she slept in a dugout shelter with the other girls, and she was scared.

The head taicho was a tough, seasoned soldier of war. He was tall, thin, and dark, with a scarred face and a wispy gray beard. He was sometimes referred to as *Batbudu*—bearded. As the commanding officer, an authoritative position he relished, he was ruthless, and there was no question that women should be servile.

Mariquita had first gained his attention by her physical charm, her grooming and femininity. He delighted in having her do his bidding. Frequently, he told the Japanese interpreter in charge of the girls to send her to be his handmaiden. What captured his attention was her apparent willingness to serve him, and soon the other officers knew that she was reserved for him. He did not know that Mariquita's passivity was only the result of the acceptance of her fate in order to protect herself and the other girls.

There was something, however, that disturbed the taicho. No matter what she was doing, she appeared detached, indifferent to his existence. Just having her work for him was not all he wanted from her. She was there to please him, and he desired her.

Each day, the taicho tried to impress upon her that he was not only the commanding officer of the camp, but her master. And each day she disturbed him more by ignoring him.

He began to slap her for mistakes, real or invented, to forcefully demonstrate his power over her. Her bow was not correct. She did not serve his food properly. She forgot to say "san" (Mr.) after "taicho" when addressing him. And she was happy about the American planes. But since Mariquita was conscientious about everything she did in the presence of the taicho, she knew the real reason for the criticisms and reprimands: he wanted her.

There were many things the taicho would do, but he would not physically force a girl to have sex with him as some of the other soldiers did. He was an officer and from a distinguished family, reared with a strict sense of honor, and he would not dishonor himself in this respect. Also, he had never had to; those in his past had willingly accepted his advances because of his position. He wanted Mariquita to submit willingly to his superiority, and sex would be the ultimate proof of this submission.

From the beginning she had rebuffed every sexual move he had made toward her. At first, he had only shown displeasure, but soon he had begun to slap her, and now, his anger mounting, she expected the brutal slaps she received and stood still for them. The taicho did not know Mariquita. With each offensive act, destined to make her relent, her determination to die rather than accept his sexual advances was strengthened. What she did not know was that part of his rage was due to the recent success of the American forces in the Pacific. As the days passed, he sensed that she would not yield. Her scorn infuriated him, and every day, with each touch of her unfeeling hands as she massaged him, he became angrier. He was also plagued with the thought that he was losing face with his fellow officers and had lowered himself by making her so important.

He began making her life more miserable. While the Americans were bombing and shelling the island in earnest, he felt his position further weakened, and he thought he detected a look of challenge in her eyes. The battle of wills continued, and as the bombardment by the Americans increased, so did his passion.

Now, he began to make her life unbearable. He would have all the girls slapped, hit, and kicked for anything she did to upset him. Mariquita, who so wanted to help them, was now the cause of some of their pain.

The other girls had their own struggles to cope with, and each would bear some scar or ache in the future as a reminder. For the time being, though, they were managing to survive, and they could do nothing to help Mariquita.

The taicho began to hate this girl, Mariquita, who he knew was married to an American prisoner of war in Japan and was now waiting for the Americans to return. At last, in desperation, he challenged her with force and she violently pushed him away. He hit her, knocking her down. Oh, how he hated this disrespectful dog!

"She will pay for saying no to a Japanese officer in the Imperial Japanese Army!" he said to himself. He called the Japanese interpreter and ordered him to tie her to the lime tree next to the hut and beat her with a bamboo stick.

"Ha! At last she is crying," he gloated. "She is calling her mother."

The next day he had her tied again to the tree, this time denying her food and water.

She wept. She cried for her mother. She could see the horror in the faces of the girls as they moved by. To each one she said, "Don't give me water or they will kill us both." At least she had the satisfaction of knowing that the taicho never wanted her to serve him again.

What kept Mariquita from succumbing to the many outrages? It was her faith, her children, and the hope of Eddie's return.

Between the punishments, Mariquita moved about the camp in a state of terror, frightened for her life. She had thought of running away, but she knew that she would be killed if she were caught. And what would happen to the other girls if she attempted such a foolish thing? She prayed continuously, asking God to forgive her for anything she may have done wrong in her life and begging for His help.

From *Cheffla gi i Manglo*

Peter R. Onedera (Guåhan)

Editors' note: Set in the middle of World War II, the novella tracks one family's experiences during the Japanese occupation of Guåhan. The brief narrative begins with preparations for the huge island celebration of Our Lady of Kamalin, follows the family as they flee to their lanchos (ranches) to evade the occupying forces, and mourns with them as they are forced to witness the violent deaths of loved ones.

Chapter 25

Out of this motley group of villagers and displaced ranchers, a young man of about twenty soon distinguished himself as a joker and a daredevil. His name was Kalistro. He kept everyone's spirits high as he would laughingly mimic the mannerisms of many of the soldiers. He had an uncanny way of sounding like the commander, who had a good command of the English language, as well as a lesser officer whose name everyone knew only as Komatsu. Komatsu's use of the English language was terribly distorted and his strong accent and his bow-legged walk were the focus of Kalistro's comedic parodies. Because the name Komatsu tended to sound like the Chamorro name Camacho, Kalistro nicknamed him "Empachu Kamachew," and neither the commander, Komatsu, nor any of the soldiers were aware of Kalistro's antics. Only the villagers knew and, especially in times of despair, would request spur-of-the-moment portrayals, which would send everyone into stifled hysterics.

Although the commander appeared to be stern, it soon appeared he also had a heart. He did not allow his soldiers to prey upon the young women, and he allowed frequent rest stops along the way so that the elderly and infirm could have moments of respite. Komatsu, on the other hand, was synonymous with the word *cruel.* He enjoyed belittling the weak and injured and, if given the chance, would force them to walk for miles and not allow them to rest. He was also given to abandoning the sickly ones on the side of the road.

Once, he almost got away with the abandonment of a newborn whose mother had died en route due to massive loss of blood. The commander had allowed the

Previously published, Peter Onedera (self-pub., 2006).

brothers of the young woman to bury her beside the road immediately after her death. It was only after a second glance that he noticed movement in a pile of banana leaves and realized the infant had somehow survived but had been wrapped loosely and left to the ravages of nature. He ordered that the infant be given to a woman who was still nursing.

During one rest stop, the villagers were huddled together tending to one another. The commander and some of his troops, including Komatsu, were huddled over some maps contemplating their route to Manenggon. Other soldiers assigned to watch the group did so while smoking cigarettes and passing around what someone said was a bottle of *sake*.

It was a hot day, and many people had fainted from the walk. Looking into the distance, Kalistro noted that the next mile or so of road would bring them among huge trees that shaded both sides of the road. This place was ideal for a rest break, as there were coconut trees where they could pick young coconuts and drink their juice, thereby quenching their thirst. He also knew that many of the soldiers drank coconut juice and found it much to their liking.

In his best commander imitation, he shouted, "It is time for us to go. Everyone let us go!" Villagers, soldiers, and the commander himself, along with his tight little group, assembled and proceeded down the road. Only those close to Kalistro knew that it was he who had called for the continuation of the trek and not the commander.

As the group entered the tree-lined road and felt the welcome relief of the breeze afforded by the shade, Kalistro again let out a loud commander-like pronouncement: "Let us now rest here."

Again, as before, the soldiers broke rank, the villagers let down their loads, and the commander and his group again huddled together. Kalistro had gotten away with his parody, much to the benefit of the villagers.

It was Komatsu, however, who alerted the commander that it was not he who had issued the first and second commands. It was then that the commander realized that Komatsu was right.

Going over to the villagers with Komatsu close on his heels, he barked, "Who issued those commands?"

Not getting any answers, he walked into the group and planted himself among them. The soldiers who had earlier broken rank sauntered into their positions.

"I said, who issued those commands?" the commander asked again.

Kalistro said, "You did."

"I did not."

Turning to the Japanese soldiers, he asked them in Japanese who had issued the commands. Judging from their responses, none of the soldiers knew either.

"I know I did not issue those commands. Somebody did," he said again.

This time, total silence met him and no one dared to move.

Suddenly, the sky became alive with planes. This time, they were flying low and the sound of gunfire began popping all around us. The villagers all scattered into the undergrowth as the soldiers sought positions for firing back.

Momentarily, no one seemed to pay attention to us as the commander and his troops concentrated on returning the gunfire that rained down on us.

We all recognized the American planes as before. It was difficult containing our excitement, and our feelings of fatigue, hunger, and fear were forgotten. In the distance, planes continued flying low above us and coming back shooting as hard as before. Somehow, not one American fighter plane was hit, but some of the soldiers started dropping like flies. We remained huddled together and someone kept repeating above the noise, "*Grasias, adios, Si Yu'os ma'ase.* Thank God. Thank you."

We began hearing explosions and many in the group noted that other planes not firing guns were also dropping bombs. The sounds around us were deafening, and soon I found myself underneath our grandparents, who had decided to shield us with their bodies. I learned later that many adults did this unselfishly so that infants, toddlers, and young children were spared from any injury. I also learned that many in our group died as they were caught in the crossfire. Sadly, some were children too.

And so for the rest of that day, we remained huddled together, simultaneously praying and crying. Explosions and gunfire continued ceaselessly, and I wondered fleetingly if this was to be my end.

As nightfall came, flares brightened up our surroundings and the sounds of gunfire and explosions diminished. I imagined that other areas in the north were being bombarded with gunfire and explosions.

Soon I fell asleep as a huge feeling of exhaustion swept over me.

From *Nasarinu*

Peter R. Onedera (Guåhan)

Editors' note: In 1912 the island's naval government transferred the first group of Chamoru with leprosy to an existing leper colony on Culion Island in the Philippines. Most of these never returned from that exile. The heartbreak of those forced to leave and those remaining behind is captured in Onedera's play I Nasarinu.

Scene 3

(A week later. It is night. Marikita is sleeping on the cot. Tomas and Filomenia are seated at the table talking.)

Tomas: It's getting closer and closer to the day we leave, Filomenia.

Filomenia: I know. I am so afraid of that day, Tomas. It's only because of Marikita that I made that last-minute decision to join you and the others.

Tomas: How do you mean?

Filomenia: If the *mediku* say the treatment is being given at Culion Island, then it might not be too late for Marikita. It might be late for me, but at least there's hope that Marikita will be cured and come back home.

Tomas: You think so?

Filomenia: I hope so, Tomas. That's the only thing that keeps me going. Marikita must come back and tell everybody in the family about you and me. Nåna and Tåta must know what becomes of us.

Tomas: Since we haven't yet begun losing our skin or parts of our body, maybe there is also hope for you and me, not just Marikita.

Filomenia: Oh, Tomas. I pray every hour of every day now. If it's the last thing I want, it's to see my husband and children. We've been here for eight months now and I'm afraid my baby will forget me.

Tomas: I don't think so. Your husband is a good man. I know he loves you and I'm sure Nåna and Tåta are right there for him and the children.

Previously published, Peter Onedera (self-pub., 1998).

Filomenia: *Ai che'lu-hu*, I'm sorry for all the things I've done to you when you were growing up.

Tomas: There's nothing to be sorry about. You are my oldest sister and you do have a mean streak but you only meant well.

Filomenia: You are *ågauguat* and you've had your share of the *kuåtta*. As a matter of fact, all nine of us had our share of Nåna and Tåta's strict upbringing.

Tomas: I kind of miss Tomasa, Leoncio, Jacinta, Prudencio, Maria, Concepcion, and Felis, but they have families now. I hope they are there for the children, your husband, and Nåna and Tåta.

Filomenia: Isn't it strange that only the two of us have *chetnot nasarinu?*

Tomas: Everyone says that people get it because of being dirty. My goodness, if it's anyone in the family who is so *areklao yan gasgas*, it's you. But, like Nåna would say, "*Nina'en Yu'os*. God has given."

Filomenia: *Kilu'os-ta.* It's our cross to bear.

Tomas: I wonder what will go through the minds of our families when they hear that we're the first ones to leave.

Filomenia: It's bad enough that everyone was torn apart when they took us from our homes, our lives, and our families with the threat of guns and violence. Many people will repeat the same ordeal again.

Tomas: I know. We may be the first ones to leave and we aren't the only ones who have come down with this disease, but I know this is not the last of this whole thing. It is so heartbreaking.

Filomenia: I try not to think of it. I tell myself it's just a nightmare that we'll soon get out of.

Tomas: Will we ever get out of this, Filomenia?

Filomenia: How can it get worse? It should only get better.

Tomas: Then, we die.

Filomenia: If and when the time comes, I must accept it, Tomas. You should, too.

Tomas: Filomenia . . . Should I die first . . . please make sure you are there?

Filomenia: *Ai che'lu-hu.* And if I should go first? Will you be there?

Tomas: *Siempre.* I will be there for you.

Filomenia: Have you been praying, too, Tomas? You need God in your life now. I have been including you in my prayers.

Tomas: Just because I don't carry rosary beads with me doesn't mean I'm not praying. It's all in here [*touches his heart, then cries*]. I'm so scared, Filomenia. I'm scared of dying. I can't bear the thought of dying all by myself. Even now, I wish that Nåna and Tåta were here. I wish I had never grown up so that this thing wouldn't have happened to me.

Filomenia: [*She gets up from her chair and cradles her brother's head.*] Hush, Tomas. I, too, am very scared, but like Tan Rosario says, we will all be together at the very end.

Tomas: I've never told you this, *che'lu-hu, lao hu guaiya hao.*

Filomenia: [*Sniffing*] *Hu guaiya hao lokkue' I che'lu-hu.* I love you, too. [*Both cry miserably as the curtain closes.*]

Scene 7

(It is daylight out in the open yard. Through a barbed wire fence, Frederico is yelling at a crowd of people. The priest is at the head of the group.)

Frederico: You know the rules, Påle'. No one is allowed in here.

Påle':   These people have just now been told that their loved ones are being sent. Please, have mercy on them, Frederico. Let them see their family members now.

Frederico: I do not make the rules, Påle'. I have been instructed to shoot anyone who steps beyond the sentry gate.

Påle':   Have you no sense of pity? These are your people, Frederico.

Joaquin: Perhaps we should, Frederico. No one will know but us. The military officers are at the naval station right now. They won't be back until this afternoon.

Frederico: What? And risk our jobs? We can't do that, Joaquin.

Joaquin: Then I will let them in.

Frederico: You do that and I'll shoot you too.

Påle':   Can they at least see their families right where you are?

Frederico: They'll get a chance to see them tomorrow on their way to the port harbor.

Påle':   Come on. I know they won't even be allowed to speak to one another.

(Crowd murmurs and shouts are heard above the din.)

Joaquin: Yes, why don't we at least summon the patients to come out here and see them? Both sides can stay where they are.

Påle':   Please, guards, this is the one last chance they can be together if only in sight and sound.

Frederico: No can do, Påle'. I can get court-martialed for this.

Joaquin: Come on, Frederico, please, just this once.

(The crowd's pleas become louder and louder as Frederico continues to shake his head. Filomenia and the others come out from their places and rush to the barbed wire fence. Frederico rushes ahead of them and, with his back to the fence, brandishes his gun at them. The crowd becomes silent.)

Frederico: One more step and one of you will die. I will shoot. I mean it.

Filomenia: Go ahead—shoot, Frederico. Show our Chamoru people that you are brave and will die for the country that has not shown us mercy.

Frederico: Shut up!

Påle':	Frederico, please, this doesn't have to end in violence.
Frederico:	You, shut up! I don't have to listen to you. Joaquin, get over here. You have a job to do. Or I will shoot you, too.
Bisente:	Our families are out there. They mean no harm but to see us.
Tan Rosario:	*Ma'åse' put fabot, lahi-hu.* This won't take long. Some of us will never see our families again.
Frederico:	Joaquin, get over here now. I will file insubordination charges against you and you will be court-martialed. *(Joaquin hesitantly takes his place beside Frederico. He is shaking his head in uncertainty.)*
Joaquin:	Please, Frederico. Just once. What else can happen?
Frederico:	And have someone disappear again, like Tun Jesus and Gertrude? We have been reprimanded for that, Joaquin. Have you forgotten?
Påle':	Alright then, Frederico. Can the families leave the food and other items they've brought for them?
Filomenia:	I know you are cruel, Frederico, and this is the real you. You will regret it someday.
Frederico:	No one in my family has *nasarinu*, so I have nothing to worry about.
Tan Hipsia:	Isn't Tun Jesus your uncle? Isn't he your mother's brother?
Filomenia:	He has forgotten. He only cares about himself. But watch yourself, Frederico. You might get it yourself, soon.
Frederico:	No. I will not, because I am clean. I keep myself clean.
Filomenia:	And you are the only one clean, you say? Well, your soul is dirty. That's worse than what's on the outside.
Påle':	Frederico, I will instruct each family member to leave their gifts right there on the barbed wire area.
Frederico:	*(Momentarily turns and addresses the priest.)* Go ahead, but they are to immediately turn around and leave the area. Hurry.

(Påle' talks to the family members. A few at a time come up and deposit their gifts on the ground beneath the barbed wire. They look forlornly at the patients, who look back at them silently. They wave to each other and the family members slowly exit. As they finish, Pale' steps forward, gives the sign of the cross, looks back once, and slowly exits, too.)

| Joaquin: | They are gone now, Frederico. |
| Frederico: | Take every single bundle and throw them out to sea. |

(Filomenia and the others stare in disbelief. They mutter indignantly amongst themselves as Joaquin stands there, not fully comprehending his instructions.)

| Joaquin: | What? |

Frederico: You heard me. Every single one of them. Weigh them down with rocks until they sink to the bottom. Make sure nothing surfaces or I will report you.

(Joaquin picks up the bundles, looks at the patients, and exits.)

Filomenia: You have thrown away the grace of God. How could you? Go to hell, Frederico.

Bisente: Now I know that you don't have God in your heart at all.

Frederico: I can't wait for all of you to leave. Then this island will be rid of all *nasarinu*, once and for all.

(He brandishes his gun, aims it skyward, and shoots. Filomenia and the others drop to the ground in fear as the curtain closes.).

Nauru Women Picket a Government-Sponsored Flight to London for the Stage Play *Leonardo da Vinci*, May 27, 1993

Maria Gaiyabu (Nauru)

On that day, we women of Nauru made a stand. That morning we voiced our dissatisfaction at the government's continued misuse of our people's money on poor investments, in particular, Duke Minks's stage play called *Leonardo da Vinci* . . . We women picketed the flight taking the VIPs to Melbourne and thence to London to attend the inaugural opening of our government-financed play. This is our unforgettable story of we women who organized and took part in an effort to stop the plane from taking off from Nauru Airport.

It was about 7 a.m. The roads came alive with the roaring of cars and buses carrying people to work. The airport began to fill as passengers traveling to Fiji checked in. Everyone went on with their business, never suspecting what lay ahead. The men in blue uniforms (police) grew in number as their big van dropped off another load of officers.

"Someone has betrayed us," I said. "Those blue-skinned men knew our strategy. That is why they are assembling here in designated places."

Several of the men in blue surveyed our cars. "What are these stupid women doing here at this early hour when they should all be at home with their husbands and getting their kids ready for schools?" they commented among themselves, but loud enough for us to hear.

We eyed each other and smirked. There they go again, we thought. Reminding us of our house-wifely duties and that they are the Lords and Masters. "This is a

Previously published, Pacific Islands Forum Secretariat, *A Woman's Place Is in the House—The House of Parliament: Research to Advance Women's Political Representation in Forum Island Countries*, 2006.
Excerpt from "Women Finding Their Place in the 'Sea of Islands': The Case of Nauru," paper presented at a conference at the University of Hawai'i, April 18–20, 1997.

Matrilineal society," I wanted to shout. "It is the women who bear the children. We will continue the clans and expand the twelve tribes of Nauru."

A few of our young girls stood at the side of the road with placards. The written messages on them swayed in the air so people could read them clearly:

"Don't party on our inheritance! Party at your own expense!"

"Politicians are getting richer and fatter. The people getting poorer, our children skinnier!"

"Where are our millions? In Duke Minks's pocket?"

The girls sang and danced, making sure they were seen by everyone.

Our group moved in closer towards the tarmac. It was time, the moment we were waiting for. There were thirty of us. My knees wobbled. My heart pounded faster. Butterflies fluttered in my stomach. I wanted to turn around and run. I realized I was scared. Like a coward, I sneaked amidst the other women and hid. A couple of young girls giggled as they pushed and tugged me out of the circle. An elderly woman in a wheelchair shouted crossly, "We mean business here, so be serious." She was the bravest of all.

We clung closely together, more frightened than ever as we marched forward toward the plane. The Director of Police commanded us to stay within the marked boundary where several policemen stood. Others were busy directing the traffic on the road that ran alongside the airport.

Thousands of people swarmed the airport property. Some clustered on the rooftop; others were outside, crammed into every available space. There were even some on top of the rock pinnacles in the bush area of the airport, looking down at us. We stood under the shade of a narrow rectangular landing of the building that stretched out onto the road. One of the women spoke to the people about our concerns and asked them for their support. Someone led a prayer, a plea for the government to answer our cries of worry that the future—our children's future—was at risk. Shaky voices rose, tears flowed as we sang songs that expressed our love for our homeland. We cried, and our husbands, our families, and other bystanders cried as they looked on. Even the policemen—men who were our brothers, nephews, uncles, husbands, and grandchildren—cried as they pleaded with us to go home. . . .

We moved towards the tarmac. The police blocked us off. We fought, pushed hard, and pulled the hair of the policemen who stood in rows to keep us off. Old women and young mothers with their wailing babies straddling their sides, pushed and pushed. Some of us, in a frenzy, ran to the sides to avoid the men in uniform. Everyone ran crazily here and there as we tried to break through the barricade of police lines. Shouts and frustrated screams filled the air. We forced the line with all our power, but they were too strong.

Suddenly, we were free. We ran wildly onto the tarmac and plonked our tired bodies onto the cement in front of the big airplane. Several women raced toward the stairway and clung to it. A couple of them reached the wheels and held on tightly. The captain looked down at us from the cockpit. I am sure he felt sorry for us, but what could he do? This was not his battle; it was ours, the Nauruans'.

People everywhere were running wildly, with the poor policemen chasing madly after them. There were so many of us that we filled the whole area, even the road. The police had stopped the traffic, and the line of vehicles stretched from one end to the other and around the airstrip. A lot of people had abandoned their cars and had joined us. The Director of Police begged our leaders to control our group.

Someone handed me a red loudhailer. I grabbed it and called the group together. A couple of men brought some Air Nauru umbrellas for shade. The sun was certainly not very kind to us at all that day. We sat for three hours under the burning sun. I yelled in the red loudhailer all sorts of things about the ministers going off to London, each with several thousand dollars as a per diem to keep them alive, while our children, widows, and widowers were living on only a pittance. I cursed and cursed. I said all sorts of things under the sun that I knew were wrong.

I can't even remember some of the things I said.

The ministers were nowhere in sight, but we knew that they were across the road peeping through the windows at the spectacle we were playing out on the tarmac.

Finally, the Director of Police and someone in the Aviation Department approached our fearless leader and asked her what we wanted. She relayed the question to us. We demanded that the passengers to London be offloaded. I accompanied them into the ticketing office to cross their names off the passenger list. The Director of Police assured us that the *Leonardo da Vinci* guests would not be flying out.

Later, we let the ordinary passengers onto the plane. After the stairway was pulled up and the side door of the plane closed, we dispersed. I felt sorry for the passengers. One was my closest friend, and others were relatives of protesters. But no matter: we had to do what was necessary. It was our day of victory in the history of Nauru.

Egade

Lucia Itsimaera (Nauru)

The sun had almost disappeared below the horizon. For a brief moment, night and day mingled together. The display of colors in the sky was spectacular. The evening meal had already been consumed, but the aroma of fish cooked on the open fire still lingered.

It was Sunday evening, and all the local picture theaters were closed. But the children didn't mind. They knew their mother Eigunamwi would use the opportunity to tell them a story. The young ones sat themselves around their mother, eager to hear yet another fascinating tale about their ancestors and life in the old days. When Eigunamwi was certain she had all their attention, she began. Apwenemek me epwenemeto . . .

A long time ago, there lived a woman called Egade. She was not married, and she had no children of her own. Being a childless woman did not bother her because the people of the island all looked up to her as their mother and they treated her with great reverence. You see, Egade knew our culture well, and, in those times, culture played a major role among the people. Egade enriched the children with knowledge of their culture. She taught them tribal traditions and decorations. She educated them in customary laws, recited ancient chants and songs with them.

So it was for many years. The people knew their identity and were proud of their rich cultural heritage.

Down the years, however, change began to take place. This change came with the arrival of the white people. They were very charming people who asked only for a little hospitality in exchange for all the wonderful goods they offered. The white people gave our people magical potions that made them happy, cute little "candies" that had healing effects, beautiful fabrics that they could wear. They even had tasty food in little tin cans that would keep for days without going bad. Slowly, the people stopped wearing their grass skirts and gave up fishing and hunting because it became too much hard work.

As the years went by, the white people called all the chiefs of the island together to negotiate a deal with landowners. They said they wanted to dig up the

Previously published, *Stories from Nauru*, University of the South Pacific Nauru Center and Institute of Pacific Studies, 1996.

"dirt" from the land and ship it back to their homeland, where they would use it. At first, the chiefs were a bit reluctant, but when the white people told the chief they were going to pay the landowners' money for the "dirt," everyone consented. After all, you couldn't get a better bargain than that.

Not long after, they began chopping down the great big tomano trees topside to clear the land for mining. Egade was furious with the chiefs. She reminded them that the tomano trees were needed to build canoes and huts. But they ignored her, saying that the tomano trees were abundant.

The landowners secretly laughed behind the white people's backs. They thought they had outsmarted them. In return for phosphate (the fancy name they gave for the dirt), the white people were paying each landowner large sums of money. Very soon all the landowners were going to be rich men.

Several more years passed; by this time, every landowner was a millionaire. More white people came, bringing with them abundant supplies of merchandise and goods. The locals could take anything they fancied; however, this time they had to pay for the goods. The white people assured them that they could afford anything they wanted. After all, they had been paid great sums of money for all the phosphate that had been dug up from their land.

So all the people "went to town," spending their money on just about everything they fancied. They bought gadgets that played beautiful music, motor vehicles that transported them around the island, wristbands that told them the time of day. They even tore down their little thatched huts and replaced them with houses brought over from the land of the white people.

In a few years, the people had changed dramatically. They had replaced their tribal decorations with gold and silver necklaces. They studied the fascinating tongue of the white people. Egade was very much forgotten. Her customary laws were replaced with political laws. Her ancient chants and songs were considered "uncivilized" by the locals; rock-n-roll music soon took their place.

So it went, on and on. As years went by, the islanders struggled very hard to adopt the fancy ways of the white people. The people said they were happy because with the white people came education, a new system of government, hospitals, airplanes, industry, and so on.

"And what has become of Egade?" one of the children asked.

"Well, Egade is still alive," replied the mother, "but gone is the beauty and pride that she once possessed. Instead, she has grown into a very sickly, frail old woman."

Eigunamwi looked around her and found that most of her little ones had fallen asleep. All except one.

"Is Egade going to die, Mama?" this one asked.

Her mother looked down on her with loving eyes and said, "Well, if Egade dies, then I'm afraid our culture will die too."

Even as Eigunamwi spoke, the little one drifted off to sleep.

The First Woman in Parliament
Ruby's Story

Alamanda Lauti (Nauru)

Ruby Dediya was Nauru's first and, up till 2006, only female MP ever elected to parliament. She was born on Nauru in 1949 and brought up in a family that regularly debated at home, although even her own mother discouraged her from speaking against her brothers. She was educated in Victoria, Australia, where she attended high school in Sale, Gippsland, at the Church of England Grammar School. At high school she participated in public speaking and drama and also joined the Interact Club, a Junior Rotary Club. After high school she trained as a nurse at the Epworth Hospital in Richmond, Victoria. She attended the University in Christchurch, New Zealand, where she graduated as a midwife.

Ruby secured one of the Anetan/Ewa seats in 1986 and held this until 1992. She regained the seat in 1995 and held it until the next election in 1997. Ruby first stood unsuccessfully for election in 1983, after being approached to do so by a group of women from both within and outside the constituency. Through their extended families, the women organized approaches to household after household requesting backing for Ruby on the grounds that she was educated, strong, and capable of addressing women's and children's issues in parliament. Ruby faced criticism and ridicule from the sitting member, who insisted that only Ruby's brother, not Ruby herself, should take up politics. Frustrated at facing such abuse in 1983, Ruby decided to stand again in 1986, this time successfully. But even victory proved upsetting when her aunt cried in sympathy with Ruby's defeated male adversary. The aunt never came to congratulate her, asserting that it should instead be a man representing the constituency in parliament.

When Ruby, now an MP, first went to the members' room, the door was closed in her face. When parliamentary staff were not around, male MPs would often ask her to make the coffee. But Ruby was elected to represent her constituency, not to make coffee. So she put her foot down and refused. At

Previously published, Pacific Islands Forum Secretariat, *A Woman's Place Is in the House—The House of Parliament: Research to Advance Women's Political Representation in Forum Island Countries*, 2006.

first, she was inexperienced and did not know how to follow Standing Orders. But she gradually built up her experience. During her period in Parliament, Ruby served as Minister for Health, Speaker of Parliament, Minister for Finance, and Acting President. She did not believe in dishing out money or personal favors to constituents; instead, she would bring them copies of the Government Gazettes and sit down with them, going through the job vacancies and assisting them with the completion of their application forms.

Ruby believes women have difficulty with becoming involved in politics. Despite formal equality, women regularly face problems at home. "Politics can take control of people's lives," she says. "If [a politician] is a woman, the stress will double. A woman has to be very strong-willed and prepared to learn, for there is a lot to learn about being a Member of Parliament."

She acknowledges that her path to politics was eased by being single rather than married. "If you have a husband, your roles double; whereas for males, their clothes are pressed and food is prepared for them. If a woman is married she must have the full support of her husband. She would need to balance her political activities and home activities, especially when she has children. Without her husband's support, it could drive her crazy and she will burn both ends of the candle."

She thinks that having reserved seats for women, perhaps one seat for men and one for women in each constituency might offer a way forward. She believes that "God picked the rib of Adam so that men and women could work together in politics."

Ti Mamaigo Si Yu'us— God Never Sleeps

Victoria-Lola M. Leon Guerrero (Guåhan)

The tide is low and the crescent moon high above Two Lovers Point. Though it rests at the tip of Tumon Bay, the sliver of moon paints the entire sky a pale purple and leaves a path of light glistening through the water. A salty breeze drifts from the ocean to dance with a young woman's violet dress. It flirts with the canopy of satin that falls mid-calf as she sashays to a table close to the out-door stage of the Tropicana Club. The woman steals the shine of the moon. On the table is a small sign that reads in calligraphy,

Reserved for Candelaria.

Candelaria has two apple-blossom-white orchids, violet at their tips, pinned to her curly black hair. Her cheeks are cherry pink. A waiter greets her and pulls out a chair for her as Desi emerges from the orchestra on cue. Desi is dressed in a white tuxedo, white creased pants, and white pointed shoes. His thick black hair is slicked back with pomade. Candelaria smiles as she notices the perfect proportions of his black bow tie and finds allure in the care he must have taken tying it. She gracefully places her small sequined purse on the table and gives the waiter a subtle nod that says she is not ready to sit. She wants to dance.

Desi returns Candelaria's smile before bringing a gold trumpet to his lips to play the intro to her favorite song, "Cherry Pink and Apple Blossom White." She holds the sides of her gown with the tips of her fingers and sways along, eyes closed, allowing the music to fully enter her. It's the song she first heard him play, the song they make love to, and the one she'll keep in the background long after he leaves her.

Candelaria opens her eyes as Desi lowers his head in a humble bow at the end of the tune. He winks at her with the whole left side of his face, from lip to high cheekbone to eyelid to eyebrow. She dances with a grace so tender he wants to abandon the stage to stand in the lull of her. She dances and everyone but him—her Desi—disappears. Candelaria spins and the drunken American sailors around her fade away. She lets her head roll from shoulder to shoulder, and the war that killed her baby sister just six years before rolls off her.

Excerpt from *Of a Tree of People* (a novel in progress).

For a moment.

There is no mud on Candelaria's face to make her look ugly; she no longer has to wear Papan Biho's dirty old work shirt to be disguised as a boy; there are no Japanese soldiers to hide from. There is just the moon, her dress with thirty buttons traveling down the side of her torso, and the trumpet player from the Philippines.

To dance this way is a luxury, her soft steps and confidence a peace she has longed for since childhood. The dress, the shoes, the lipstick are all new—gifts from Desi. Candelaria, the eldest daughter in her family, the middle of twelve children, could only imagine these things when she was younger, before the war. She had daydreamed a dress like this to match the orchids in her hair as she walked in the jungle behind the sweet potato patch to pick coconut shells and tangantangan twigs for her mother's fire.

🐝 🐝 🐝

Unlike most girls raised among boys, Candelaria refused to dress like one. She wore only dresses or skirts and would not leave the house without her hair brushed and styled. She learned to sew at six and would make herself outfits using leftover fabric from her mas dudus older cousin, Rosita Mateo.

As a teenager, Candelaria pretended she was a fashion model. When Rosita would visit, she'd give Candelaria makeovers and take her picture with the camera she'd borrowed from her sailor boyfriend. Once she asked Candelaria to sit on the log of a fallen coconut tree and took her picture with a row of kalamansi trees and an aged 55-gallon drum in the background. Candelaria posed gracefully, her long homemade dress printed with big pink flowers covering her legs, her hands draped over her bent knees.

"Ay, Candi," Rosita sighed as she looked through the camera's lens. "Gof bunita na palao'an hao."

🐝 🐝 🐝

Candelaria had a classmate in the ninth grade named Wendy, si Wendyen-Americana, who would show off her *Vogue* magazines filled with orange- or yellow-haired women drawn in bright dresses made to fit their curves and flow about their calves. Models with perfectly blushed cheeks, long eyelashes, and lips so defined and bright that Candelaria would save two cents a day from her tips delivering Nanan Biha's bread until she could buy a fifteen-cent tube of lipstick from Wendy.

"*Oh.*" Wendy sounded perplexed as Candelaria tried on the lipstick. It was the first tube that was only hers, that wasn't worn to near bottom from daily use by Rosita. The red was much more crimson on Candelaria's lips than on Wendy's. She took more naturally to the deep tone, more beautifully. But she couldn't see it. Wendy wouldn't let her.

"Oh, it looks kind of dark on you. Here, let me show you a trick."

Wendy applied some of the lipstick on Candelaria's finger and told her to rub the red into her chiseled cheekbones.

"See, now you have blush. Now it blends better. That'll have to do."

"Okay. Thanks," Candelaria said quietly, trying to find her reflection in a dusty, rust-spotted silver napkin dispenser in the girls' restroom. Wendy walked to a sink to wash her hands and Candelaria finally saw herself, smiling.

When Candelaria got home from school she reapplied the lipstick with excitement. She didn't have to pretend to be cool or unmoved. Wendy wasn't there anymore; she would never come to Candelaria's house. Her father wouldn't let her. Candelaria grabbed a handheld mirror from her sister Catalina's drawer and, along with the tube of lipstick, placed it in the front pocket of her dress. She poured a glass of water, then went out the door and through the back kitchen to find Nanan Biha squatting in the shade of a tronkon lemmai, picking pumpkin tips. The sun, though its rays only peeped through the leaves of the tree, left circles of sweat in the fabric at Nanan Biha's fa'fa' and made her muumuu stick to her body. Candelaria noticed a rusty nail just two inches from her mother's everbare feet and bent to pick it up.

"Hafa adai, darling Candi," Nanan Biha greeted Candelaria. "Maolek i eskuelå-mu?"

"Maolek gui."

Nanan Biha put down her small machete and plopped her dagan on an open patch of warm, soft grass. Candelaria gave her mother the glass of water and a big kiss on the cheek, then planted herself on the earth next to her. Nanan Biha took a giant gulp as Candelaria pulled the mirror out of her pocket and brought it to her mother's cheek. She noticed the lips Candelaria left there and playfully grabbed the mirror to shine it back at her daughter, illuminating the crimson fullness of her smile.

"Nanalao," Nanan Biha teased. "Mampos dudus i haggå-hu. Na'chagi yu'."

Candelaria reached back into her pocket for the tube of lipstick and handed it to her mother. Nanan Biha ran the lipstick once, twice, three times over her lips, for extra shine, extra color that would last. She liked to make things last, so she took her time. The result was lovely, like adding cinnamon to coffee, and the red matched perfectly with the plumeria petals printed on her yellow muumuu.

"Gof bunita hao," Candelaria complimented her.

"Ei adai, hågu lokkue haggå-hu."

Nanan Biha sat quietly with the daydreaming Candelaria for a few moments and listened to the rough voices of her sons echo in the jungle where they played. She eventually got up to look for Papan Biho and kiss him with her red lips. Candelaria grabbed the machete to finish off the picking of pumpkin tips.

❧ ❧ ❧

"Candi, Candi, come see." Dung ran the jungle trail so fast to get to the pumpkin patch that he pulled air in loudly through his nostrils as he spoke to his sister. "Come, Candi, come."

"Come where, neni?"

"Back. Backin da jungle."

"In *the* jungle, Dung."

Four-year-old Dung was Candelaria's youngest brother and student. She had started teaching English and reading classes in the American-run elementary school when she reached the eighth grade. She practiced her lessons on her youngest siblings every evening as the sun went down, and constantly corrected their mistakes when they spoke.

"Let's go in *the* jungle Candi. Hurry, you have to see."

Candelaria let Dung take her hand and lead her through the trail. At the mango grove the bitter smell of death crept above her and forced Candelaria to look up. She turned her head from the tip of her shoulder back to her chest to greet a half-dead frog smack in the face. "Ah! Ah-aha-ah!" One of the frog's legs was tied to the branch of a mango tree with fishing line. Candelaria slapped it away from her and bent over to frantically rub the potential for warts from her face with the skirt of her dress. "Ugggh!"

Candelaria looked up again and saw at least a dozen frogs hanging from the branches. Some were black and a few days dead; others squirmed in hunger with their eyes bulging out and occasionally flung their bodies in attempt to free themselves. But worse than what they looked like was their smell. The stench of the decaying frogs lodged itself in the receptors of Candelaria's nose, souring everything she ate or sniffed for weeks.

"Hayi chumogui este?" She squeezed Dung's ear lobe. "Hayi, Dung?"

The little boy pointed to another tree in the jungle. Candelaria could see a moving shadow and followed it to her brother Inocencio, who stood behind the tree shaking in silent laughter.

"Inocencio! Inocencio! *Hafa* na chumachalek hao? Kao kaduku hao?" How could he be laughing, she asked. Was he crazy? It was this tinge of madness that embarrassed Candelaria and left her constantly imagining herself in another life.

"Ti mamaigo si yu'us, Inocencio. God *never* sleeps." She flicked her fingers at the cartilage of his right ear in a strong deska that made his eyes shut in pain and left a sound ringing in his brain. "Cut them down, right now! Ti mamaigo si yu'us."

❦ ❦ ❦

Since he was a child, no one fully understood Inocencio. He didn't say much except what was asked of him and was always with a smile. When he'd smile, there's no telling who would come running his way. He had intense appeal to a certain flock of people, who could talk about themselves for hours. And since he would just stand there and smile, they loved him. It was a smile that wasn't exactly bright and shiny. His teeth crashed into each other, giving him a jagged lisp, light as mist, that made his rare words even more of an art. He was not ashamed of his colliding teeth and the food that got stuck in between them, because no one seemed to mind. And for this, he felt loved.

Unlike most fishermen, Inocencio did not tell giant stories of sharks and marlins and the spears he drove through them, or how he had first discovered the might of dynamite. How it sent shock waves through the ocean, ruptured the coral reef and blew schools of fish to the water's surface for him to collect. No one knew that Inocencio thought the dynamite was a gift from the war, just for him. He had learned how to fish this way from the Americans and bought M-80 firecrackers at the Acme store in Aniqua. Within minutes of a blast he'd have dozens of fish that would have taken him days to catch otherwise.

Why would he do this? A *pescadot* who loved the art of his work and the hours spent walking the ocean—why would he destroy it? Love. Inocencio was in love with Chilang. He could think of nothing but her while at sea. The echoes of her laughter and her moans floated in the waves as they rushed about him and swirled between his legs. He'd dig his toes into the tangled seaweed on the ocean floor and imagine they were his fingers locked in her curly hair, lightened by the rays of the sun to a hue of deep flames. He couldn't even remember a time when fishing was about the catch. A time of waiting for the right moment to toss the talaya or shoot his spear or feel a pull on one of his lines resting against the rocks. The more time he spent with Chilang, the less he wanted to be at sea.

Chilang was a woman of the land. In the mornings, she roamed the jungle behind their small shack with bare feet, found leisure in simple walks that led her down red dirt hills lined with short trees, using branches to guide her. Walks that led to streams she'd sit by and listen to but never jump in. Water was meant to wash away, she believed, and she didn't want to get lost in its flow. This made Inocencio restless: the two things he loved most could never meet. He was so addicted to Chilang that he wanted her there with him in the ocean, pulling his end boat as they walked the low tide, out past the reef to fish their food. But she would never join him, and all he could do was long for her at sea. Until the dynamite.

The speed with which it produced his catch meant he could walk with Chilang in the jungle, or work at the post office in the afternoon. And he could make more money than he ever imagined. He caught enough fish and octopus to feed Chilang, bring some to Nanan Biha's house, and sell what was left to the grocery stores. Families of fish, enough to feed an entire village, could be blasted in just seconds. So could his hand. In just seconds, a life changed like that. A part of you gone forever. One day, in just seconds, he was rendered handless, fingerless, useless. Inocencio blew off his right hand and three of his left fingers. And thus began his decline. His blatant madness.

❧ ❧ ❧

Inocencio was in the hospital for a week while his stubs healed. He didn't speak to anyone, except to ask for Chilang, who never came. He didn't know how to explain what he had done. He was stupid; that's what he thought everyone thought of him. He hadn't been planning to do it for a long time, the blast fishing. It was meant to be just until he made enough money to save, to ask

Chilang to marry him, to pay for the wedding of her dreams. But it had all blown up before his eyes.

☙ ☙ ☙

Chilang didn't even love him. She thought she did at first, when he was quiet like her, when he would get lost at sea for hours and let her be by herself in the land. But once they were living together, she got bored. Smothered. Since he never spoke to anyone, Inocencio seemed to pour out all his words on Chilang. And most of the time his stories did not make any sense to her. But she'd learned to listen and nod, to laugh at the same jokes he told over and over. This she could deal with. It was his possessiveness she could not bear. Chilang was not one of those people who got attached. Inocencio was. He wanted to know where she was all the time and tried to fit himself into all those places. Chilang had grown irritated with his constant presence. Always there, waiting for her, like nothing else in his life mattered. Waiting for her, who could go days without seeing a soul, who was happier that way.

Chilang was a rare only child. Inocencio was one of twelve. Most Chamoru families were large like his, but Chilang's parents had gotten married when they were older, after they had lived a life of religious celibacy. Her mother had been a nun for eighteen years, her father a priest for twenty-two. They had fallen in love in their forties at Mt. Carmel Church in Agat, in the second-to-the-last pew on the right side of the church. Chilang was their miracle child, so they had kept her away from the world. She had fallen for Inocencio because she saw him as an escape from the confines of her overprotective parents. She admired his skill as a fisherman because it meant that she would have space to roam while he was out making his catch. Instead, she ended up trapped in his net.

☙ ☙ ☙

Candelaria realized all of this as she sat with her brother in the hospital, and watched him look out the window for Chilang, who never came. She understood instantly why he was there, why he had used the dynamite. She cursed his stupidity and what she had known of him since he was a child, that he was selfish and crazy.

"You've always been the kaduko one," Candelaria says under her breath and wonders if she ever loved him. Of course, he was her brother, she had to love him, but there was no denying the hate. Love works that way. You never know when it will turn to hate. But it doesn't matter. With all that hate, Candelaria was the only one sitting there, loving him, wondering what he was thinking. What was Inocencio ever thinking?

IDENTITIES

Sun Burns

Teresia Teaiwa (Kiribati and Fiji)

"Mad dogs and Englishmen," the Korean man muttered.

She smiled, quizzically. "What?"

"Mad dogs and Englishmen," he repeated, and tilted his head towards the white man walking away from them.

"What does that mean?" she asked, still smiling, but now with a furrow in her brow.

The white man had a T-shirt on, but nothing on his bottom except a pair of Speedos. He had a wide-brimmed hat on his head, the kind only ladies should wear, and funny sock-like shoes on his feet. He had a bucket in his hand.

"Mad dogs and Englishmen go out in the midday sun," the Korean man elaborated. "It's a line from a Noël Coward song."

"Really?" She was impressed.

The Korean man liked her. He liked her because she didn't speak fast like the white people. And this was the first time ever that she'd asked him to repeat himself.

She liked him because he was brown. A nice brown. The glowing brown of a young coconut. And he reminded her of her father. He and her father had the same kind of hair.

It was indeed midday, she noted, as the white man became a miniature doll on the reef.

She and the Korean man only went swimming in the afternoons. The lagoon on the other side of the Atoll Hotel was warm then, and the fish nibbled a lot. He would call her to join him out in the deep, but she never would. She liked the shallows.

On Sundays they would go to mass together at Tearoaereke. He would sit on the men's side. She would sit on the women's side.

One Sunday, it was a special feast day: the feast of Corpus Christi. The congregation crawled on their knees on the coral around the church in the burning sun. She wanted to ask the Korean man what he thought about that. But she didn't.

He was a devout Catholic. And was working on his penance. She was not so devout. And hated confession. She loved the sun, but not on her knees.

Her aunts in the village would tease her because she got black very easily. Just walking from one coconut tree to another, she became a darker shade of brown. Either the equatorial sun had it in for her, or her skin was really sensitive. She didn't mind being black. She just didn't like getting burned.

Once, on the beach at Ala Moana, she and her Samoan 'afakasi friend lay out in their bikinis. A black man called out to her, "Sistah, you don't need to be gettin' anymo' sun!"

"Fuck you," she muttered, and slapped more Hawaiian Tropic dark tanning oil on.

In Fiji, the women put charcoal on their faces when they go out fishing. If she was a fisherwoman, she would too. Sunburns aren't nice. She can't sleep if she's burned. It feels like a hundred thousand ants under her skin. And she cries. Nothing will soothe it. Not baby powder, not aloe vera, not a cool, damp washcloth. Not her mother, nor her sister, blowing on her back. Nothing soothes her sunburns. But mad dogs and Englishmen make her smile.

crash

Kathy Jetñil-Kijiner (Marshall Islands)

by the side of a sagging mountain
i staggered away
tiny and scared
from a silver beast smashed to glass pieces
cold mortality dripping down my forehead
sliced skin flapping against my palm

flannel-draped samaritans blew budweiser smoke in my eyes
threw camouflage hunting jackets on me
hollered
WE
pointing to themselves
calling 9/11! YOU
pointing to me
bloody. Cold? Shiver shiver? How many fingers?
Dos?
Traayas?

in a rolling ambulance a sugar blond nurse
asked me how to spell my name
seven times
giggled. every time
eyed me suspiciously
Are you Indian?

in the hospital a male nurse
strung stitches through the blooming wounds of my wrists
his blue aloha shirt reminded me of home
i wanted to tell him i wasn't from here

Previously published, *Iep Jāltok: Poems from a Marshallese Daughter,* University of Arizona Press, 2017.

i wanted to tell him i missed my mom
i wanted to tell him i was scared
of dying in someone else's home.
he yanked the black thread
just a little tighter
as whimpers escaped from my lips.
at my friend's house
i leaned against a porcelain shower stall
yearned
to be diluted
into waters clear of color

when i turned the knob of the shower
i remembered my friend's
corn-blond family and desperate
searched the entire bathroom
swept
wiped
scooped
gathered
my swirls of long curly black hair
weary
of leaving any ethnic trace

Juan Malo & Da Real Chamoru

(a malologue)

Craig Santos Perez (Guåhan)

On behalf of the leaders and the people of the "sing-song" community, the "real Chamorros," I encourage you to pay us a visit. Locals in general are called Guamanians, but I am speaking for the real Chamorus, 'cause I am a true Chamoru myself and I care a lot about what is happening to my people. History and anthropology dictate that the real Chamorros, or "ancient" Chamorros, died centuries ago; the rest of us live outside this temporal wall. They say there are no real Chamorros; we're all mutts from centuries of changing hands. They subscribe to the belief that there are no real Chamorros left because of that very concept! But for anyone looking for a fun, lively, and real Chamoru Island–style Liberation Fiesta Celebration, we will salute you with gratitude in the real Chamorro way, as we do all those who served in the U.S. Armed forces, with music (house and trance) and the latest in the ancient ways (hip-hop, of course). One of my friends wants to start a "real" Chamorro band, which will create sounds more indigenous than just translating English lyrics. Now that's a real Chamorro dish! Has to be. Because who's heard of it? Come to think of it, who's heard of "Chamorro"? Either I have no real Chamoru pride or just no real knowledge of our "roots." Man, I was starting to feel like a real Chamorro. But if you're a real Chamorro, pass this on to 15 true Chamorros u know including the one that sent u this. Come and put yourself on the map, che'lus! Keep da brown pride umbe'!

My Blood

Marianna Hernandez (Guåhan)

Their blood
Is thick and full of
Long nights listening to stories
Of a time lost to me.

Their blood
Carries a history and tradition
That mine only has
Traces of.

Their blood
Beats through veins made strong and clean
By songs and a tongue
I cannot hear.

Their blood
Flows beneath skin made smooth and brown
By the love of the sun
I cannot feel.

My blood
Washes clearer than theirs,
Their blood I once thought
Was mine.

Téétéén Kúen

Myjolynne Kim (Chuuk)

About ten years ago, in the village of Kuchua, Tonoas Island,[1] two young men (one of whom was my cousin) were drinking together. An argument broke out and they started to fight. Taking out a knife, my cousin stabbed his drinking friend. Fortunately, the wound was not deep enough to be fatal, and the victim survived, but the incident initiated anger between the extended families of these young men and bred fear. The victim's family was furious, and my family was distressed and humiliated, and for days, people feared the incident might trigger violent disputes between the kin of both devastated families.

After getting together, my relatives decided to approach the victim's family to perform the customary gesture of *omwusomus* (reconciliation) called *téétéén kúen* (to creep like a lizard). *Téétén kúen*, a customary practice in Chuuk, is carried out during disputes, and in the past was performed on the battlefield. When one side petitioned for peace, the women would gather and advance to the enemy's homes. As per tradition, this movement would ultimately result in a partnership and peaceful agreement between the two opposing sides. Today, even with the absence of Chuukese warfare, this conciliatory gesture is still practiced among many Chuukese families, including my extended family.

So, after the stabbing, my relatives gathered and encouraged the *mwániichi* (firstborn sons), *fiinichi* (firstborn daughters), uncles, and aunties of our *eterenges* (extended family) to participate in this conciliatory movement.[2] My cousin, along with his parents, also took part.

As they sighted the victim's house, all the participants quietly knelt down, moved forward onto their stomachs, and started to crawl towards the house over mud, dirt, and rocks. When the victim's household witnessed this, they were stunned but understood immediately that it was the gesture seeking

---

1. Chuuk is an archipelago of high islands within a great barrier reef (Chuuk Lagoon) and all low islands (atolls) beyond the barrier reef. These atolls include the Mortlock Islands group and Northwest Islands. For further information and names of islands, see Alton Higashi's *Getting to Know Chuuk*, Chuuk State Department of Education, 2008. For more information on the Federated States of Micronesia (FSM), see Francis X. Hezel's *Strangers in Their Own Land*, University of Hawai'i Press, 1995.

2. In Chuukese culture, the firstborn take leadership of critical incidents, and it is offensive to decline their requests.

omwusomus. It was a heartfelt and emotional scene. My agonizing family was crying and sobbing for several reasons—not least of them being that their knees and legs were aching from crawling. But they also cried because they were ashamed and humiliated, and anxious as to whether or not the family would accept their gesture. They were crying not only for the physical pain but also because they were deeply apologetic about what had happened.

When members of the victim's family saw my family's tears, they also began to cry, and they welcomed my family into their home. They realized that my family respected them greatly by performing the *téétéén kúen*, a practice of *omwusomus* (forgiveness) and *afféér* (peacemaking). Although the victim's family members were upset and perhaps wanted justice done, they also realized that forgiveness was more important. Their welcome symbolized acceptance and forgiveness.[3]

I share this story to emphasize an important aspect of Chuukese culture that differs from the conventional narratives given about Chuuk and its people. Among the island groups in Micronesia, Chuuk had the reputation for making the most frequent attacks on foreign ships, and Chuukese were often referred to as fierce warriors and a treacherous race.[4] As a result, Chuuk has acquired a reputation for hostility and violence—a reputation that I feel is exaggerated but that persists to this very day. Stories like this one emphasize Chuukese cultural values that transcend "violence" and "warfare," and display a more positive aspect of the Chuukese people.

---

3. Myjolynne, Kim, "Combating 'Dreaded Hogoleu': Re-Centering Histories and Stories of Chuukese Warfare," MA thesis, University of Hawai'i–Manoa, 2007.

4. Francis X. Hezel, S.J., "The Beginnings of Foreign Contact with Truk." *Journal of Pacific History*, 8: 51–73: 1973; Francis X. Hezel, S.J., "Chuuk: A Caricature of an Island," in *Pacific Places, Pacific Histories*, Edited by Brij Lal, Honolulu: University of Hawai'i Press, 2004, 102–119.

The Micronesian Question

Emelihter Kihleng (Pohnpei)

For those who
Think they know
Wonder
Don't care
Or haven't given thought to . . .

WHAT IS A MICRONESIAN?
No, not a POLYNESIAN
Not a MELANESIAN

MICRONESIAN
MICRONESIAN
MICRO-NESIAN

Micro
Small
Miniscule
Invisible
Ignored
Isolated
Distant, "tiny islands"

MICRONESIANS
Migrating
Moving
Island hopping
On Continental Air Mike
Departing from our islands
Descending upon the U.S.
who gave us
permission
back in '86

Previously published, *Tin Fish Net 2*, Tinfish Press, June 2005.

slowly getting noticed
across Honolulu
FOB MICRONESIANS
women wearing
colorful,
bright,
long skirts
Pink combs in long hair
Walking by the road
On TheBus
With babies
Accompanied by
other women
With babies
Dangling gold earrings
Crammed into apartments
Movin' on up
Stereotyped
Misrepresented
Speaking "MICRONESIAN"
If you read the news
You'd think we were
Invading legal aliens

Newspaper Headlines Read:

"MICRONESIAN BILL TOO LONG OVERDUE; THE ISSUE: THE
FEDERAL GOVERNMENT OWES HAWAII NEARLY $100 MILLION
FOR SERVICES PROVIDED TO IMMIGRANTS FROM MICRONESIA"

"MICRONESIANS: THE INVISIBLE MALIHINI"

"HAWAII MAY GET HELP IN HELPING MICRONESIANS"

we are a **"BURDENSOME"** group
of more than 10,000
50% living below
federal poverty level,
relying **"not only on educational services but on social-
welfare services, health care and safety-net programs"**

CAYETANO CLAIMS:

**"WE SIMPLY CANNOT ABSORB THE EXTRA COSTS OF PRO-
VIDING SOCIAL SERVICES AND MEDICAL AND FINANCIAL
ASSISTANCE NEEDED BY SUCH POOR MIGRANTS"**

Are **MICRONESIANS** the only **"POOR MIGRANTS"** coming here?

Are **MICRONESIANS** guilty of consuming all
food stamps
invading all
KPTs,
Mayor Wrights,
and Palolo housings
Using up all
QUEST,
WIC,
MEDICAID
and welfare on island???

I DON'T THINK SO.

So where are all these "MICRONESIANS" coming from?
Who are we?
What are we?

MICRONESIA
POLYNESIA
MELANESIA
colonial constructions
colonial creations
imaginations
configurations
divisions of Pacific Islands

MICRONESIA in the Western Pacific
between Hawai'i and the Philippines
And YES, Guam, the U.S. Territory,
is located in MICRONESIA
And the people there, Chamorros,
are MICRONESIANS in denial

the term "MICRONESIAN"
Was first coined on Guam
To distinguish Guamanians from
Their non-U.S. citizen, inferior neighbors
migrating to Guam
MICRONESIAN became a means to
Discriminate and target a vulnerable population

At George Washington High School
On Guam

MICRONESIANS
Are discussed on a daily basis

Those fucken MICRONESIANS

I'm not sitting by stupid Trukese

*I would never go out with a fucken Trukese. I'd shoot her if she tried
to kiss me*

my school
segregated
MICRONESIANS in A and B wings
in the cafeteria eating free lunch
Filipinos in C and D wings
Chamorros in E and F wings
And everyone else around someplace
Chuukese, AKA Trukese
not allowed
To wear red
The school
Said that was
The Chuukese gang color

MICRONESIANS don't identify as MICRONESIANS
We were given that identification after leaving home
Upon coming to Guam and Hawai'i
Each of us unique like
Tongans,
Samoans, and
Hawaiians
Who do not merely identify as Polynesians

WE ARE:
Pohnpeians
Palauans
Chuukese
Chamorros
Kosraeans
Nauruans
Yapese
Gilbertese
Marshallese
and More

WE SAY:
Kaselehlie
Alii
Ran Annim
Hafa Adai
Lenwo
Mogethin
Yokwe

So what is a **MICRONESIAN**?

Can you tell me what is a **MICRONESIAN**?

An outside invention?
A misconception?
A location?
A population?

MICRONESIAN lacks concrete definition
An inadequate
Insufficient
Identity
Misplaced
Bestowed wrongly
Upon a large and diverse
Pacific Island population
Who are not under one flag
Who do not speak one tongue
Who do not eat the same food
And most of all who
Do not want to be recognized as One

Micro-Eye-Class

Jelovea Seymour (Kosrae and Chuuk)

Looking through the eyes of an islander
Hitching that eye glass on the tip of flat nose
Makes me look smart and hip
Are you really blind
Too many encyclopedias ventured
Too little time to close them atron muta?[1]
Walking into the room
Pushin your nose in the air
Mouth smartly pouted
Kusel kom oralah![2]
Scholar! Wannabe they say
Click, clack, click, clack.
Me no comprehension
Work on that EN 110 paper
Teacher said that too many grammatical error
Click, clack, tick, tock
Udahn ke pahi suksukuhl UOG.[3]
Nod, flip that dark hair, chest heaving, nose in the air
Adjust 'em fashion eye-glass
You Micronesian eye-Class
When will you learn it's not
About the ngetnget pakomotom![4]

---

1. eyes
2. Oh, you've really accomplished something.
3. You're so lucky to be attending UOG.
4. to feel sorry for; empathy

Kaki se (a coconut)

Jelovea Seymour (Kosrae and Chuuk)

Kaki so brown, so plain,
So insignificant, backward, indigenous
thick skinned,
Hollow shell, hard, useless.
Kaki—What's your nationality?
"I'm Kosraean!" almost defensively . . . Oh?
Redeem self: "I'm not Chuukese!"
Chuukese this, Chuukese that
"Kosraean, Chuukese, whatever! They're all the same."
Look Kaki up and down
Hmm . . . you need serious pedicure treatment,
MACY'S—no, Ross is cheaper . . . Ever heard of hair salon?
(Pei mac ma uh!)
No signs of powder and lip gloss; just plucked eyebrows
Yew! So filthy smell of Kaki and sweat,
So Ghetto. Kaki you no belong UOG
Thrift backward island coconut.

Echukeison in Maikronisia

Alex Rhowunio'ng (Chuuk)

Did you just say, "Echukeison in Maikronisia?"
I know exactly how you spell it.
But just how, precisely, did you mean?

I wonder, 'cuz, see,
When u pointed high-powered telescope heavenward,
I raised my head and gazed skyward.
When you looked for life . . . way, way out there,
I looked within, 'round here . . . up there.

When u reached for your surgical knife
I snaked my fingers, delicately,
'round tender swells of twisted flesh . . .
 mangled bones.
You cut open to mend,
I closed cuts to heal, to set in places
                              bits of broken bones

When you linked-up to *your* satellites,
I called up *my* rolling thunder.
And when you downloaded from the web . . .
through the thunder, I chatted with a calling relative
far, far away.

You proceeded to study the ocean
I felt the ocean
You studied the soil
I was one with the earth
You studied the weather
I tasted the rain,
listened to the winds . . .
                    and felt the calm stillness afterwards.

When you taught a kid,
I raised a young man,
        a young woman.
NOW, you're studying a disease
And, what do you know,
I am the disease!
        Thanks to you.

So, you're still going to echukeit me in Maikronisia?
What for?

I am Maikronisia!

My bones are of my ageless family stories,
          my clans' epics.
My words melt into the tide of my waters
And spring up on the mountains of my islands.
I was born with the stars and the ocean!

U still think you'll echukeit me?
For me . . . for my home . . . for *my* Maikronisia?

Echukeit me and you'll take Maikronisia out of me.
Echukeit me and you'll take me out of my Maikronisia.

Teach me only
to breathe
to taste
to see
to feel;
To live . . . to love; but leave me be . . .
a Maikronisian!

Bomb the School System

Melvin Won Pat-Borja (Guåhan)

One of my students was arrested today
He skipped my 4th-period English class to fill
An empty gray space under a freeway overpass
With spray-painted dreams
And even though I'm phenomenally pissed,
I'm more upset about the class he missed;
We were reading poetry today and I think he would have dug it
Taylor is definitely the most colorful character in my classroom
The classic cut of the ADHD profile with a capital "H"
I like to say that it stands for "hilarious"
But the experts say it means Attention Deficit Hyperactive Disorder
That he can't pay attention
But it's not that he can't pay attention, it's that he can't NOT pay attention
He is skin, bone, and attitude rolling in on a skateboard
5 minutes late every afternoon yelling, "Whatup cutty?!"
I think he thinks I'm a pirate
He was the orphaned student that no one wanted
Drifting through campus looking for learning in all the wrong places
In textbooks that teach him nothing he needs
In lessons that leave him left out
Absent from the equation
He always seems lost in the hallways
Taylor does not have a seat in my class
He just wanders from desk to desk
With an occasional pit stop at the dry erase board to tag his name
As if to say, "I was here Melvin. Don't mark me absent minded. I'm still
    listening, but
these legs need to move and that desk is a prison. Teach me something."
And so I do
Lessons hidden in Hip Hop soliloquies
He says a lot of things,
But he truly speaks with his hands
Aerosol cans drop bombs on urban canvases

More precise than government missiles
He paints a thousand pictures with a word
Parallel pigments painted priceless
While pig-men pound pavement to place metal bracelets on adolescents
For the defacement of barren walls
I can just imagine him thinking, "These walls could really use some color."
I wish there was some other way for him to get that shit out
Without winding up in juvie
I'm sure his parents wish he would do something more constructive
I wish he owned The Great Wall of China
He is Picasso with a spray can and
No one will ever really appreciate him until he is gone
He is misunderstood
Which is why he fits right in with the rest of the vagabonds in my class
Labeled academically handicapped and intellectually inept
He finds himself in Special Ed. meetings
Surrounded by experts with more labels than solutions
They say he can't focus
But they've never seen him
finger pressed on a fat cap, bringing a lifeless wall back from the dead
never seen him resuscitate concrete
I swear I've seen him make brick breathe
And it's days like these that make me feel like I've failed him
Like I couldn't give him the tools to express himself
But he was given a gift at birth
He makes paint speak like a poet
I wish they could *see* his language
They charged him with defacing government property
But he should charge them with illiteracy
Their literature is ill—literally
Taylor is a surgeon and this city is in need of emergency surgery
I mean seriously, how do you deface a faceless fallacy
Built on stolen land anyway?
And where did I go wrong?
What could I have done to keep him in my classroom?
How do I deny that I sympathize with the rebel that pulses in his veins?
I can just see him afraid that these streets will forget his face
And so he tattoos his name on an abandoned building
That's been forgotten just the same
With lonely walls wishing they could only be so lucky
as to become a masterpiece someday
The experts say that he'll never become a productive member of society
But he hates this society anyway
And I can't blame him
This urban wasteland is run by a man who wants to tame him

But "not I" said the cat

See, you can take rap out the concrete jungle, but you can't take the concrete jungle out

the rap; and he is Hip Hop

But what do I do now? Where do we go from here? How do I make sure he doesn't get

pinched again? These questions don't have answers without chains.

There are no simple solutions

this is not a problem about truancy or delinquency

But when deficiencies are made to be disorders

The student spirals downward in this order:

Self-confidence is shattered, trust doesn't matter, the system fails again, and all that's

left is anger

Sometimes these things look like graffiti

Sometimes they look like Virginia Tech

Somewhere down the line, someone failed him

Even worse, no one ever taught him HOW to fail

Never taught him that our struggles are fingerprints

They make us unique

Never taught him that a disability is not an inability

It's just reality reminding us that we all do things differently

So Taylor, if you're listening, don't let anyone tell you any different

You can never be anyone better than yourself,

so might as well get comfortable

And if anyone ever tries to change you,

remember that you put the FUN in dysfunctional

"unfit"

Melvin Won Pat-Borja (Guåhan)

On Monday mornings I drag my lazy ass out of bed and prep my head for
    another day
without a dollar
Wrap my words in compassion to create scholars out of students hungry
    enough to meet
me in the middle
And then there's Lawrence:
Five foot six, about 170 pounds plus the weight of the world on his back
He looks a lot bigger than he is
The other kids either fear him or respect him
He is like family I've never met
A long-lost relative divided by opportunities
He is proud like our people have always been
Brown skin that blends like earth
Brown eyes that bend to no one
He is 16 years of defiant aggression
Born with everything to prove and
My lessons fall on ears deafened and disillusioned by low expectations
    and premature
violence
a descendent of warriors
thick flesh wraps wide palms and
flat knuckles to form fists fit for breaking,
But when open, they offer gentle security
He is a walking contradiction just like me
And I hate the similarity
If makes me feel weak and incompetent
I know that he was sent to me for a reason but I still question my ability to teach
Sometimes I preach hysterically and wonder why no one listens
Some days I feel like I am running a marathon by doing the cha-cha: I am
    moving, but
not forward
Lawrence looks at me like a friend in need

I study the insides of my eyelids searching for answers to give him
And I keep coming up empty
He is searching for sympathy in me, a hand out, some charity
Because we are both bred from the same bloodline
Pump pressure
The veins like vines
It reminds me why I'm here; I want to help him
plant hope inside his ear like a seed that he can hear
To remind him that we were more than just warriors
We are the oldest civilization in the Pacific
But sometimes explicit screams louder than dreams
And my patience is busting at the seams
He is as stubborn as a hangnail
Playing hangman with butterfly knives and gram bags of weed stuffed in
   deep pockets
with shallow vision and half-baked ambition
I'd be a liar if I said I've never packed a weapon or gotten high,
Which is why, sometimes, I just wanna take him out back and slap the
   shit out of him
My composure snaps like guitar strings under the weight of heavy metal
Thunder clap and just like that,
We are identical typical brown,
Pacific Islander drowned in his own anger
Push panic to automatic crabs-in-a-bucket syndrome
and here we are locked expressionless
I second guess myself twice and give advice that I never listened to
I've fallen face first flat into fallacy just to see the bottom
I've gotten caught up in my own racial profile more than once and
   I wonder what gives
me the right to lend this young man even a little bit of advice?
Besides, these days, I'm not too big to admit that I'm a piece of shit like the
   rest of them
I smoke cigarettes and teach poetry like a hypocrite
A part-time participant and example-setter when it's convenient
These students need me like Ozzy Osbourne needs a double dose of heroin
I am not the answer
Just another problem with problems overflowing like bullshit from the
   idiot tube
When our leaders lube their nuclear weapons in preparation to fuck the
   world
How am I any different than them?
But what I do know is that, someone stood up for me so that I could
   return the favor
Because if no one ever taught me to stand up for myself
like I had a forest fire underneath my ass,

I would have stopped, dropped, rolled over and died a long time ago
So Lawrence, I may not be the role model that you need
But I will carry you barefoot across the desert in search of a heater
Because I'm not just your teacher I am family
And you are not heavy, you are my brother.

English Only Law Impact

Angela Hoppe-Cruz (Guåhan)

Part I **Ekungok, pot fabot . . .**

Guela yan Guelu, what meaning do our words have if we cry to you in English?

Part II **Broken**

Guahu
    si
chaggi I
       fino
Chamorro
    Dispensa yu,
guahu
    si
fino
            Chamorro
sa
m
aj(y)
a
ma
k

English Only Law: Impact 1

Part III **Beware** (enunciate as you read)

surprised, you compliment my english
while my sister laughs at the perfection with which my tongue
enunciates

and my elders laugh at my feeble attempts to speak in our native
tongue.
what is it about my english that impresses you so?
hmmm . . . is it the color of my skin that caught you off guard?
did you not think it possible for a brown-skinned woman to
art-iculate
            post-ulate
                    to not be consumed by the colonizer's hate?
beware of the {micro} brown-skinned woman
for we are broken, yet full of surprises.

Language with an Attitude
Palauan Identity with
an English Accent

Isebong M. Asang (Belau)

"Arc had ra Siabal a uchul eyak mengededuch a tekoi ra Siabal. Kmal mle mer-ingl e mekngit a omerelir meng diak el sowak el mesub a tekoi ra Ngebard. Tis a frree cuntree."
    "Haalo," my mother yelled into the phone. "Sorrrie, no speekie Englees."
English. Speak Good Standard English. This is my story, my journey, my search.

Leaving

My father migrated to Guam from Palau in the late 1940s. My mother fol-lowed in 1951, with me straddling her left hip and a box of bento tucked under her right arm. I was only six months old. We boarded the MV *Gunnersknot*, a cargo ship that embarked out of Malakal and sailed for about eight days before docking at Apra Harbor in Sumay Bay, Guam. For the duration of the trip, we slept under a makeshift tarp that protected us from the wind, the rain, and the sun. The days were hot, and my mother ate corned beef, smoked fish, sliv-ered sea cucumber (bêche-de-mer) fermented in lime juice and soy sauce, taro (yellow and purple), and billum (ground tapioca wrapped in coconut leaves), and drank warm coconut juice from the boxed bento packed for this long trip.

I entered the school system speaking Palauan, which was the only language spoken at home by both of my parents. While I speak and write Palauan, it is not because of any formal education in the Western sense, but because I grew up in a family in which Palauan was the only language used. To my parents, language was the means by which cultural values and beliefs were transmitted and mediated both in the home and within the Palauan-speaking communities both outside and on the islands of Palau. "Speak and learn the Palauan way of life," they admonished.

Both of my parents spoke Japanese, from the brief education they were allowed under the Japanese regime. But the only time I heard them speak

Japanese was when they wanted to talk about something they didn't want me to understand. I learned to recognize little words such as *kodomo* (child), *onna* (girl), *mizu* (water), and *takai* (expensive). "Ohhh, you no see me last night," crooned the female Japanese voice out of the megaphone held up by a little white dog attached to a manually wound-up RCA phonograph. The 33 1/3 RPM records were thick and heavy, but they were my mother's prized possession, brought from Palau to Guam. I never learned to speak Japanese from them.

Returning

I am a migrant. I have been to several Asian countries, from Japan to the Philippines. I have lived mostly on Guam since that hot November day we boarded the cargo ship at Malakal. I have visited and lived in several states—Washington state, Pennsylvania, Oklahoma, Texas, and California. I now live in Hawai'i. I have been to Mexico and Cuba. But the most profound memories I have were the summers my mother sent me home to Palau to live with my grandmother, and eventually my grand-aunt.

I had a love-hate relationship with Palau during those long hot summers. I missed eating Spam. I ate fish—smoked fish, fried fish, dried fish, pickled fish, raw fish, soup fish, reef fish, deep sea fish. There was fish for breakfast, fish for lunch, fish for dinner . . . fish, fish, fish! I missed eating rice. I ate taro—yellow taro, white taro, purple taro, boiled taro, mashed taro, pounded taro, land taro, patch taro. Taro for breakfast, taro for lunch, taro for dinner . . . taro, taro, taro! I missed the running water to wash dishes, to take showers. I missed simply opening a faucet and filling water receptacles. I had to lug pails of water from one of the many screen-covered 50-gallon drum catchments to wash dishes and fill the drinking receptacles. I had to take cold showers at a runoff stream from an underwater spring that was located in the middle of nowhere, with only the leaves and the scent of the wild gardenias separating me from the rest of the world.

But I loved the open fire that smoked the fish and warmed the bamboo-floored kitchen. It was a place to perch and watch my grandmother and sometimes my grand-aunt grate and boil coconut milk, extracted from the shredded coconut, to make oil to sell at the village market. I loved eating the crispy dregs left at the bottom of the black cauldron when the oil was drained into recycled Coke bottles and capped with a coconut-husk cork. It was under this tin-roofed kitchen that I began my journey into the many paths of my genealogical community. It was through the eyes of my grandmother and then my grand-aunt—when my grandmother journeyed to the land of her father—that I learned to "see."

It was in this community that I learned that the self existed in relation to and was dependent for its very being on the lives and experiences of everyone in the community. I learned that the self is not a signifier of one "I" but the coming together of many "eyes." The self is seen as the collective realities of the past and present, parents and children, family and clan. Social construction of self meant that I would be in touch with the voices that spoke to me from the past, and that from the present I could "see" and touch my genealogical story. However, because I didn't grow up in a Palauan community, these voices have been suppressed, silenced, and it is this collective voice that I struggle today to recover.

"Speak Good Standard English"

"No one will want to give you a job. You sound uneducated. You will be looked down upon. You're speaking a low-class form of good Standard English . . . [Y]ou'll go nowhere in life. Listen, students, I'm telling you the truth like no one else will. Because they don't know how to say it to you. I do. Speak Standard English. DO NOT speak pidgin. You will only be hurting yourselves." [1]

Although this passage appeared in a novel portraying fictitious Japanese American families in Hilo, Hawai'i, these words and its explicit message are real, and they resonate throughout the Pacific in ominous waves of militarism, expansionism, educationism, Englishism—"isms" that have never ebbed. I can still see Mr. Wilkinson, a balding, middle-aged white man, standing in front of my fifth-grade class promising us the good life if we learned to speak good Standard English.

"Speak good Standard English," he commanded his little regiment of one brown Palauan and 23 mestizos and mestizas. "English will civilize you. It's 'th,' with your tongue pressed against the top of your front teeth. 'T-th-three,' not 't' as in t-t-tree."

English was mandatory in the classrooms and on the school grounds, with detrimental consequences for offenders. Being paddled with a chiseled plank of plywood that resembled a miniature oar was the punishment of choice. If paddling didn't send the message home, expulsion did. I was glad that I was never expelled; I would have probably gotten a worse beating than with the paddle. My mother would not have understood, and her coconut-rib switch would have splintered. To her, education was the vehicle to enter this foreign world.

English. This one word has shaped my cultural identity as a second-generation Palauan migrant compelled to speak, read, and write in good Standard English. It is a word that has become a journey, both complex and full of contradictions, into the constantly shifting world of cultural identity construction. My perspectives are those of an insider-outsider, who has been raised outside of Palau searching for some meaning in this sustained voyage home. Although other colonizing tribes exhausted their presence in Micronesia, the American educational system and English as a medium of instruction have etched the

---

1. Lois-Ann Yamanaka, *Wild Meat and the Bully Burgers* (Farrar, Straus and Giroux, 1996).

most profound impression—complimenting, altering, and adding—onto the complexity of my Palauan cultural identity.

See Jane Run

"Speak and write Standard English."

See Jane run. See Isebong run? Jane must not see too much sun where she lives. She is so pale, even her eyes are blue.

See Spot run. See Buta run—hmm. Buta is sooo lazy; he loves to dig his snout in the slob and laze under the lean-to tin in the midday sun. Buta cannot run. He waddles like a duck and occasionally his huge pink belly rubs against the coarse gravel that lines his bed.

The ubiquitous *Dick and Jane* readers are but one example of the tools used to teach the English language in the tiny village of Sinajana. The method of instruction, the curriculum, and the artifacts (books, teachers, media, technology) are English. Palau today is no different. Woven through the various institutions, most of which are foreign to the Palauan culture, English has been the second official language of the Republic for the past fifty years and continues to be into the twenty-first century. English is a language without borders, with an overreaching grasp.

This morning I was so nervous about how my presentation would read and sound.[2] I was nervous because I didn't know if it would be comprehensible to a room full of academic professionals. "Speak and write in good Standard English" rang in my ears all night, so that I did not get much sleep. I arrived early and, to my relief, I saw Dr. Karen Peacock (curator for Hamilton's PACC collection). I have spent countless hours with Karen discussing these very issues that I am sharing with you today, so I asked her to read my presentation just to make sure that it made sense. Although she had to leave early, she reassured me that my key ideas came through, but she told me I had crammed too much history into such a small space. Her one suggestion was that I inject my own personal experience into it.

"It will add the personal touch and bring you closer to your audience," she wrote in the margin.

My Children

Joshua Fishman (1998), a distinguished professor in language and linguistics, estimates that one-third of the world's population, or about 1.6 billion people, speak English in one form or another on a daily basis.[3] The English language has

---

2. This article was originally presented Oct. 20, 1999, at a conference entitled "Out of Oceania: Diaspora, Community, and Identity." The conference was hosted by the Center for Pacific Islands Studies, UH Mānoa.

3. "New Linguistic Order," *Foreign Policy* 1, no. 113 (26 December 1999).

crossed national borders and, without prejudice regarding ethnicity, has created faceless cultures mirrored in the following six "worlds": transnational companies; internet communication; scientific research; youth culture; international goods and services; and news and entertainment media.[4]

I have five children. My older sons and daughter speak and understand Palauan. Growing up, they were privileged to have my parents on Guam. And when my father retired and both of my parents moved back to Palau, my children, too, began spending the summers with family. The two that I have at home now are not so privileged. My 13-year-old daughter understands when I speak to her, but never replies in Palauan. My 9-year-old son knows only *sulang* (thank you) and *alii* (hello). They live in Hawai'i, and my middle son lives in Germany. And regardless of whether they know and speak Palauan, my kids—from the oldest to the youngest—all converse in English and reply in English when I speak Palauan to them. They crave and thrive in the "six worlds," obliterating their Palauan world.

Pennycook explains my family's phenomenon with his linking of "discourse" with power and knowledge. "Discourses," he argues, "are organizations of knowledge that have become embedded in social institutions and practices, a constellation of power/knowledge relationships that organize texts and produce and reflect different subject positions."[5]

In other words, Pennycook's "discourse" institutionalizes the English language so that its usage for my children has become natural, neutral, and beneficial, and prevents them from recognizing the relationship between the spread of English and the inequitable structures of international relations.[6]

I Pledge Allegiance

"I pledge allegiance to the Flag of the United States of America and to the Republic for which it stands" could be heard every morning at precisely 7:55 a.m., drifting through the concrete halls of Sinajana Elementary School. In the courtyard, semi-enclosed by a two-story building that has now been renamed Carlos Taitano Elementary School, we were required to stand at attention in front of the American flag, flapping over the Guam flag in the Pacific breeze, and pledge allegiance. Back in the classroom, Mr. Wilkinson started the day by calling each one of us to stand in front of the class and recite, "Four score and seven years ago, our forefathers brought forth to this country . . . ." I always wondered what happened to those distant ancestors whose skin was as white as the wigs they wore. I thought I must be what my science teacher told me I was—an aberration of the gene pool.

---

4. Ian Seaton, "Linguistic Non-imperialism," *ELT Journal*, vol. 51, no. 4 (1 October 1997): 381–382.

5. Alastair Pennycook, *The Cultural Politics of English as an International Language* (Longman 1994), p. 104.

6. Y. Tsuda, "Critical Studies on the Dominance of English and the Implications for International Communication," *Nichibunken Japan Review* (1998): 219–236.

Leonard Mason, professor of anthropology at the University of Hawai'i, advised the Navy in 1951 that "[i]n the future there will be fewer rather than more contacts between the mass of Micronesians and the English-speaking people."[7] Mason also felt that the teachers recruited locally by the Navy to teach English taught "poor English which has no value whatsoever" because they did not speak English as a first language. Consequently, he advocated teaching in the vernacular language in areas that would be *good* [emphasis mine] for the islanders such as in health and hygiene, subsistence activities, social studies and the basic skills that would create *good* [emphasis mine] providers and mothers of the young men and women of Micronesia.[8] "Good" meant that it was imperative that these ancient societies learn social skills from a nation that had just soaked their sandy island shores with the blood of thousands of its good young male providers.

Woman as Savage

"As part of the requirement for Speech Communication 210, you will be required to write and talk about a topic you choose to the class. Choose a topic of interest to you and to the others in the class as well. A topic that we don't already know about," instructed the professor of speech communications at the University of Guam. "It must be written and delivered in good Standard English."

I chose to write about the naked facts about women of Palau and how the culture encourages the practice of marriage as a means of wealth acquisition. From my native perspective, I began, "In Palau, a woman's body is a form of collateral to gain access to land, money, and wealth."

An irate Professor S. wagged his finger in my face, yelling, "Young lady, in this society we do not say 'woman's body.' It is 'womanhood'! 'Woman's body' is savage. It is the language of the uncivilized, especially depicted in such primitive acts."

The difference, I surmised years later, lay in the Belauan woman's matriarchal right to land, money, and division of properties in her clan of origin vis-à-vis the social welfare systems targeted at women and children in the U.S.

Differences

This inequitable structure of international relations, particularly as it relates to the morality of language, sanctions the desire of the Other to access English. However, this desire is not always to the benefit of the colonizer. Denial of access to English and the promotion of education in the local languages were as critical to colonialism as was the insistence on English,[9] as in the case of Palau.

---

7. Quoted in Karen M. Peacock, *Maze of Schools: Education in Micronesia, 1951–1964, "The Gibson Years,"* dissertation, University of Hawai'i, 1990, p. 26.

8. Quoted in Peacock.

9. Pennycook.

On Guam, I was forced to speak English at school. In Palau, the debate over English, as it was with the rest of Micronesia, was disguised and centered on financial constraints and on the lack of properly trained teachers. Consequently, the students in Palau learned to read and write in the vernacular with the aid of mimeographed text in the early years. Today, the vernacular is used to teach in the primary grades (one to three) in Palau. Then English and Palauan are used from grades four to twelve. However, the textbooks are predominantly in English, and a student is required to take four units of English and one unit of Palauan for high school graduation. Guam, on the other hand still has an English-only curriculum from preschool on up to twelfth grade, with Chamoru immersion programs and bilingual education available. Both Guam and Palau use textbooks that are written and printed in the United States by American authors. Although there has been an effort to develop textbooks written by local writers, it has been slow and sporadic.

These early debates on language in Palauan history under the U.S. are rather benign when compared to the Kennedy administration's aid targeted at the "disadvantaged and poor." Under his administration, an accelerated rate of development was encouraged so that the people could make an informed and free choice as to their future. Operating within the discourse of expansionism, the Kennedy administration not only hired Americans as contract teachers to teach in the rural areas of Palau but sent Peace Corps Volunteers (PCV) in later years to replace contract teachers. There was also an explosion of educational aid funding that funneled huge sums into the island's coffers and increased the enrollment of young men and women in institutions of higher learning in the U.S. and abroad. Palauans did not always possess the cultural capital to take advantage of this rapid deluge of educational aid funding, designed to increase Palauan dependency on the U.S.[10] Not all students who went away to attend higher institutions of learning succeeded. Consequently, these unsuccessful ones were forced to work at entry-level jobs, forming small diasporic communities in host countries such as Guam, Hawai'i, and the continental U.S. Those who did return, impregnated with the values of the conferred degree, found adjustment back into their island culture not only difficult but plagued with tensions between them and the stay-at-home Palauans. Today this juxtaposing of differing cultural values has contributed to complex issues of identity.

Omelengmes

Palau is historically an oral society; its values and cultural expectations socialize the youth into a highly stratified hierarchy of behavior. The ways of knowing in the Palauan culture are embodied in the language of *omelengmes*,

---

10. Donald Shuster, *Islands of Change in Palau: Church, School, and Elected Government, 1891–1981*, dissertation, University of Hawai'i, 1982.

the language of social and economic order for Palauans. It is delineated by some researchers as the culture of the word, which "expects the youth to be quiet, to know its place, to respect elders, to be satisfied with a subordinate role and to accept Palau as it is."[11] These Western perceptions are inaccurate, reducing *omelengmes* to stereotypes that generalize a complex way of life. Intrinsic to *omelengmes* is the relationship between Palauan and nature, between Palauan and the rest of humanity, and Palauan and time.

Omelengmes is and continues to define the relationship between Palauans and their natural environment. It determines the boundaries of personal consumption and limits each Palauan's harvest from the environment. It is an environmental control that ensures a continuous supply for all and recognizes that nature is not as quick to replenish its largesse. Thus, survival has meant that Palauans maintain a close relationship with nature to ensure that its bounty will be here tomorrow. For Palauans, this bounty is possible because the weather assures supply in its pristine form rather than by preservatives. Antithetical to the exploitative ways of the cold West, where nature must be tamed to ensure survival, *omelengmes* involves maximizing natural resources without artificial interests.

Omelengmes is woven into the Palauans' respect for other living beings. This ensures the survival of the species through the agglomerate sense of mediation that creates and maintains the social order of Palauan society. Accustomed to having a lot of space for mobility and intermigration, Palauans respect and honor community space. Thus *omelengmes* nourishes politeness even if it means forfeiting immediate gratification based on the perceived need of another. In a capitalistic society in which the competing needs of the consumer surpass the need of the needy, *omelengmes* is seen as being lazy, unproductive, and backward.

At the root of *omelengmes* is the belief that there is a time and place for everything. Patience becomes a virtue. The generalized Western view of *omelengmes* is that Palauans expect that "youth need to be quiet and know their place," that Palauan children learn primarily through observation, and that teaching/learning interactions favor demonstrations more than verbal rationalization. While there is some truth to this, it is theoretically reductionistic. In reality, not only are Palauan children expected to observe, but they are pushed toward adult standards of speech, behavior, and responsibility at a very young age. Children are constantly engaged in cognitive and interaction skills that promote comprehension and inferencing and draw on the creative use of metaphors, all these essential for effective performance and recognition as an elder. Thus, education is a lifelong journey that is "graded" by the language of the elders in the community and by their collective and complex cultural perspectives. *Omelengmes* venerates the aggregate body of knowledge culled and modulated across generations and legitimized by Palauan elders. *Omelengmes* establishes

---

11. Shuster, p. 216.

the borders that articulate language and action within the Palauan community. To a linear society, however, in which life is governed by a day planner, *omeleng-mes* is construed as precarious and fatalistic.

By contrast, the English language, as taught to non-native speakers, is not only pervasive, it is invasive and individualistic. As taught, "good Standard English" objectifies the English language. In other words, English becomes "an object that is disconnected from all the other political and cultural forces around it."[12] Dramatizing a society in which "first impression is important" not only in what you wear but in terms of what comes out of your mouth, Standard English is a struggle in which speaking is a matter of "isms" rather than a communicative tool. Prescriptivism consequently is a mask behind which hidden messages that speak to power reside and the voices of Other are silenced.

Omelengmes is symbolized via English lenses such as museums, reservations, national parks, and social safety nets. But to native Belauans, *omelengmes* is the dynamics of competitiveness fed by the thirst for wisdom. Today, English is the second official language in Palau. It is also the institutional language of business, law, government, and education. Those who have access to the English language dominate and maneuver within these foreign institutions. English, unfortunately, is the language of power and status. Education in and acquisition of the English language are seen not only as a means to comprehend and discern the ways of the foreigner, but also as a vehicle by which to appropriate status. This is problematic when juxtaposed against language and knowledge acquisition in the Belauan society. Foreign artifacts and technology have now replaced the "eyes" of the elders in the community.

I am not arguing against development. My concerns are the hidden curricula and the hidden messages that accompany the acquisition of the English language. These must be brought to the fore and discussed in the classroom. As I have evidenced in my journey through an educational system that is predominately English, as a Palauan, my voice, my genealogical history, my ways of knowing have been and are silenced in the English curriculum.

Exposing the Hidden Curriculum

Paulo Freire speaks to a hidden curriculum that operates in classes as a "culture of silence."[13] Traditionally, the language of knowledge in Palau as a means to the eventual acquisition of power is usually shared between mentor/mentee and parent/child in ungodly hours of the night when the public is asleep, or in remote places away from the ears of possible appropriators. The economic, political, and historical bonds between the U.S. and the Palauans have watered down this way of living. The hegemonic position of English has pushed *omelengmes* to a second-

---

12. Pennycook.
13. Paolo Freire, *The Politics of Education: Culture, Power, and Liberation* (Bergin & Garvey, 1985).

ary position. This is further reinforced by the fact that those elders who traditionally would have been the mentors and "graders" of the up-and-coming young leaders of the community do not necessarily possess the cultural capital of the incoming foreign institutions. Consequently, education in the broadest sense of the word is relegated to the classroom, to artifacts and technology, and to the teachers who wield the power to mold the minds of the future of Palau.

Who I Am and Who We Want to Be

Although I was raised outside of Palau, my cultural identity is predominantly Palauan. However, I find that my views are an agglomeration of Western and Palauan ideologies. I view Palauans at home as a source of authenticity. For me, as a Palauan with an English accent, there is an unstated expectation that I have to constantly strive to retain my Palauan accent and cultural values to be viewed as Palauan at all. My Palauan cultural identity is then placed in the context of the competing "I" as defined by the many Palauan "eyes," which is both complex and at times problematic and which requires code switching as a necessary skill and tool for survival.

I feel fortunate that my parents had the foresight to anchor me in the Palauan language and ways of knowing. It is through their "eyes" that I stand today. Mine is a voice that seeks to move away from the margins, from being an "object" to a "subject" defining its outcome and its future. It is a voice that issues a caveat: that while there is a need to embrace the English language and educational system as a bridge to the global society, perhaps somewhere in the genealogical past of Palau lies buried the key to the educational enigma faced by both Palau and the U.S.—how to improve Palau's poor performance in the English educational system while still maintaining the birth culture.

Culture for Sale

Joseph Borja (Guåhan)

I bought a Sinahi at Chamorro village
The carver/salesman told me I could be Chamoru for just $300
Once you wear it
He said
Everyone will know
That you are a Chamorro
Cultural security
For just 300 bucks
I could have back everything I've lost
Language
Spirit
Identity
I asked if I could trade
Like it was done in the old days
But he said he took cash only
It sounded like such a good deal
That I ended up buying it anyway
And the next time I went to the Chamorro village
I wore it proudly around my neck
And thought to myself:
Now I am a real Chamoru
I stopped by the booth of the artist/salesman
To thank him so much
For the newfound identity
He afforded me
But I saw him conversing with an American Marine
Telling him that for 500 bucks
He could become a Chamoru
I was shocked
And felt like a fool
To be a Chamorro was supposed to be something special

Since when was culture for sale?

Since the cultural leaders turned capitalists

The Sinahi hung heavily around my neck
Like a chain
And I couldn't bring myself to take it off
Now I wear it all the time
Cause it reminds me
That the culture I seek
Is now for sale
To anyone with money
At discount price
Available every Wednesday
At the Chamorro village
Cash only

In Search of What Matters . . .

Vidalino (Vid) Staley Raatior (Chuuk)

If you have come to help me, you are wasting your time. But if you have come because your liberation is bound up with mine, then let us work together.

—*Lila Watson*

Raatior: Reclaiming my native name was a personal protest against the injustice of foreign domination on indigenous rights. Sadly, I am the product of a long history of colonialism in which our identities have suffered greatly at the hands of overzealous foreigners. They arrived uninvited on the shores of our pristine islands in many forms, with many causes and agendas—all with the same misplaced notion of "helping" us by displacing our native names, our spiritualities, cultures, traditions, governing structures, diets, and our lives in the name of their foreign gods, ideologies, self-proclaimed governments, and unjust economies, and their social and physical illnesses. While Micronesia has since reclaimed its sovereignty with several outward legal documents with the U.S. and the United Nations, we as a collection of varying languages and cultures continue to struggle to find our true identities. We have been dominated so long by foreign governments that we have to reclaim our histories, reconnect with our spiritualities, recalibrate our self-understanding, revisit our roots, reclaim our traditions, reclaim our innate goodness, and remove our dependency syndrome.

My own family name has been marred by this history of foreign domination. My paternal grandfather Raatior (named after a navigational bird—so I'm told), a well-respected chief on the island of Onoun, was baptized Ionas by overzealous missionaries who desecrated ancestral names with European ones, as though only Euro-centric names guaranteed entrance through the Heavenly Gate. Then, as if that wasn't enough, a Peace Corps volunteer on Onoun back in the 60s decided that Ionas was better pronounced in its American form on his class roster. So, at the stroke of his number 2 pencil and with a high dose of cultural insensitivity, he forced my older siblings to take the name Jones as their

Previously published, *Raatior Ventures: Powering Social Good & Innovations in the Pacific*, Raatior Ventures. No date.

last name. And there began the story of Maggie and Damian Jones and the subsequent line of Jones kids in the middle of the Pacific without a sliver of Jones DNA in any of us.

I carried that last name for 30 years of my life, even though I've never felt comfortable having to explain its American origin. Exactly 30 years later, while at graduate school in Berkeley and with the support of my older siblings whom I respect greatly, I decided to stand up and legally reclaim my native family name of Raatior. Ironically, the legal system in Berkeley, California—the bastion of sixties radical liberalism and countercultural protests in support of civil rights—reversed the wrong done by one of its own sons in the Peace Corps. While I respect my siblings' decision to keep Jones as their own surname (or perhaps their indifference to the whole matter), I consider this little feat of reclaiming my indigenous name to be my shield of honor and the roots of my pride.

Chuuk: I was born into a family of eight siblings on the island of Tamatam, raised on Onoun, and moved to Houk, where most of my family now live. Although I live in Northern California now, I embrace my Chuukese identity with everything that accompanies it, good, bad, and ugly. Growing up in those outer islands in Chuuk State was a real privilege. There, I learned the valuable lessons of living simply and respecting others, which have proven to be wonderful ways to counter the complicated life in the United States. I really do believe a variation of that saying which goes something like this: You can take the boy out of Chuuk, but you can never take Chuuk out of the boy.

Micronesia: For the sake of those in the global community who prefer to generalize people's citizenship by nationality, then I am proud to say I am a Micronesian. While that "Micronesian" label is limiting because it was historically created by foreigners to label a variety of unique people, cultures, and identities, it is what it is. I am a proud citizen of the Federated States of Micronesia (FSM), which includes the four states of Chuuk, Kosrae, Pohnpei, and Yap. When traveling the world as part of my job, I proudly carry my FSM passport, my Micronesian roots, my history within the larger context of a struggling yet proud people, and take every opportunity to be a good citizen ambassador for the country I love, Micronesia.

Pwaraka and Alengeitaw: I value and take pride in my roots and history. I am proud to be part of a matrilineal society in which our lineage and roots are traced through our mothers' clan. As such, I am a proud member of the Pwaraka clan and secondarily (*afakur*) to my father's clan of Alengeitaw. Pwaraka has linkages either in name or history with Ketemang, Houpelai, and others throughout Chuuk and in some of the outer islands of Yap. The clan was legendary back in the day, so they say, for having the fiercest warriors, who conquered lands throughout Chuuk. The Pwaraka clan members gave the land known as Winiku to the Catholic Mission, which became the site for Xavier High School.

While the clan has diminished in numbers in the lagoon areas, it continues to thrive in the outer islands; its roots are firmly planted on the island of Tamatam, where the majority of the population are Pwaraka clan members.

My Alengeitaw clan has a sadder history written in blood. While it has roots in Arhaw or Achaw, the name Alengeitaw (the name means "reef of the ocean") itself originated on a section of Onoun's reef called an aleng, where the last survivor of a massacre was rescued. It was on that sliver of reef that a little girl escaped the murder of her entire chiefly Arhaw clan by another feuding clan that wanted the seat of power. In a well-executed plan, the men, women, and children of the Arhaw clan were herded to shores where they were massacred. But that one little girl swam out to the aleng to escape the carnage. There, out on that reef, naked, cold, and lonely, this little girl cried for days and nights until one courageous man from another clan paddled out and rescued her. He raised her as his own daughter until she later married and bore many children, whom she called the Alengeitaw clan in memory of their roots on the aleng of Onoun. The Alengeitaw clan thrives especially on Tamatam, where we hold the chiefly title; on Onoun, where our history was written in blood; and in some areas of the Chuuk lagoon.

International Education: I am blessed with an international education that has shaped my own vocation in life. That education began at the nondescript one-room Houk Elementary School (Houk), which led to Wei-Pat Jr. High School (Onoun), Chuuk High School (Weno), the University of Guam (Guam), Manresa Jesuit Novitiate (Palau), Fordham University (New York), the Jesuit School of Theology at Berkeley (California), the University of San Francisco (California), and University of Hawai'i at Mānoa (Hawai'i). While those many years as a student formed me intellectually, it was my years teaching and serving as a Jesuit scholastic at Xavier High School on Chuuk that inspired my passion to be an educator. I am blessed to have had a career in international education at Santa Clara University in which I helped to advance world peace through the development of leaders of competence, conscience, and compassion. Today, I am proud to serve as a Pacific-focused educator, consultant, and social entrepreneur dedicated to the advancement of indigenous rights and educational equity particularly for Micronesians locally and globally.

Spirituality: My Christian faith with a Catholic flavor plays a hugely important role in my life. But my 10 years of training as a Jesuit in the Micronesia Region of the New York Province of the Society of Jesus formed the core of my Ignatian spirituality, a journey of deep faith for which I will forever be grateful. The Jesuits truly formed who I am today, my spirit of service, and my capacity to love unconditionally. They deepened and stretched my once conservative Catholic faith by grounding it in the liberally based Ignatian spirituality of "finding God in all things" and "all things in God." That simple yet profound worldview directs what I do with my life, my decisions, my relationships both personal and professional, and how I relate to the world. I am blessed with this foundation of my heart that respects the dignity of humanity and our responsibility to the Earth. It matters less to me to what particular faith community a person belongs, whether Catholic or Protestant, Jewish or Muslim, Rastafarian or atheist; what matters to me most is that each person's faith life enables him or her to see the goodness in others. And when that goodness takes over one's heart, no act of injustice is ever acceptable anywhere, any time, to anyone.

Political Activism: I was born into a culture that embodied humility as a virtue, and of which silence was the hallmark of respect. As such, the less one said, the more respectable one was. Sadly, those same values have been exploited by elected officials in Chuuk to keep people quiet, thereby silencing the voices of justice, all under the guise of respect. Politicians have exploited the culture of silence to advance their own corrupt and selfish ways. Chuuk has plenty of politicians and many more emerging to carry on the same dirty, self-serving politics. People are stuck in the rut of treating politicians as chiefs rather than the public servants that they truly are in a democratic government. In that traditional role, we the People are somehow expected to listen quietly, meekly, silently.

Chuuk desperately needs more political activists who have a burning desire to make a difference, but more importantly to embody those solutions themselves without always blaming and vilifying political leaders. It is important to understand the root causes of the problem to find solutions, but true political activists must understand the power of their minds, the strength of their character, the courage needed to persevere, and the commitment to lead by example. It is not popular to be a political activist, but it is a necessary calling for new generations of Chuukese.

While others aspire to be politicians, I feel the call to the "road less traveled" of a political activist, a gadfly, a nuisance for corrupt politicians.

kul

Emelihter Kihleng (Pohnpei)

you call us roaches[1]
invasive
dirty
brown
smelly and ugly
come one roach come plenty
some of you scream when you see us
crawling out from under the kitchen sink
but we are quite harmless
only thing is
we are hard to kill off
no matter how much you hate us
we keep on reproducing and thus
reappearing
in the laundry room, dining area, even
your bedroom
and worst of all . . .
some of us grow wings
and fly!

---

1. Micronesians are often called roaches by racist people in Hawai'i.

FestPac neni

Johanna Salinas (Guåhan)

I see her
Like a heroine in a young adult novel,
she's always staring off into oblivion
As if the universe is telling her its secrets.
Yet she's just tired of technology and the world news
Eyes like lost light in a dark ocean,
Defeated frown like a dead dream.

Steven said meditation and philosophy go hand in hand,
Like how you cannot float without a purpose or think without a dream.

I'm seeing what happens when philosophy eats the mind of a modern girl.
What happens when one questions life instead of lives it.
Does she belong to our culture,
Our island?
"What we had is gone," she mutters.
"What's still here is ours to share," I try to soothe her.

But she fights the otherness with creativity and passion.
Her path to self-discovery is lit by museum lights and fiesta nights.
Writing half-stories and flashing blurry photos to give herself a voice.
With her magic words and images, she saves herself from self-doubt.
She saves us, she saves me. Amen, amen, my FestPac friend.

Kao siña hao fumino' Chamoru?

Jacob L. Camacho (Guåhan)

I'll be damned if I died today and the world didn't recognize
what fucking burns in my chest so passionately. Fuck my name—forget it.
 Fuck who I am as a man—forget it. Fuck my soul and all the rosaries
 you can utter for it.
Fuck accomplishments and goals—fuck it all.

Let me tell you a story.

A Chamoru man awoken in his spirit, asked me with his chin to dirt then
 to sky,
  –Kao siña hao fumino' Chamoru?
The answer he was looking for was No.

And in Chamoru he turned to others around me and spoke. Loud and
 laughing.
How confusing and empty it can be—to be an outsider even amongst my
 own people.

I am Chamoru.

When I was 7, I would line up for food in San Vicente cafeteria and Grandma,
 from behind the large glass pane, with her black hairnet, would say,
 Make sure to eat your vegetables, ah! Sah I'm watching you—here,
 extra green beans and corn.
She was making me mahe'tok. I hated green beans.
Her smile stretched across her face, wrinkles at their ends.
Her eyes heavy behind bifocals hiding a deep sorrow I didn't yet know or
 understand.

I am Chamoru.

When I was 9, a boy beat me atop a hill at an island land rights meeting.
 In the sun.

After Al Robles's A *Thousand Pilipino Songs: Ako Ay Pilipino.*

Several feet from the canopy shading around 100 people. He beat me
   because he didn't like how I looked. Dark and doknus.
He broke my K-Mart sunglasses in half on my face.
He didn't like my face.
We wrestled until rolling off a cliff together—bouncing off limestone and
   dirt all the way. My zori kicked itself free from my foot into sakate—our
   bodies pummeling to the earth.
The boy disappeared. My primu laughed at me from top the cliff; when I
   looked up
squinting thru blood.

I am Chamoru

When I was 12 I got off the school bus and a white boy pulled me down
   by my collar at the back of my neck, in front of the latte stone bus stop.
   Near a rusty Japanese WWII pillbox; it's roof folding in on itself.
   The white boy shouted in my face. He reached for a rebar from
   under the bus stop—he always hid his weapon there.
Everyone in the neighborhood knew it.
He was mad because I'm Chamoru.
We fought each other with fists.
With rocks same size as our tiny guava palms.
We picked up trashed bottles of miller lite from the road. Broke it.
And flung it into each other's bodies.
My jeans were so stiff with blood; walking home afterwards felt like I had
   cardboard pants on.

I am Chamoru.

When I was 16, I walked thru a jungle in Yigo as the sun set. Once I was
   deep to where I couldn't see the highway—every bush, shrub, and tree
   along my right side shook violently. There was no wind. Nobody with
   me nor near me.
I didn't start taking heavy drugs yet. I was sober.
From a knee high donne' plant. To a papaya tree. To meshes of
   tangantangan—I walked—they shook. I stopped. It stopped.
What was this? Taotaomona? Why? When I came to the exit I said, You
   won't scare me. What do you want from me?
Then the jungle stopped swaying.

I am Chamoru.

When I was 17, my Sunday School teacher said Catholics added books
   to the Bible and whosoever adds or takes away from this book is
   condemned to go to Hell.
Looks like we're going to Hell.

I am Chamoru.

When I was 18, I learned to speak Japanese better than Chamoru because all the local girls around me liked light skinned athletic boys and I was too much of a nerd. And fat.
I was sociably awkward—anxious and nervous just to make friends.
So I set out with my dick and selfishness to learn how to become a fool. Lost in his own island.

I am Chamoru.

When I was 21 my kickboxing coach kicked me in the throat and I threw up with my head hanging off the edge of the boxing ring. Everyone laughed. I laughed too, once I picked my balls up off the floor.
I'm still laughing.

I am Chamoru.

I am—the kind of Chamoru that doesn't make it onto the cover of *UNO Magazine* cuz my skin isn't light enough and my body carries too much SPAM, Sapporo Ichiban, McDonald's, Ruby Tuesdays, Fuji Ichiban, Globe & Club USA.

My body is layered in too much MSG, Kikkoman Soy Sauce, fina'deni, RedBull, Assam black tea, Assam strawberry milk tea, Jack in the motherfucking Box, KFC, Kings and Shirley's.

I am Chamoru.

Watch me carve my body free out of this latte stone, with the same nails that hammered Jesus to His cross. Look at how all the limestone crumbs off my lips, my shoulders, chest, and hips. Chunks of black and grey porous stone anchoring into sand. Watch me shake it off and raise my knees through the latte stone; breaking it without hesitation. Look at how my skin peels open when it kisses against the latte's rock. Watch the dust spray off my black hair when I nod left to right. Listen to me step deep into the sand—loud enough to wake all our ancestors angry.

I am Chamoru.

Come again.

Maila' *magi*.

And ask me if I can speak Chamoru.

Memory Revising, As My Diasporic Queer Self

J. A. Dela Cruz-Smith (Guåhan)

And just like that our fingers dusted in a fine residue   our lips glossed   and
frosted   We bite into it again   What exactly is the taste of a dessert outside of
indulgence?   I will start with the flavor of accompaniments   Accoutrements
Chocolate marshmallow   Mousse   Says something about not eating too
much   Silken like the pudge on my stomach   How I keep doing this
          Taking you out to eat all over town   Alone   and just feeding

I like treating you to things

A year ago this part didn't exist   therefore   our conversations and laughter
          over   the sweetness   on my tongue   There's our simultaneous guilt and
enjoyment   uncontained and elsewhere like a preposition   or in the process of
performance   Another space somewhere in the heaving of a city   our city just
outside   a window's landscape   the booming cranes blasting up the sky's
spine   Or is that you?   You want to transfigure yourself into such heights
          Towers above   When we were little didn't we think the highest our necks
could give us was a crucifix marking our home's doorways?   Or once   there
was an off-colored orange because its segments were exposed of its skins outside
in our grandparents' yard   just dripping   forming into the rest of the flowering
backdrop   Construction sites   You peeled my thumb   trying to peel a
pear without asking for help   and flap laid there   you couldn't stop staring   but
your mother pulled me into the bathroom and washed your bloody mess
Bandages and one or two blood spots left on a stinking sink   Those are going
to be sleek apartment homes someday   And all the bones   the pipes I picture
punctured and spraying like opened veins   The sun wiping across all its
chemical fume   Shoe polish   Still   those momentary dark streaks left
from a damp towel to your wet abdomen in a summer

One day   you loved the curves swelling beneath a wave's inhale—   The torture of
our diasporic heart   The conundrum   of   a definitive romance   or
sense of whimsy   Maybe   fucking a colonizer   Looking back   My guess is
that there is a love story somewhere   Crushing beetles for paint   how black its
blood was   Why the hell did we do that?   The certitude in all the forgetting
that history does   and how in childhood I hadn't thought about fucking yet

bringing us both in motion   A set of fleeting kids trying to make a kiss for
someone

If our lives were a conglomeration of points and this was the beginning to a linear
range   in innocence   different sets of ranges   perhaps(?)   what were our functions?
        What of our practices?   What of our last meal?   I hope it is as tasty
as a perfect relic   For an instance of you   Memory gives me the physical
perception of you   attenuating curiosity   The taste of it (a hint of)   What
is putting food in the body   or what a friend is   or the contexts   the coincidences
on curves?   Today   I will give myself entirely to the silly sound of a kiss
        Chuckle   Out   from the slim membrane of time   I feel lightheaded and
satisfied   And savor   its closeness

as if it were you   Substantial pieces of bread kept from my starving insides . . .
        Ahh   I remember now   Mae and I must have had a nice time
together   Were you there?

I watch you both   Like the grass grow   Excommunicating myself
        For wanting anything other than loving   in the childishness of a first shame
        You went home wanting to ask what the word Fag meant   but never asked
anyone   The smell of the playground

The smell of grass and dirt (on an island) is alarmingly similar to the smell of a city
like Seattle on a day like today   Or trapped underneath my soccer cleats at one
time   before you knew the answers   Or in a gigantic set of jaws above a field or
farmland stuck in low   slow swinging somewhere in Spanaway   where your
closeted teacher made eyes at you   and the canons on JBLM blowing off   How
I ever came to memorize this smell   of what playing with another boy on the
team   and getting caught was like   As if tomorrow there was an examination of
both our penises to prove what we had done   Finish the food in your mouth
first   as I look over at us glaring each other in the eyes   like two windows   and
I'm in a tar   Smashed in your mouth before swallowing   Just watching us
    for our running   Lifts a cup to your first love's mouth   sets it back
down   turns to her   turns to him   and asked if they want anything else

If you want to be masc today   be masc today   If you want to be femme
tomorrow   be femme tomorrow   *Kids are fluid*   I say to you

You are about   Two animals stumbling out into a beam of sunlight   taking
root and giving it to each other   I always enjoyed taking care of others   tasting
bitterness

And our bums coming from sitting on chairs with no backs   The wooden seats
contouring an undulation   somehow fitting our bodies right next to the other
        The hands do this well when placed in back pockets   When reaching for a
dollar bill in a lunch line   When gathering water like a bowl   Or for a pack
of cigarettes on the sidewalk   the burning   standing in for time   and its minor
stressors   A Chapstick because there is such thing as dry air   A lipstick
too   you think you might try   Our skin against   Cold blankets   Our hair

follicles perking up out of instinct   Fear contacting us from the realm of
delusion

From here   the day can still look bright and a restless fish against the full force of a
river   Against everything   Opposing the stream like stick caught in between
stones   Our mouths   The way you pull the fish out of water   Gaping
      Gaping   There it is   (and you slip the knife back in your trousers)   All
colored like dragon fruits   Laying in the riverbeds   During different parts
of the year these shrink and widens   How you necessitate experiencing
everything all at once   Insisting on tasting anything   eating like a horizon
before another empty   hot sky   You know what I mean

You think you're hungry   How a line devours the sun every day at a certain time
      There is a laughter again coming in and out like the scent of marmalade and
heavy whipping cream sticky   on your chest   drifting by   You reaching for
the knife   and other means to bring it into my back   And I give you my
back   *Spread to me*   We bring our head up to a clear day   Someday it will
rain   And what else is that?   Some vanilla   lemon verbena   Somehow
the grease like fried dough and sticky fingers   You ferocious   No mannered
deviant   is like this   Woozy   kneading oxygen into my tired chest   I felt
full   My belly hurt   Your belly hurts

Grass

Lynnsey Sigrah (Yap)

Showers come from the heavens
Nourish my roots with water.
Sunlight of the morning star
Sends colors up my sleeve.
But when there is no water
I dry up.
The sunlight shining from above
Sends heat up my sleeve.
After a few days I will wither
And be like the dust of this earth.
But don't lose hope
For again I shall rise, with life within me.
As green as the coconut leaves
As lively as the birds flying with the wind.

Paan

Ma'anang uu tharmiy nga buut'
Ea bea piq gelngin likngig.
Rama'en ea yaal' ni bea yib ko ngaek
Ea bea piq rama'en dowaag.
Machne napan ni dabi yib ea raen
Mug malik.
Ma napan ra gaal ea rea yaal' ney
Mug guwaal nggu muduldul.
Napan iin ea raan nga' mea maq gelngig
Mug boed ea buut' ko rea fayleng ney.
Machne dabi kirbanum
Ya baay gusuul, nge yib ea yafos ngog.
Ni ri gub gulunglung ni boed rama'en yuwan ea niiw
Ni gu boed ea arche' ni beau un ko nifeng.

Paan

Rag thamiiy ea nu'uw,
Mug gel nigeg nggu suwoon.
Ra maat ea yaal',
Mug gaq nag rama'en dowaag.
Machne kug ma lamach,
Ni faqan ra yoqor ea raan.
Ma kug ma mororoyu,
Ni faqan ra kaygi gal ea yaal'.
Machne ra guum' nggu chuuw,
Ma damruus.
Ya napan ra thiil biyay ear ran
Ma kug ra suul
Nggu leqeg likngig, mu ku suwoon biyay.

Grass

When I feel the rain
I strengthen myself to stand.
When the sun shines
my color goes brighter.
But I will drown
If there is too much water.
And I wither
If it is too hot.
But when I die
Don't despair
Because when the next day comes
I will come back
To take hold of my roots, to stand up again.

English Major

James Perez Viernes (Guåhan)

They tell me to read
them good ol' boys
  billy shakespeare
  eddie poe
too many to name
the noise
of their canons
numbs my tired ears

that crave
MY good ol' boys
their stories cry out
from those years
nearly forgotten
  Grandma's jungle tales
  Grandpa's latte legends
they are my canon
their noise so sweet

  No white words
  No white paper
  No white publisher

Just brown "oral traditions"
or so they call them
but not any less than those
pages from the west.

Previously published, *Storyboard: A Journal of Pacific Imagery* 9, 2006.

VOYAGES

Raiarecharmoracherchar

Valentine N. Sengebau (Belau)

I'm going to relate this epic legend
about the original tribes
of courageous men, women and children
who in the darkness of time
dared to dream lofty dreams
of adventures and discoveries
and so following the current
of the mighty seas
and direction of the trade winds
of the sky
and guided by the moon, sunsets and fixed stars
set sail from their distant land
braving gales and thunder storms
amidst the towering and malevolent swells
and mercilessly tossed about in the foam
suffering the scourge of heavenly torches
and the chilling and freezing night winds
accompanied by the mounting pangs
of hunger and thirst,
survived the herculean ordeal
safely arrived on these thousand isles
in the golden sun where no man abided.

They were decreed to inherit these lands
not by hostile act of force and violence
but by the guiding lights
of good fortune, skill, and endurance
and the blessing of their god and ancestors.

They became the first men
to inhabit these lands of a thousand isles.

Previously published, *Microchild: An Anthology of Poetry*, Northern Marianas Islands Council
for the Humanities, 2004.

They tamed and tilled the soils
built dwelling houses, canoe huts and bais
enacted laws for peace and harmony
and shared the bounties of the land and sea.

A new society was born
and the inhabitants called it
"BELUMAM," our homeland.

And so thru the eons of time
while peace and comfort prospered,
commuting and migration ceased.
However, an occasional expedition was made
and some drifters from afar rescued.

When the isolation became acute
variance among the brethren
dwelling in the sun emerged
and thus evolved the differences
in cultures, customs and languages
with time blunting and eroding
the oneness in the beginning of time.

Then the epoch of intruders came.
on their monstrous and gigantic canoes
with many huge sails, they appeared
where the sun went to sleep
at the end of the western sky.

They plundered and raped
the inhabitants, land, and sea
and further claimed the thousand isles
in the name of their god and kings.
There were inquisitors to save the heathens
and Kaiser's boys lusting for minerals and copra
and children of the rising sun to colonize
and stars and stripes for international peace.

They all left deep and permanent scars
and each scar was deeper than the last
until the entire populace
of the thousand isles in the sun
became the nation of sheep
without the shepherds of old.

Then a pack of wolves descended
among the herd and devoured a good meal.
slowly and silently the prey and predator
became one through digestion.

There was no other sound
except the lapping and swishing
of the waves hugging the shore
and the rising of the new moon tide
bringing the broken zories, plastic bags
and aluminum coke and beer cans
to the immaculate beach.

There are a few tracks on the sand
and scattered skeletal remains
bleached in the golden sun
await resurrection or reincarnation
await a new genesis for the building.

What Grandma Sinsilmam Knew

Dickson Dalph Tiwelfil (Yap)

We arrived and soon departed, Tiwelital and I.
Nothing much to tell about this point of time—
We did not know how Grandma felt when she kissed our necks,
our stomachs, and almost every single part of our selves
as her expressions of longing love for us,
when we left Topwat, our beautiful village.

Our relatives cried and chanted local songs
as they were saying good-bye to us;
Mother could not bear the thought of our departure,
tears running down her face.
My young brother cried but I didn't.
I didn't show any expression of sadness.

Who did I think I was with no tears,
not even a single sign of sadness.
When my brother couldn't even handle
the running tears on his face,
I kept my thoughts to myself.

The silent *kesaisei* paddling toward Gapilmwogal vessel
amidst laughing and smiling
and whispering in my mind
allowed much time to think things over—
that was when a sudden reality fell upon me:
We were leaving Wottegai, our island home.

Two weeks in the island of stone money, Yap,
awaiting onward travel—
Home news comes—
Sinsilmam is sick.
We were not ready for this.
We roamed around with old friends,

seeking comfort and understanding;
finally more news appears,
with tears, cries, discomfort—
our loved one, Sinsilmam, had left us.

Nothing will ever be so vital as that moment—
I was filled with unhappy thoughts and ideas,
"Where to go? What to do? How to be?"
This new reality sinking in—
I would never see Grandma Sinsilmam again.

Flying to Makiki Street

Kathy Jetñil-Kijiner (Marshall Islands)

night lights peer into your oval window and you, cousin
are crouched on the edge of your seat
you bury sobs beneath an itchy blanket
leavemealone stinging my palm from your shoulder
evaporating slow
in this arid airplane cabin
cradling us across the pacific
from majuro to hawaii with my family

and my 9-year-old mind is desperate
contemplating if sticks of juicy fruit gum could chew away
the raw ache in your heart
or maybe if we peel the wrapper
of some ametama
wrap our teeth in sticky coconut flake rounds
we could find some way
to peel away the loss of your home Rita
a town that looked like
a patchwork quilt sewn together by squares of tin roofs
boxed in by plywood and cement regrets
the sea hushing peace at your slippered feet
your father placid drunk in his
blank wooden chair chanting
fluid family histories and black magic tales
an oil lamp glow bleeding
into thick black nights

cousin lets stretch those nights to hawaii
makiki street with bunkbed whispers and bruised van cruising
jawaiian music saturating damp rainbows

Previously published, *Iep Jāltok: Poems from a Marshallese Daughter,* University of Arizona Press, 2017.

over a lush manoa valley
crushed under family straight
"A" expectations band practice tennis practice rotc college advisory
   and your
mcdonalds uniforms
folded starched
every night so
neat

our lives folded
starched every
bare night so nice and
neat
it won't be so bad cousin

trust me

Tomorrow

Tutii Chilton (Belau)

tomorrow   i gotta get a drink

monday: gotta do my internship
turn in my reaction paper by 12
oh man, forgot the damn poem
what to write?
childhood memories, revolution
love stories, colonization
damn, roses are blue, violets are red
come on get it right.

tuesday: gotta read, write for 6pm class
okay, review the assignment again
nah, I'll wait till thursday
"hey bro you wanna get a drink?"
nah, I gotta get ready for class
"just one drink at manoa gardens before class"
aight, one, two, three, four, five
it's six p.m. I'm late for class.

wednesday: prepare an outline, choose a poem
lunch at east side grill
"what pitcher would you like?"
gotta get ready for wednesday nite seminar
just thinking about that girl at magoos
sustainable development
economic development
another drink, another drink
where is she?
last call, it's 2am
we gotta close
I'll do the outline later.

thursday: alright, read before saturday
             be ahead, finish it and . . .
             "bro don't forget, dollar drinks at red lion"
             yeah no cover charge before 7:30
             last call, it's 2am
             we gotta close
             I'll do the work tomorrow by noon.

friday: "10 am, you coming to work?"
             damn, I start at 7:30
             hurry up, eat, shave, shower
             don't forget your teeth
             make your smile nice for work
             got my ass chewed out by da boss
             gotta catch up
             my reading
             my papers
             my assignments
             my project
             what mid-terms next week?
             my proposal
             my committee
             to hell with it
             it's kava night.

The Monkey Gate

Kathy Jetñil-Kijiner (Marshall Islands)

I.

my light-skinned uncle tells the story
of being lost in the honolulu airport
how he fished out a wandering airport employee
and asked him if he knew where the Micronesian gate was
the man smirked through blue uniform
you mean the monkey gate?

my uncle tells the story
of the blood rushing beneath his
face calm as stone as he turned
and jogged in the direction the man had pointed

months later my cousin told me the story and i
sat stunned
wondering why
would they call it that?

II.

alarms sound off
three o'clock in the morning our bodies buzz
from cramped beds pull-out couches and flowery futons
we rise
shove swap meet t-shirts fresh tuna
macadamia chocolates and extra cases
of our lives into solid trustworthy
coolers snapped shut and bound with luminescent strands of tape
we pack

Previously published, *Iep Jāltok: Poems from a Marshallese Daughter*, University of Arizona Press, 2017.

everything
into battered minivans and bucking SUVs
and as we sail along blank roads
we watch the landscape of apartment complexes
that loom above dozing bars, blinking 7-11s and mini-marts

karuji leddik ne. wake her up.

our eyes flicker open to muttering cousins
the harsh lights of the Honolulu airport
flood through the milky translucence of the window
as we drain our belongings from slide and shut doors
we chatter away nerves
rumbling and rolling in our bellies
At the check-in gate

gold teeth Kosraeans argue over coolers that weigh too much
a Ponapeian suit urgently checks his watch while
bony-kneed brown children run   leap across
carts and piles of suitcases coolers boxes guarded
by graying Chuukese and Marshallese women in flowing guams
whole families crouch and recline on the linoleum floor
we slide our slippers off
we make ourselves comfortable prop up ashy feet
the line to check in is long and
bag check even longer
saying good bye are one arm hugs and tears
sweating slow off our skin
and we are sad to see each other leave
and we are happy to see each other leave
and linking arms around the handles of our baggage
we wave to the airport employees
we thank them
for handing us our tickets and carry-ons
and with upright backs we smile
and stroll past security.

Moon Sickness, Green Cards, and the Taro Patch

Isebong Asang (Belau)

1963 was a very tumultuous year for me. An unknown sniper assassinated President John F. Kennedy a year after he declared Guam a major disaster area in the wake of Typhoon Karen, and the dreaded moon sickness (*smecher ra buil*) arrived.

The year began with concentrated efforts to recover from and rebuild in the aftermath of Karen, a murderous lady who had stormed over Guam on November 11, 1962, packing winds up to 250 mph.[1] The tin roofs of our home and those of my friends speckled the hillside of Sinajana. I was excited when Governor Manuel Leon Guerrero declared all the schools closed indefinitely, but then it quickly dawned on me that we did not have water or power, and no power meant no *Ed Sullivan Show* on Sunday nights. Made of concrete and sustaining minimal damage, Sinajana Elementary School, as it was called then, provided shelter for the many homeless families in the village. It also served as the nerve center for the Red Cross, Navy hot meals, and potable water distribution.

A year later, the village had undergone a major cleanup, families had returned to reconstructed homes, and school was once again in session, making up for lost time. November was an unpredictable month on Guam; it was what the weather lady called tropical depression month, ripe for typhoons,[2] and on this Saturday afternoon, it was particularly hot and muggy. I sweated and squatted behind home plate in my catcher's mask, waiting for the ball. We were no professional team, just a group of village girls getting together after our chores to play a little game of softball.

Instead of pitching the ball, however, my girlfriend yelled, "Isebong, you are bleeding!" I looked down and, for a moment, I felt dazed and disoriented.

"Moon Sickness, Green Cards, and the Taro Patch" is the preface from the author's disssertation, *Epistemological Implications: Blebaol, Klomengelungel, ma Tekoi er a Belau*. In it, Asang explores the methods and resources Palauans use "to solve their problems and acquire knowledge."

1. J. S. R. Coye, 1963, "The Typhoon," *Glimpses of Guam*, vol. 2, pp. 13–56.
2. The word *typhoon* comes from *tai fung*, Chinese for Great Wind.

I slowly stood up in what seemed like an eternity. My heart started racing, and my mind reeled with questions of how I could have injured myself *there?* Coming to no logical conclusion, I dropped my glove and the mask and raced home. We lived not far from the schoolyard we used as a softball field. Like the cold blast preceding the winds of a typhoon, it hit me—I had the dreaded moon sickness! I tore through the house, making a beeline for the bathroom, when I realized half of the team was at my heels. I was the first of our group to get *it,* so it was an extraordinary moment for all of us. I took cover in the bathroom, blocked out my friends, and tried desperately to remember my mother's words of advice about when and if this day should come. She was still at the taro patch.

🦎 🦎 🦎

It is the year 2000 and I am back in Ibobang, a small village in the state of Ngatpang on the west coast of the big island of Babeldaob in the Republic of Belau archipelago. As I sit looking out from the air-conditioned library of Ibobang Elementary School, two *mechas* (elderly women), soiled from a day at the taro patch, amble. They are carrying *sualo* or *oruikl* (woven coconut baskets) packed with freshly rooted taro atop their heads, swaying gently to the rhythm of their steps, and each has an *omsangel* (basket used by women to store personal effects) under her arm. Their appearance brings back memories of a similar vision I saw the first time I sat in this very library reading to a young girl called Ngeluul Karine Taro.

Today, as before, I cannot help but wonder at the inimitable yet poignant picture of the two *mechas,* who, through their soiled physical appearance and the objects they carry, embody a culture and its beliefs many centuries old. But, for a brief moment in time, they are captured and framed by a glass window encased in a concrete building, floored with synthetic tile, cooled by air conditioning, and furnished with computers that are linked to the larger global society by the internet, all products of the twentieth century. In an instant, centuries collapse and time seems to warp as the two worlds elide into one another. Mesmerized, I recall my mother's pleasure in her taro patch, my mother who during her life had three passions: her admiration for John F. Kennedy, her green card, and her taro patch.

🦎 🦎 🦎

I was still in the bathroom when I heard my father's car pull into the driveway. My friends had all gone home. My parents came into the house—no, their voices came in first. My mother was exclaiming about the injustice of everything. How could anyone kill such a wonderful man, she asked my father. What about that beautiful wife of his—was she hurt? Their children, are they okay? I could hear their voices, but absorbed as I was in my own heady mix of dread and excitement about the unknown, I was more or less oblivious.

"Mamang!" I screamed. No response.

I called her two more times before she finally came to the bathroom door to see what I wanted. I explained my predicament, and after a few moments she returned. She handed me the feminine articles I required, explaining their functions, reminded me what I needed to do, and then she was gone. The death of a man she had never met overshadowed my rite of passage into adulthood! I grieved into the night.

🪶 🪶 🪶

It was early in the fall of 1998 that I first met Ngeluul. On most Sundays, you would find her playing Nintendo with her 12-year-old sister, Sheena, or visiting her cousins, who lived next door. Today was a special day. though. It was Sunday, the 27th of September, and the *kebliil* (clan) was celebrating her aunt's *ngasech*.[3] Her aunts and uncles, cousins, grandparents, and other relatives had come from afar to celebrate and welcome the new baby into the family. At eight years of age, Ngeluul was anxious and excited to visit with her cousins and the other children with whom she did not have daily interactions. Sometimes sheltered behind her long, straight black hair, Ngeluul's dark brown eyes quietly observed the preparations and excitement that marked the birth of her baby cousin.

Ngeluul had participated in many celebrations with her cousins. They all knew that the birth of a new baby is a very special occasion for both the birth mother and the birth father. The baby is a living, breathing sanction of the relationships and reciprocal exchanges between the families of the birth parents, a cultural practice dating to the pre-contact period.

Ngeluul's great-grandmother, one of my mentors as I worked on my Ph.D. dissertation, had invited me to live my research by engaging in the life of her village. "Place is important to knowing," she had explained. "The smell, the spirits, the feel of the place all influence how one comes to know the world" (Dirrababelblai Emesiochl, 1998, personal conversation). She had arranged with Ngeluul's mother for me to live with them that year. "*Ngeluul, mei e bo mo chotii a blai ra Isebong,*"[4] her mother called to her as I arrived.

It was just after noon and celebrants filled the village. The new mother was married to a European and so his friends attended as well. Ngeluul came out from behind the outdoor kitchen where she was visiting with a group of young boys and girls her age. I noted that it would be one of the few times I would see Ngeluul participate in any activity with a group of girls and boys outside the classroom. In the traditional education structure, children are encouraged to matriculate in groups comprised of the same gender and developmental age. During my stay, I observed that Ngeluul and the other young girls who belonged

---

3. A Palauan word that literally means "rising," but here it connotes the ritual surrounding the celebration of the health of a mother and her newborn baby after the mother has gone through a regimen of hot baths and drinking herbs. It is a ritual usually reserved for a married woman after she has given birth to her firstborn.

4. "Ngeluul, come and show the house to Isebong."

to her age group emulated the behaviors of her older sister, Sheena, and her group. The older girls taught the younger girls, honing and refining how they completed their tasks and developing their critical thinking skills.

Growing up on Guam, I did not belong to any social group because there were no other Palauan girls and boys in our village of Sinajana. My primary source of and only link to the understanding and usage of the Palauan language, knowledge, and cultural values and beliefs were my parents. So my mother believed it was critical for me to spend my summers in Palau to connect to my cosmological roots and breathe the essence of being a female, a Palauan female. The importance of place, like a bull in a fine porcelain shop, pushed its way to the forefront of the "Isebong must learn" list.

In preparation for that inevitable return home, cultural practices based on a cosmology and ontology of being a Palauan female filtered into my everyday life. My grief over the onset of my moon sickness competing with the assassination of JFK was short lived. To my dismay, my mother curtailed my movements so that I no longer had the freedom to go fishing with my father, fix cars with him, play softball with my friends, or take part in any other activity deemed by her to be men's work or domain. My diet suddenly changed, and my mother prohibited me from eating extremely ripe fruits during the moon sickness. "It will give you bad body odor," my mother would hiss at me if I hinted at throwing a tantrum. Our conversations were private, away from my father and the other males in the house, and often took place at the taro patch. Yes, the taro patch! Every day that I was not in school, I now had to accompany my mother to the taro patch, to observe her work, but more for those "private" conversations.

In 1951, my father settled our family in Tamuning, a small village in the center of Guam. Guam, an unincorporated territory of the United States, is 700 miles northeast of Palau. Home to overseas military bases representing each branch of the United States Armed Forces southwest of Honolulu in the Pacific, Guam developed faster than her Micronesian neighbors, who were devastated by the ravages of World War II.

The end of the U.S. Naval Administration of Micronesia, including the passage of the Organic Act of Guam in 1950, opened a small window that enabled a few Micronesian migrants to apply for a green card from the U.S. Immigration and Naturalization Service. The green card, or permanent resident card,[5] allowed the holder to seek employment and "a better way of life," but they could not own land or vote in local elections. This was a right reserved for U.S. citizens, namely the Chamoru people of Guam, civilians, and active-duty military personnel and their families. Chamoru distinguished themselves from other Micronesians due to their special political relationship with the United States.

---

5. Younger Palauans entered Guam on student visas for educational purposes and lived with host families or sponsors. Some who entered on student visas went on to join the armed forces.

Through my mother's unswerving faith in the virtues of respecting the first people of the land, descendants of the *maga'lahe* and the *maga'haga*,[6] I remain a green card holder today.

My father was the oldest son of a Chinese migrant laborer brought to Palau by the Germans at the turn of the twentieth century and a gentle woman from Pelelieu. It was no accident that he was also a green card holder the day he passed away in 1995 at the age of 78. In 1947, he worked as an engineer on board the many vessels that traveled the waters of the Pacific, connecting the islands of Micronesia, with occasional stops at distant ports of call along the coast of Japan. His last voyage ended in 1951 on board the MIS *Reliable*, a reefer-type seagoing vessel with a gross weight of 163 tons. You could say he followed his father's footsteps and looked for adventure on the high seas, but I know better. Grounded in his identity as the oldest son in his family, his leaving home was to provide a means for goods to flow back to his family and a route for others in his family to foray out into the world.

For my parents, the green card represented something deeper than its primary purpose of allowing my parents to live and work on Guam. Over the years in the course of their travels, each had been encouraged, asked, and sometimes prodded to seek permanent status in the U.S., ultimately citizenship, by the Immigration and Naturalization Officers at each port of entrance into the United States and its territories. However, to them the green card represented their last tangible link to their roots. To replace it with a more permanent status such as citizenship would seem to sever all possibilities of returning home and access to whatever land or property they still had in Palau. While my family had lived on Guam for close to five decades, the green card represented a provision that not only were we transients, we would go home one day.

This is a common belief, one that has perplexed researchers wanting to anchor movement to a statistically tangible quota. The green card suggests a transient state of mind; it provides an aperture into the cultural values and beliefs of home thereby transcending time and borders. It is not simply the physical manifestation of a body's mobility, or merely something that the Immigration and Naturalization Officer checks as one crosses a border.

Similarly, home is not only the physical space that one inhabits; it is also the cultural values and beliefs that shape and guide how one sees and understands the world. It involves knowing that you are a guest, and therefore transient, whether the place be a physical one such as a country or someone's home, or a nontangible one like this world or the next; and it dictates that you respect the land and those who walked before you.

Finally, for my parents, the green card symbolized the cultural values and beliefs they brought from Palau. Leading the list was the notion of *omengull*, or respect for the first people of the land. *Omengull* is applicable to a variety of

---

6. Highest-ranking male or female, usually the oldest brother or sister of a clan.

cultural contexts, but in the context of my story, it is fundamentally a deference to those who have come before you. For my parents, that translated into showing a respect when entering someone's home or alighting on an island. It is the sense of respecting the essence, cultural values, beliefs, and cosmological origins of the Chamoru people, all of which are intimately linked to the ownership of their land and, according to my parents, to Chamoru identity itself.

❦ ❦ ❦

Ngeluul acknowledged my presence with her eyes, then took one of my bags and started walking up the dirt road towards what would be my home for the next six months. We were preceded by a truck carting two coolers of frozen goods I had brought for Ngeluul's family in reciprocity for allowing me to live with them. It was the first time we had met, so we walked in silence and stole guarded glances at each other until we reached the house. She showed me to my room and asked if she could help me unpack before we headed back to the celebration.

"*Ke kmal mesaul, eng di becherei e dorail mor seriou eng sowak lomes a bol tobed a Freida, adang,*"[7] I replied. I was not only excited to witness this momentous occasion but also humbled by the graciousness of this family and needed time to reflect on the arrangements. Ngeluul nodded and we left the house with the doors and windows wide open.

Unlike the homes of my friends at school, our home had a revolving door. I grew up with aunts, uncles, cousins, and distant family members sharing our table. It was always exciting to come home from school and find someone new there. I remember my parents sending needed items to Palau whenever someone sailed or flew home. It was also inevitable that visitors brought with them all kinds of Palauan goods, mostly fresh fish or seafood that was not available or too expensive on Guam. Sometimes their stay was short—a day or so. Other times they stayed for years. It did not matter how long they resided in our house; what stayed with me were the stories and the knowledge that they brought with them, including the cultural practices that they exhibited. I looked forward to each new arrival partly because of the gifts that they brought—for instance, I delighted in the pickled *eremrum* (beche de mer, trepang, or sea cucumber) bottled in recycled mayonnaise jars—and partly because their arrival gave me a reprieve from my mother's gaze and the taro patch. Like well-oiled machinery, each person knew their place and what was expected based primarily on their biological ties to either my father or mother, and whether they were male or female.

My journey into this gendered land of knowing took place the summer after JFK's assassination on my thirteenth birthday. That summer, I accompanied my mother to Palau. She deposited me at the doorstep of her only

---

7. "Thank you, but why don't we go down? I want to watch when Frieda comes out, okay?"

living maternal aunt so that I could learn the many ways of being a Palauan woman. I began my journey on the hills of Ngerkebesang, the land that birthed my mother's mothers. Through my great-aunt, I observed the sites where traditional knowledge emerged. I carried her baskets as we climbed the hills of Ngerkebesang to her cassava plots at Ketund. I also carried her organic compost to the taro patch at Ultil a Dub, where, submerged to her waist, she turned the sludge to cover the compost and prepare the *mesei* for future taro cultivations.

Historically, environmentally based communities flourished around these taro-cultivating sites, putting an end to the nomadic gathering society. Categorically speaking, taro serves more than a utilitarian purpose. It and the taro patch exemplify specificity, place, time, space, and Palauan women's cosmology. Men, on the other hand, culled specific knowledge that spoke to death and the life beyond. This is not to say that all truths passed through these two paths. On the contrary, the way to knowing is complex and esoteric, an intricate labyrinth with many layers.

On Guam, my mother cultivated a taro patch and a cassava farm to supplement the starch requirements of our growing extended family. She believed that the cassava plant did not hold the same ontological significance as the taro because of its short history as an introduced source of food.[8] As a female, and more importantly, as the mother of the house, she was responsible for the food supply, and by extension so was her family, not my father and his family. However, in her own family of origin she is the source and path from which all economic security flows. For example, during the funeral of a deceased immediate family member, her role would be a *mengol* (which literally means to carry upon shoulders). On a purely utilitarian level, a *mengol* in this sense is one who feeds the mourners. However, fleshing out the ontological facts that inform a *mengol* begins with her passion for the taro patch.

While my father's role changed slightly—he now had to work for a wage— expectations of him as the protector of the house and the oldest in his family remained the same. Each of my parents had a specific role that was utilitarian. Fundamentally, it was my father's house. However, the relationships that connect him to those who chose to appear at our doorstep are traceable through his siblings, mother, uncles, his home island of Pelelieu, and some relationships that were formed before he was born. Some of these relationships trace to the pre-contact period, a time when men initiated war and relationships were reinforced with a *blebaol,* or the decapitated head of an enemy. This is also true of my mother. However, my mother's side of the guest list provided the manual labor around the house.

⁂

---

8. It is believed that the cassava or tapioca was introduced as a commercial product during the German administration.

"Ngeluul, morrechedau el melcholb eked duob ra skuul,"[9] cried Sheena from the kitchen door. It was 6:30 in the morning and a haze hovered among the betelnut trees surrounding the house. We had returned from the *ngasech* after everyone had left, and Ngeluul had gone to bed very late. Although they each had their own rooms, the two girls preferred to sleep on futons on the bright yellow wooden floor in the living room, which was furnished with a television and a Nintendo on top of a beat-up desk in one corner.

Very early into the ways of knowing their world, young girls care for and educate their younger siblings. In addition to teaching Ngeluul basic chores around the house, Sheena is obligated with the larger task of easing Ngeluul into adolescence. Traditionally, as young women enter adulthood, the subject of sexuality becomes an important aspect of their education. Equally important as part of this education is knowledge about procreating, about being a sexual partner, and about the wider world in relation to their roles in the many relationships they will nurture throughout their lives. However, this is not a topic that is freely engaged in between mother and daughter, and this communication gap becomes extremely pronounced at the onset of the moon sickness. A third party, a mentor, either an aunt or a grandmother, will be sought to ground the young woman in the fundamentals of biology; at the same time, the girl-clubs consisting of young women of the same age and physical development (and for some, a trip to the men's *abai* or meeting house as a *mengol*[10]) will provide the balance of information for the inquisitive mind. When asked to share their personal stories, most mentors spoke about learning from an elder of the same sex. For the men it was a father, uncle, grandfather, or *cheldebechel* (men's or women's club), but few cite learning from a parent beyond adolescence.

The concept of *mekull* (the forbidden or taboo) prohibited me from sitting and discussing sexual topics with my mother; it is considered even more *mekull* to discuss these things with one's father, or with male siblings or cousins. Elders took extreme care to deter any form of incestuous behavior between siblings and between parent and child. Women as the *luuk* (nest) had the task of preventing at all cost genetic aberrations resulting from incestuous behavior. The birth of a deformed baby was either a sign of a calamity waiting to happen, or a revelation of a past transgression.

It was *mekull* for the young adolescents to socialize publicly with the opposite sex. Most of those interviewed told stories of warriors and *mengols* learned as children, adolescents, and as descendants of a complex socio-cultural learning society. These narratives linked these mentors to organizations that separated the men and the women into distinct groups of socialization and knowledge production. There is no more pronounced way to separate young women from young men than the onset of the moon sickness.

---

9. "Ngeluul, hurry and take a shower or we will be late for school!"

10. Throughout her dissertation, Asang's focus is to move cultural concepts away from reductive definitions, in this case of a *mengol* as a mere concubine, to a more culturally layered, complex understanding.

Given these obligations to the spiritual world on the one hand, and to the physical world in the possible consequence of defective genes on the other, young women and men's education in the ways of sexuality and the responsibility that come with it ranked high in priority. The taro patch provided a rich learning site for such an education, constructing for young women the ontological framework of their womanhood.

Most homes in Ibobang[11] village have running water pumped from the Ngebeduul River, but none have water heaters. Therefore, on a cold morning, in a society that prides itself on personal hygiene, everyone has to endure a cold shower—something that did not sit too well with Ngeluul. Like all showers, the family's was located in a separate, smaller building. The shower building located *dimes* (south) of the main house had corrugated tin walls with a wooden door and poured concrete flooring. Directly outside the kitchen was the outdoor kitchen sink. In the *ongos* (east) corner of the property stood the outside *benjo*.[12]

After some prodding, Ngeluul finally finished her shower and got dressed in her school uniform, consisting of a long-sleeved white shirt and a navy-blue jumper skirt. She completed her ensemble with a pair of white socks and white walking shoes. Her black hair, tied tightly behind the nape of her neck, left a wet shadow on her uniform as she struggled to sling her backpack full of books over her shoulder. Sheena handed her a cinnamon roll (bought in the main town, Koror) as they left walking *diluches* (north) toward the main dirt road that would take them to Ibobang Elementary School at the *ongos* entrance of the village. While they walked, they ate their breakfast and talked quietly. One main road intersected the village from *ongos elmo ra ngebard* (east to west), with homes on both sides.

This morning, Ngeluul who is in the third grade, arrived at school at 7:30 with her sister. They were accompanied by a group of girls of the same age that they had picked up along the way. The school is coed, replicating the educational system borrowed from the West. However, outside the school, Ngeluul and Sheena continued to keep within the traditional gendered groupings. It is mandatory for all the students to attend the morning gathering, which starts promptly at 7:45 am. The principal makes important announcements after the students sing the Palau national anthem. When the bell rings at 8 a.m., the younger students go home to do their chores before returning to school in the afternoon. Because her mother is the school cook and her sister attends the morning session, Ngeluul comes to school early and stays for the whole day.

Ngeluul's father lives and works in Koror as a boat operator for the Department of Education. The family does not have the means to buy a car so he does not commute between Ibobang and Koror, an hour's drive on a good day due to the jagged road. Instead, he stays in Koror at his sister's home and visits on weekends when he can.

---

11. A hamlet of Ngatpang State built by the members of the Modekngei religion.
12. Japanese for toilet.

On most school days, Ngeluul helps her mother in the cafeteria or runs errands for the teachers. Other times, she goes to her grandmother's house, about three doors down from the school, and visits or runs errands for her. Today, however, was different. Because I tagged along with her and Sheena, we decided to spend the morning at the library. Before leaving for work, her mother had informed me that Ngeluul had not had the time to study over the weekend because of the *ngasech* and asked if I could see to it that she reviewed her schoolwork.

At the library, Ngeluul looked over her notebook. After we determined that she did not have any schoolwork to do, I asked, *"Diak el sowam a donguiu ra tara cheldecheduch ra ikal babier er tial library?"*[13]

Her eyes lit up and she squealed, *"Ochoi! Sebechek el mo ngiltii a sowak?"*[14]

"Ochoi," I replied. I read *Mother Goose's Nursery Rhymes* with enthusiasm and in some parts we sang the songs. The oral traditions of Palau use *cheldecheduch el chelid*[15] to both entertain and teach traditional knowledge to children. Reading aloud is not a practiced activity in Ngeluul's life, and the novelty of it delighted her.

After lunch, I accompanied Ngeluul to class and sat in the back observing. The teacher taught in Palauan, but the books and the contents were in English. The course followed the national curriculum, which included four basic subject areas: language (Palauan and English), mathematics, social studies, and science. In addition, the curriculum sometimes included health, agriculture, community education, population education, and special education programs. During my stay, except for an occasional softball game on Friday afternoons, the main courses offered were language, science, social studies, mathematics, and health.

Classrooms mirror the common classroom in the U.S., and teachers arrange desks in rows and columns facing the blackboard. In contrast to U.S. classrooms, these walls are bare, and if you glanced through the window you would see a woman or two returning from a morning at the *mesei* (taro patch) or *sers* (garden). The contrast between traditional education and the formal education that takes place in the classroom is stark in Ibobang. Ngeluul's experiences in the classroom are not too different from mine. However, Ngeluul has the advantage of living in a community that anchors her in the ontological threads of being a young Palauan girl.

As we walked home that Monday afternoon, women and smaller children tended their cassava *sers*. The children played by imitating their mothers carrying plantings, weeding the garden, telling stories, or just exploring. Some mothers were talking in the shade; another was taking down her laundry from the clothesline.

---

13. "Would you like it if we read a story from these papers in this library?" *Bahier* is the Palauan word for paper, letter, or book, from the German *papier*.

14. "Yes! Could I choose what I want?"

15. Story, folktale, myth, legend. Literal translation: story of the gods.

"*Ngeluul morchedau el mo remuul a urrerem!*"[16] Sheena called as we approached the house.

"*Choi*" ("Yes") Ngeluul responded with a grunt as she dropped her schoolbag on the kitchen floor.

Their mother had already gone to the *mesei* and Sheena was preparing the evening meal.

With their chores completed, dinner dishes washed, and another cold shower, Ngeluul and Sheena settled in to do their homework. Lying on the floor with her books and papers scattered about her, Ngeluul attempted to read a story about a squirrel lost in some city park in the United States, to the humming of the refrigerator.

"Auntie, *ngara* (what is a) squirrel?" she asked, turning to me with tired eyes.

"Yes, indeed. What is a squirrel?" I asked myself as I listened to the gecko chirping under the blanket of a starless night, remembering another night many moons earlier.

I remember the early evenings, when I would sit across from my father at the dinner table, after my mother and I had just returned from the taro patch. He would tell stories about the old days. He would tell a short story or two that his mother had told him, also at dinner. The quiet time at the end of the day just before nightfall provided the perfect ambience for family storytelling. With food in their mouths, children were apt to listen to the lessons that meshed together with the tales and were swallowed with the food. The place, the smell, the time, the taste, and the speaker all add multiple and complex dimensions to these forms and sites of knowledge production and exchanges.

I am decades from those evenings, but my quest is more urgent than it was then. My parents, gone for several years now, are not here to guide this current journey of mine into my people's way of knowing, so my journey is at the hands of the mentors in whose paths I have been placed for guidance. Perhaps it is coincidence or chance that leads me to write about a way of knowing linked to a cosmology and ontology obscured by a departed time, but I would like to believe that it is my destiny to be here at this time, foreshadowed by the moon sickness and my mother's passion for her taro patch.

---

16. "Ngeluul, hurry up and do your chores!"

Bare-Breasted Woman

C. T. Perez (Guåhan)

"For a moment
she had forgotten
where she was,"
the daughter said
of her mother
who, earlier that morning
had walked past convention
past the waiting cover-up shirt
into the garden,
in to the sun,
in, to the greens,
and the feel of the breeze.

She worked with breasts swaying
like her arms in color and swing.
There was grace in her stoop
and art in her till.
She worked, stooped, tilled
and planted,
even after
neighbors' gazes
called her
naked.

They could not see
that her skin
was their skin,
color brown
colored earth.

The sight of the woman
squatting,
close to the ground,

too close to the color
of their own skin,
stripped them
and left
them standing
naked,
brown
as the day
they were born.

Perhaps
they had forgotten
they were born
of this land
the color of earth,
born of salt sea
and born of salt air.

They
must have
forgotten,
for
as neighbors gazed
out pretty-picture
windows,
a dark
bare-breasted woman
was all
that they saw.

Homes of Micronesia

Yolanda Joab (Pohnpei)

From the rolling hills of Yap
To the low shores and landscape of Majuro
To the serenity of Kosrae
To the booming mountains of Pohnpei
To the everlasting lagoon of Chuuk—
I've lived, I've worked
I've taught, I've learned
I've shared and received
And I've listened
To these people, their stories
My people, my stories.
I used to live in Yap
Where the rolling hills bleed red dirt
The same deep red we get from chewing betelnut but will never see on the
    clean streets
Where the winding road to Maap sneaks you between unbothered villages
Where the talk is quiet and the boast is scarce
Where thuws are worn in peaceful pride
And colorful vibrant grass skirts swing in the March sun
For hundreds of curious and awed onlookers on their name day
Where life is carried in a basket
Yap was home
Yap is home
I used to live in Majuro
Where the ocean greets you with a blunt first impression
Where the horizon stares you down in the face
And then blesses you with a peace offering of the most glorious sunset
    you've ever seen
Where to conquer the highest peak in all the land is to jump off of a
    bridge
Where songs are sung in gifted spirit
Always in unison
Always in perfect harmony

As if rehearsed for a lifetime
Where celebration of life is always the celebration of a lifetime
Because it needed to be
Where it still needs to be
Majuro was home
Majuro is home.
I used to live in Kosrae
Where the dewy fog settles you in and nestles you down beneath the
    sleeping lady's bosom
Where the green runs into green and then blends into more green
Only interrupted by the halting blue of the encroaching ocean
Where the days are quiet and the laughter is loud
Where the mangroves form mazes for you to get lost in
Where the pace reminds you
That life is not a race
But to be appreciated
Kosrae was home
Kosrae is home
I used to live in Pohnpei
Where I was born
Where I was born a Lasialap woman taking after my mother's and her
    mother's and her mother's before hers clan
Where in our municipality only a Lasialap woman can give birth to a king
Where the mountains boom and demand the sky's attention
Only to surrender back down to the land with waterfalls as if blessed by
    the heavens
Where the sakau is strong
And the culture for it stronger
Where the stones of Nan Madol raise up from where our history and
    heritage collide
Where my ancestors fought
Where my children will live
Pohnpei was home
Pohnpei is home
I live in Chuuk
Where the lagoon scatters us like stars in an ocean sky
Where the island warrior mentality is ever present only to succumb to the
    humility required of us
Where the women form rainbows of colorful muumuus and skirts that liter-
    ally brighten up your day
Where our reputation proceeds us in the same way every movie you
    thought you were gonna hate but ended up loving does
Where family is life
 And if you come for one of us
You come for all of us—

The hundreds of us

Where if you ever wanted to learn what "don't judge a book by its cover"
 literally means

Then I suggest you call up United flight 155 and ask for my in-laws

Yeah, Where I found love

Where I found family

Where I found a home

You see

These

Are my homes

Of Micronesia

The common thread of coconut fiber that weaves it all together?

One. In every single one of these places our livelihoods, our livelihoods,
 our livelihoods—

Our names, our history, our legacy, our blood, our bones, our breath—

Is anchored in our oceans and burrowed in our land

Two. For us conservation and sustainability are not just words that we
 throw around at meetings and on paper, but lived, every, single, day

Three. It's in the way my grandmother's been able to feed generations of
 her children from the fruit of her own two hands

Four. It's in the way my brothers and uncles negotiate the oceans' catch,
 while their mothers beg the oceans' mercy for their safe return home

Five. We can't afford the luxury of denying science that proves climate
 change puts all of THIS into a ticking time bomb that we have our
 fingers on

Six. Because for us when we turn a blind eye we get slapped in the face on
 the other side with

Seven. King tides that engulfed Majuro and Kosrae

Eight. Relentless back to back typhoons that swept Pohnpei, Chuuk and
 Ulithi

Nine. Droughts that sucked the life

And water out of all of us

Ten. Creeping sea levels that taps all parents on the shoulder like a nightmare
 that our children haven't even had yet

Ten. I heard one of your presidential candidates doesn't believe in climate
 change

Ten. It doesn't matter how much money he has, God forbid if elected, he
 can't afford to ignore this too

Ten. I once said to my students that if our islands are too small to be seen
 on a map then you make them see *you.*

Ten. *I'm saying it again.*

Ten. I'll say it for the rest of my life.

Ten. We can't afford to keep counting to 11

So ten, let's end it here.

The Cry of Oceania

Josie Howard (Chuuk)

As the western paradigm becomes dominant across the region, Micronesians are increasingly migrating from their home countries. These paradigms include universal education policies and a wage-based economy (Heine, 2008). Lifestyles are changing and families are breaking up to accommodate this new way of living. Our traditional leadership systems have been shoved under the table to allow space for the new "democratic," capital, and colonial imperialism leadership style(s). More and more island-born traditional leaders are going abroad to gain education to enhance their leadership skills in navigating this Western lifestyle imposed on us.

The songs chosen for this project were songs made for two of my grand-uncles, two uncles, and my cousins and oldest brother. They are about the migration of males from a small island in Chuuk State called Onoun, a matrilineal society, for purposes of education.

My hope is that through these songs the indigenous voices will be heard representing their own views, announcing their own epistemologies as voiced by women who are the bearers of my culture, in this case, by my maternal grand-aunties, grandmother, mother, and aunt. Most importantly, through these songs one can hear the cries of the indigenous people as they journey through their changing world of Oceania.

Song 1: *Urun Asterio Takesy*

Composed by Neli Elieisar (grandmother) and Lienkainam "Teresa" Episom (aunt) in relation to Asterio Takesy.

> Wekichime sangeilo ne, mangeto lemakurei
> Wekichime sangeilo ne, mageneto lemakurei
> Mengito lemakurei, lioromailulo ne
> Mangito lemakure, lioromailulo ne
> Lioromailulo ne, sarewichiakiniae
> Lioromailulo ne, sarewichiakiniae
> Sarewichiakiniae, morou letipemame
> Sarewichiakiniae, morou letipemame
> Morou letipemame, pwe ie ekimone

Morou letipemame, pwe ie ekimone
Pwe ie ekimone, Ochieisarepalene
Pwe ie ekimone, ochieisarepalene
Ochieisarepalene, olomo tipe tewalene
Ochieisarepalene, olomo tipe tewalene
Olomo tipe tewalene, tipeni wairhuuk o
Olomo tipe tewalene, tipeni wairhuuk o
Tipeni wairhuukune, ololamesefaline
Tipeni wairhuukune, ololamesefaline
Olo lame sefaline, o mangi rhipweirawe
Olo lame sefaline, o mangi rhipweirawe
O mangi rhipweiraw ne, tuukata mesanefale
O mangi rhipweiraw ne, tuukata mesanefale
Tukata mesanefale ne, asoso leimwamame
Asoso leimwamame.

Translation

As my body turned,
The thought floating into my head
My body feeling lethargic
Began to perspire
Feeling unhappy
Hidden feelings
You're still a child
With a voyager's heart
Longing for Chuuk,
Now you long to come back
As you missed Onoun
Rise up into the house
Resting in our house

This is a song about a young man, around 12 years of age, who left his island to further his education at Xavier High School in Chuuk. Chuuk is the center of what's known today as the Chuuk State, in the Federated States of Micronesia. The composers described him as being very young, yet already wanting to venture off. It was explained that this young man was one of the first from this island to graduate from Xavier High School, a prestigious Jesuit school known as the best academic school in Micronesia. Most graduates of this school became the first leaders in Micronesia.

During those times, when someone left the island for education, families felt a great sense of loss for the absence of the loved one and a great deal of uncertainty about what might happen to that person and whether they would ever come back. "Tipetewal" refers to individuals who don't miss home and always want to venture away. This kind of attitude naturally worries the parents and families. Education was viewed as the cause of this pain for family members.

Western education was seen as valuable to a small community like Onoun. Today, the young boy, Asterio Takesy, is the current ambassador for the Federated States of Micronesia to the United States. He formerly served as secretary of the FSM Foreign Affairs Department and the SPREP. He is also a strong advocate in the fight against global warming.

Song 2: Urun Manis Episom

Composed by Lipung.

> Mwatoiraki sangepung fini kefanei, mwatoireki sangiei pungu waluarh le ipatan
> Mwatoirakisangepung fini kefanei, mwatoireki sangiei pungu waluarh le ipatan
> Mwatoireki sangiei waluarh le ipatan, waluarh le ipatan pone ira tong
> Mwatoireki sangiei waluarh le ipatan, waluarh le ipatan pone ira tong
> Waluarh le ipatan pone ira tong, nge amwo nemeniei ena pukoi tes.
> Waluarh le ipatan pone ira tong, nge amwo nemeniei ena pukoi tes.
> Nge amwo nemeniei ena pukoi tes, ina repwe irhiitan manieweires.
> Nge amwo nemeniei ena pukoi tes, ina repwe irhiitan manieweires.
> Ina repwe irhiitan manieweires, use fang ne waluei epwe urusangiei.
> Ina repwe irhiitan manieweires, use fang ne waluei epwe urusangiei.
> Use fang ne waluei epwe urusangiei, use fange ne waluei elapo komwairhi.
> Use fang ne waluei elapo komwairhi.

Translation

> Sitting, worrying, and crying, the ladies of this island
> Sitting, worrying, and crying for our lei of flower bud
> Lei of flower bud of the love tree
> Wishing the test is under my control
> They're going to write Manieweire's name
> I refuse to allow my lei to wander away from me
> I refuse to allow my lei, the only flower bud
> The only flower bud, a first-born son

"Waluei" is a metaphor referring to a flower that is put in the hair or on a lei. In this song, the composer uses it to describe her nephew as a flower for her hair or lei. A flower is something we handle gently to avoid damaging it. A flower is also very beautiful and has scent. On Onoun, a flower is considered very important because its beauty cheers people up and its scent can remedy any ill feelings. The phrase that is often used to describe this is "e apala ai ngahangaha": it helps me breathe better and feel better. When the composer uses a *flower* to describe her nephew, she is trying to explain what her nephew is to her: someone who cheers her up, someone who makes her feel good, and, most importantly, someone she protects carefully. In this song she also expresses her refusal to allow her nephew to leave, indicating she has power of ownership as a woman.

This song is about a young man who was recruited to attend Pohnpei Agriculture and Trade School, known as PATS, located in Pohnpei, which is also where the capital of the Federated of Micronesia is located. PATS was another Jesuit school for the young men of Micronesia, and specialized in vocational trainings. These young men were learning vocational skills in agriculture, carpentry, mechanics, and electrical work, as well as training to become priests.

Manis is a teacher at the Weipat High School on Onoun.

Song 3: Urun Tosiwo Nakayama

Composed by Rosalia (mother) and Lienkainam "Teresa," (cousin of Tosiwo).

> I ono lekiareng kianai we kechilo, nge ureki sangilo
> I ono lekiareng kianai we kechilo, nge ureki sangilo
> Urekesangelo talipongono maram urekreki ne Tosiwo
> Urekesangelo talipongono maram urekreki ne Tosiwo
> U rekine Tosiwo eno pwe urhutenrei ne iananamo
> U rekine Tosiwo eno pwe urhutenrei ne iananamo
> Iananamo nee elo teokawow Merika me Sapan
> Iananamo nee elo teokawow Merika me Sapan
> Inetenanamo elo tokalong patiw me weito
> Inetenanamo elo tokalong patiw me weito
> Ekko ese pung letipei ehau.

Translation

> I lie on my mat of resting, worrying and crying secretly
> Worrying and crying secretly every night of the moon cycle for Tosiwo
> Worrying about Tosiwo, who is my precious pride, far and away from me
> Far and away, he traveled to America and Japan
> It will be long before he comes back to Patiw and Weito
> Oh, my heart is unsettled, Ehau!

"Urhutenrei" refers to someone who is a pride of the family, clan, community, or island. In this song, Tosiwo is clearly identified by the composers as the pride of the island; "teokawow" means to climb to, to conquer, to travel to. In this song the composers used this word to describe Tosiwo as a fearless leader who is brave and courageous. The word "eokawow" also indicates who Tosiwo is and what his functions are.

Tosiwo was the first president of the Federated States of Micronesia (COFA). He was also one of the key negotiators of the Compact of Free Association Treaty between the Federated States of Micronesia (FSM) and the United States. This song was composed during the time of the negotiation for the FSM's COFA Treaty.

Song 4 *Urun Keper Jos, Valentine Rosokow, and Kinsiano Aliwis*

Composed by Lienkainam (Grandmother) to Keper.

> Sorota ewe soran ulo kapwereta, nge ulo kapwereta lon imweunan
> Sorata ewe soran ulo kapwereta, nge ulo kapwereta lon imweunan
> Nge ulo kapwereta lon imweunan, ulo sarata wor ulurhai alukau
> Nge ulo kapwereta lon imweunan, ulo sareta wor ulurhai alukau
> Ulo sareta wor ulurhau alukau, nge ra monokalo ulun waluaraw
> Ulu sarata wor ulurhau alukau, nge ra monokalo ulun waluaraw
> Ngera monokalo ulun waluaraw, pungutekin ai kakai saretekin ai ma
> Ngera monokalo ulun waluaraw, pungutekin ai kakai saretekin ai ma
> Pungutekin ai kakai saretekin ai ma.

Translation

> At breaking dawn,
> I went to the Mweei [a place on Onoun].
> I came upon three young handsome boys,
> Hiding behind the tree leaves.
> I began to laugh very hard,
> Laughing so hard my tiredness went away!

Instead of expressing the emotions of sadness she felt when her grandsons left her, the composer expresses her happy memories, explaining how these are the remedy for her longing for her sons. Mweei is most northern part of the island of Onoun, and walking there is difficult and tiring. The simple act of the boys hiding behind the leaves of trees is depicted by the song's composer as something so funny that it made her forget how tired she was from the long walk. She is also describing how much she cherishes and loves her nephews: when she's sad, worn out, and longing for them, she uses these memories to cheer her up.

Kinsiano is the current mayor on Onoun.

Song 5: *Urun Masao Nakayama*

Composed by the women of Onoun.

> Achimare lepekupek, lieni Onoun sipwe amwolota
> Sippung sippeok
> Sipwe amwolota weni mwene waan, wenimwen waan Masao Nakayama
> Sippung sippeok
> Masao Nakayama, epwou sakana Patiw me Weito
> Sippung sippeok, sia wawarai ehau!

Translation

> All celebrate, women of Onoun, we must prepare and get ready
> Do it together

We get ready before his canoe, before his canoe, Masao Nakayama
Do it together
Masao Nakayama is fishing in Patiw and Weito
Do it together, we are done, ehau!

Achimare, the first word in the song, is a game usually played by children. The image of children playing and having fun refers to the happiness the women have when their sons return, and the freedom they feel to express that joy. When adults play this game, they become childish; the game is a temporary escape from the expectations of adult behavior.

As Vilsoni Hereniko and Caroline Sinavaiana-Gabbard put it, the women are free to behave in funny and sometimes inappropriate ways, to clown around— as long as they ultimately remove their "clown costumes" and return to their adult ways.

"Pekupek" means including everyone. Adults play this game only in times of celebration, and this song describes metaphorically the degree and capacity of the celebration.

Masao Nakayama came back to Pattiw and Weito atolls to educate people about the first drafted constitution of the Federated States of Micronesia. "E Pou sakana" literally means that a person is catching fish using a fishing pole; in this song, it is a metaphor used to describe the outreach education effort Nakayama provided for his people. "Sakana" is a Japanese word for fish; it is possible that this word was chosen because Masao Nakayama was part Japanese—his father was Japanese. He is also the younger brother of Tosiwo. Masao Nakayama was a former ambassador to Japan and the United Nations and was well known for his work on the fight against global warming.

◈ ◈ ◈

All of these songs are about men leaving their islands to go elsewhere for education. When I interviewed my mother and aunt while writing this piece, they told me that there have not been any songs written about women simply because there were no females leaving to go to school at the time.

Songs like these were composed by women specifically for their beloved sons as a way to heal their grief—"the cry of Oceania." For these women, expressing their feelings through songs was their own form of therapy. But most importantly, these women were creating an epistemology of a particular time.

Today, men and women continue to leave the island to obtain an education; others leave due to the effects of global warming. By studying the songs of these women, a question arises: "What will happen to matrilineal societies like this, where the land is what gives this system its meaning and its reason for existence?"

As a woman from this society, I was not given a song when I left Onoun to go to Xavier High School and on to the University of Hawaiʻi at Hilo; but I was given a song to write. This song and these stories will make a lei for the women in my family now and in the future, women whose origins are in Yap, Fanif, Ifaluk, Namotreok, and Piik. This "string" went onto Satawan, to Patiw and Weito, and now lies on Onoun in the Namwonweito atoll.

With global warming and the rising water of Oceania, this string will soon be floating. Will it survive the rising water? Will it float to a new place? If so, where will that be?

References

Graham, B. "Determinants and Dynamics of Micronesian Emigration: A Brief Discussion for Micronesian Voices in Hawaii Conference." Micronesian Voices in Hawaii Conference. Honolulu, 2008.

Hawai'i Appleseed for Law and Economic Justice. *Broken Promises Shattered Lives: The Case for Justice for Micronesians in Hawaii*, 2011.

Heine, H. "Micronesians' Contributions and Challenges in Hawai'i." Micronesian Voices in Hawaii Conference, Honolulu, 2008.

Hezel, F. "The Changing Family in Chuuk: 1950–1990." *Micronesian Seminar*, 1992.

Rosokow I., and T. Elieisar, November 24 and 30, 2012: personal interviews and recordings of songs.

We Are Human at the Wrong Place at the Wrong Time

Josie Howard (Chuuk)

In spite of our location in the world, and the size of our islands compared to the rest of the world, we are still human beings living and making this part of the world, Micronesia, our home, where we inherit our identity and the meaning of our very existence. Our lives have been disturbed many times over the years, due to foreign interest in our world. We have sacrificed our lives, dreams, and futures for the sake of all mankind. Our lands and oceans were the battlefield during World War II and many of our people died, and the living are left with scars of cultural trauma that will pass on from generation to generation.

The nuclear testing didn't happen just once but 67 times, which took the lives of our families, lands, and ocean, and the future of our children and our children's children. New ideas and lifestyles imposed on us are just as damaging to our lives and health as the nuclear testing. Out of our control is the global warming that is physically eroding and submerging our islands into the ocean.

Most importantly, our dignity, integrity, and lives as human beings are at stake, as we trusted that our relationship was sincere and mutual. Our hands are tied because the Compact of Free Association or Commonwealth were our only choices! To maintain the most of our integrity and independence, the Compact of Free Association was the "better" choice. This is another chance to assure us that, under this Compact of Free Association treaty, our relationship is based on the fact that we are human and that the responsibilities of this relationship are our common objective, and our relationship is a mutual one.

Healthcare is one of our most important needs—to heal the mental and physical scars of the sacrifices we gave for this relationship, and for our existence in this part of the world.

Imbibing Native DNA at a Pacific Science Meeting in Australia

Vicente M. Diaz (Pohnpei and Guåhan)

In what feels like ancient prehistory, in a site so far away as to seem unreal, certainly discombobulating in the present for a native who insists on politically motivated and culturally informed knowledge production in modern academic settings, I was invited to show my documentary *Sacred Vessels: Navigating Tradition and Identity* (Moving Islands, 1997) at the 19th Pacific Science Congress (PSC), which was held at the University of New South Wales in Sydney, Australia. The PSC is the oldest academic organization devoted to the Pacific; it has some ties to several antiquarian societies around the region and has tended to feature research mostly in the "hard" sciences. A good number of the presentations were by physical anthropologists. My documentary and brief presentation were received well, and I suspect that was because I am a Pacific Islander and because my own work, which tends to inhabit the liminal spaces between scholarship in the humanities, politics, and cultural production, is seen as quirky or anomalous. Certainly it is an exception to the kind of scholarship typically presented at the Pacific Science Congress. Such presumed normativity almost always makes me want to invoke for the work that I do the hardest of the hard sciences, even though the results have often led to greater erasure, the likes of which ultimately make me want to throw my hands up in exasperation and even lose myself in the most self-preserving if also self-destructive of social practices.

For example, the buzz at this particular forum, thanks to one of the conference's keynote speakers, was the recent discovery that the last specimen of an extinct Tasmanian cat (decimated by White settlers in the 19th century) had been preserved in ethyl alcohol, which as it turns out, also happens to preserve rather well a specimen's DNA. The speaker estimated that *within three decades* Australians would be able walk into any pet shop and purchase these once-extinct felines. His buddies over at the Human Genome Project were even more enthusiastic: "Try within *ten* years," they trumpeted. Apparently, there is also big corporate money already lined up for the project, and enthusiastic support from the Tasmanian government (via the museum), because, after all, the specimen "belongs to the state." I couldn't help but see this scientific project of resuscitation as also a significant act of political and cultural redemption for White Tasmanians, just as I also couldn't stop thinking about the tragic figure of Truganini, the *so-called* last "pure" Aboriginal Tasmanian, whose skeletal remains were so viciously and savagely dug up, dismembered, and even displayed, as British and Tasmanian and Australian antiquarian and scientific societies fought over her ownership—in shameless disregard of her dying request that her body not be disturbed. This case was featured in Tom Haydon's documentary *The Last Tasmanian* (1978).[1]

Anyway, after the screening of *Sacred Vessels* and delivery of my paper, someone in my own audience came up and challenged my claim about the persistence of traditional canoe culture in the contemporary Pacific, asserting instead that Polowat and maybe a few other places (like Satawal) in the Central Carolines were exceptions, that as a matter of historical and cultural fact the vast majority of Pacific Islanders had *already become* thoroughly modernized, and that traditional seafaring had long been extinct. Because he had missed the fundamental point of my presentation, it thus became necessary for me to explain it in other terms: you see, I said, as it turns out, the DNA of seafaring has been preserved remarkably well in alcohol in this tiny corner of the globe and, unlike the Australian scientists, other contemporary Pacific Islanders from across the region have already tapped the genetic material through shared voyages of revival and rediscovery in the last twenty-five years. The kicker, I pointed out, is that today one can go to practically any island in the contemporary Pacific and find a real, live traditional navigator.

I prided myself in my "scientific" retort to this person's colonialist nonsense as he walked off clearly annoyed, grumbling something beneath his breath in that all-too-familiar way in which Westerners react when their expectations of Islander authenticity are not only unmet, but aggressively repudiated by educated Natives (an oxymoron in colonial discourse). As he stormed off, perhaps in search of an authentic academic panel to compensate for his wasted time, I for my part spent the remainder of the conference at a neighborhood pub among a great mob of Aboriginal educators biding our time in an all-too-familiar form of producing knowledge in ways that at once seemed ancient and futuristic, self-preserving and self-extinguishing.

---

1. For a critical view of this film in light of contemporary Aboriginal Tasmanian land, resources, and rights claims, see Tom O'Regan's *Documentary in Controversy: The Last Tasmanian*, available at http://wwwmcc.murdoch.edu.au/ReadingRoom/film/Tasmanian .html.

A Journey of CHamoru Self-Discovery

Nikkie de Jesus Cushing (Guåhan)

For the first twenty-eight years of my life I resigned myself to knowing that I could never be CHamoru enough. I was the second generation born after World War II and could speak English better than many who lived on the United States mainland. But I could not speak my own native language. My grandmother spoke CHamoru only. My grandfather spoke three languages— CHamoru, Japanese, and English. My mother, on the other hand, went to school at a time when the CHamoru language was banned from being spoken in school. She and her friends welcomed the chance to learn the language of the Americans. She recalls the ease she had adjusting to speaking only English in school. So although her first language was CHamoru, she spoke to me in English and speaks mostly English today.

As a result, I grew up not learning my language. When I met up with the *manåmko'* (elderly) of my family, they would say something that was meaningful to the handful of people who spoke the native tongue but incomprehensible to me. Not understanding, I felt that somehow I had disappointed my mother and grandparents. I thought the cure was learning my language. So I took a college course in the CHamoru language. But while I thought I was making progress, I was being laughed at by my own family for speaking words that were not native.

"Those teachers are wrong in teaching words that don't belong in the CHamoru language," they said. "They think because they have degrees they can 'fancy' up the language. That is not real CHamoru."

Contradictory experiences like this confused me. How, then, could I be more CHamoru? Surely the answers could not be as simple as putting a sticker with the latest CHamoru catchphrase on the back of my car or shaving my son's head of all his hair but the traditional patch in the center that a few CHamoru activists proudly sport nowadays.

In a surprise twist of fate, I was given the opportunity to travel to Bali, an island that is part of an archipelago thought to be the origin of my CHamoru

Previously published, Kirk Johnson and Dianne Strong, eds., *From Classrooms to Rice Fields*, University Press of America, 2011.

ancestors. As I stood feeling ethereal in the wisps of a cloud on the mountaintop looking over the volcanoes of Java, I reflected on the Balinese and their ability to breathe life into their island culture—a culture and history not so unlike my own. It was in that feeling that I found the desire to do my part to revitalize CHamoru culture, the courage to make my blind leap of faith into a journey of discovery that would show me the strength of my culture, and the power of my own personal beliefs.

When the Spaniards invaded Guam beginning in 1521, there were at least 50,000 of us CHamoru. After giving the Spaniards food and water they desperately needed to survive, my ancestors became the targets of hostility, disease, and natural disasters. Then there were only 4,000 CHamoru. That was just the beginning of the subjugation of my culture by one colonial power after another. After the initial wars of the 1600s, subjugation became a quiet destruction based on the constant reiteration by outside forces of CHamoru as "primitive" and "savage." The result has been devastating, as it was for my grandfather.

Up until his death, my grandfather had never been able to talk about World War II, in which the Americans "saved" the CHamoru from the Japanese who had invaded and occupied Guam for two and a half years. I remember taking Guam History under Dr. Anne Hattori; her class sparked my insatiable interest in that particular war because of its domino effect on how I relate to culture in general. When I asked my grandpa about what he had gone through, his eyes watered and he said he still had a hard time talking about it. All he could say was, "I think about my mother and it hurts to talk about it." So I never broached the subject again.

Then there was American education. Being CHamoru became un-American. "Chamorros [were] blind-sided," according to educator Katherine Aguon "by ethnocentric 'American' institutions [that told them], they were . . . lazy, incompetent and part of a primitive reality . . . The people eventually accepted these distorted images. CHamoru became their own worst enemy in terms of self-concept" (qtd. in Johnson 2008, 281). As a result, my generation and I grew up thinking that being *chåd* was a bad thing. We wanted the modern and the fashionable and saw more traditional lifestyles as backward. Now, this new venture beyond subjugation has pushed me to learn why I have felt that way, has pushed me to learn about the quietly spoken, repressed histories of my people—histories that will hopefully be quiet no more.

My travel to Bali gave me the insight into something unimaginable; it opened my mind to the beauty of my own island—the island traditionally known as Guahan. A product of 300 years of being culturally dominated, I began trying to bridge the gap between my desire for modernity and my respect for tradition. I found myself asking what it was that made my CHamoru culture especially remarkable. I knew that my culture wasn't dead. Regardless of adaptation, acculturation, or assimilation, there was still a lot there. I began to notice and explore certain traditions and values that had been carried on through the years and taught to each succeeding generation, traditions and values like *inafa'maolek* that I had taken for granted.

Based on interdependence, reciprocity, and group effort *inafa'maolek* is one of the foundational values of CHamoru culture (Hezel, 1–2). As former Governor Gutierrez explains, *inafa'maolek*'s "very essence . . . is compassion, . . . caring, accepting, and helping one another with open hearts and open minds. *Inafa'maolek* is the inner strength and the treasure of our families and our island community. We live it daily in the warmth, [and] the generosity, the deep and abiding respect for our elders. It lives in the hearts of our people" ("Decision 2006"). I began to see and value the remarkable uniqueness of *inafa'maolek* and other traditions and values that composed my CHamoru culture.

In a conversation about my newfound respect for our culture, a close colleague said to me, "We are American. Why would you want to go back to a time when people wore grass skirts?" I told her that we did not have to be wearing grass skirts. Rather, my interest lay in the values that our parents taught us—the values of life, family, and friendship. We respect the elderly, the earth, and the ocean. The intricate social rituals range from kissing an elder's hand to oral recitation of legends, the trust in the *suruhanus and suruhanas*, and something as intrinsically necessary as asking for permission from the spirits before entering into the jungle.

My journey to comprehending what it is to be CHamoru has brought me to this place where I now understand the complexity of CHamoru identity that the weaving of centuries of cultural domination, resistance, and adaptation has left us. I have stepped out of my comfort zone and am walking into a kaleidoscope of possibilities. I now understand that cultures grow and change—it is this ability to grow, change, and adapt that allows a culture to survive. I no longer find it so easy to lay the blame at the colonizer's doorstep alone, to allow myself an escape from dealing with my own inabilities to cope and comprehend. Opening my mind to my own ignorance has been the key. I now understand what Julian Aguon meant when he said that we CHamoru are "not marching, but being marched, to the drums of our own disempowerment" (13).

Knowing is half the battle, so I figure that I am halfway to my goal. To Aguon's statement I can now reply, "Not me." Where I was ashamed before, I now understand that *chåd* doesn't have to be bad. It can mean embracing one's place in the culturally diverse realm of the modern mixed with the traditional. At the same time, I refuse to allow myself to believe that the only right way to be a CHamoru is to be a traditional CHamoru. Where I had once been naïve, I am now empowered. Culture is not something one can gain at the largest mall or the priciest dealership. It definitely cannot be bought or sold, traded like an inconsequential addition to a monetarily meaningless life. Instead, my cultural roots are the core of my beliefs and values, those I used to take for granted but don't anymore. This understanding is what I want to pass on to my children as they seek who they are as CHamoru people of the twenty-first century.

Bibliography

Aguon, Julian. *Just Left of the Setting Sun*. Tokyo: Blue Ocean Press, Aoishima Research Institute, 2006.

"Decision 2006: Candidate Profile—Carl Guiterrez." KUAM News. 2008.

Hezel, Francis X, S.J. "Culture in Crisis: Trends in the Pacific Today." *Micronesian Counselor* 10: May 1993. http://www.micsem.org/pub/counselor/frames/cultcrisfr.htm.

Johnson, Kirk. *Globalization and Human Dynamics*. Course Pack. University of Guam, Spring 2008.

The Five Stages of Being Micronesian in Guam

Nedine Songeni (Chuuk)

Guam is unique
geographically, it is located in Micronesia
politically, it is American through and through
physically, a tropical paradise
mentally, confusing.

Denial

You gain your US Citizenship immediately after birth, but you are
susceptible to denying your "ethnicity" to fit in amongst a sea
of others whose fates are in question in the uniqueness that
is Guam.

Guam is unique
geographically, it is located in Micronesia
politically, it is American through and through
physically, a tropical paradise
mentally, confusing.

Anger

You grow up with other Islanders and like anywhere else in the world,
you want to stand out and be better than the others. Tensions
ensue, anger grows, bitterness becomes part of your daily life.
We are constantly blaming others for anything wrong we can't
explain.

Guam is unique
geographically, it is located in Micronesia
politically, it is American through and through
physically, a tropical paradise
mentally, confusing.

Bargaining

As you grow older, you're at a crossroad in your life. You learn to hide what you can do without, adopt what you can and highlight what you feel will make you accepted.

Guam is unique
geographically, it is located in Micronesia
politically, it is American through and through
physically, a tropical paradise
mentally, confusing.

Depression

Like many, you're confused. You act out when you can't change. You stay within your comfort level because you feel like that's the only place you can be yourself. Others put on a mask to disguise their difference, hoping to be something else in order to be accepted. But what are you really losing?

Guam is unique
geographically, it is located in Micronesia
politically, it is American through and through
physically, a tropical paradise
mentally, confusing.

Acceptance

After a while, especially after many heartaches and lessons, you learn to accept your differences. Only when you turn your difference into uniqueness can you be comfortable in your own skin.

FAMILY

My Urohs

Emelihter Kihleng (Pohnpei)

my urohs[1] is an isimwas feast
with over a hundred urohs hanging
from the rafters of the nahs
swaying in the breeze

a kamadipw en kousapw
as women marekeiso the soupeidi
it shines on brown skin,
fragrant with coconut and seir en wai

my urohs is a lien Pohnpei
dancing and singing in a nahs in U
after winning a yam competition
the envy of the entire wehi

a seukala
for Likend
inviting her to lunch
at Joy

my urohs is a limesekedil
a weaver of kopwou and kisin pwehl
she has 13 children, 39 grandchildren
and 4 great grandchildren

Previously published, *My Urohs*, Kahuaomānoa Press, 2008.
For Nohno.
1. An urohs, or Pohnpeian skirt, is the quintessential dress of Pohnpeian women, especially at
events like mehla (funerals) and kamadipw (feasts). In this poem, I liken urohs to tiahk en
Pohnpei (Pohnpeian culture or custom). Urohs embody lien Pohnpei (Pohnpeian women) and
all of the things Pohnpeian women do.

a mwaramwar
of yellow seir en Pohnpei,
white sampakihda and
red hibiscus

my urohs is a mehla
the body covered in tehi
women with their little towels
bent over the deceased as they mwahiei

a kiam
of mahi, pwihk and kehp
taken home after a feast
to be devoured by family

my urohs is me
daughter of the lien wai
and ohl en Nan U
a iehros, walking slowly

The Tree

Christine Taitano DeLisle (Guåhan)

The tree
will never be
the same.
Not for the woman who planted it
thirty-three years ago,
who since then
has nurtured it,
has watched it
grow and grow.
She herself, joined in the bonds of
ma-tree-mony
with the man/the clan/the land,
placed her own roots
into the same fertile ground.

The tree
will never be
the same.
Not for the woman whose morning ritual
after a good night's sleep
consisted of—
standing in front of the *labadót*[1]
of her *kusinan sanhiyong*[2]
washing her *la'uya*,[3]
picking *puntan kalamasa*[4]
for her *kaddon mannok*.[5]
        And all the while

Previously published, *Storyboard: A Journal of Pacific Imagery* 5, 1998.

1. sink
2. outside kitchen
3. pot
4. pumpkin tips
5. chicken stew

taking in the sweet aroma of the red blossoms from
the tree
which she couldn't always see
from where she labored
but knew was there.
Familia.[6]
Familia.
Familiari-tree.

No, the tree
will never be
the same.
Not for the woman
who on the way back
from her usual three o'clock feeding of the chickens
one rainy Monday afternoon
spotted a strange fruit hanging from its fragile limbs.

Disoriented/confused/restless . . .   *Gof ma'åñao yu' pues hu ågang i
    lahi-hu*[7] . . .
Her son then called someone to investigate.
He in turn called someone to examine
what was later declared
to be a case of a sour-turned-bitter fruit
that left itself on
the tree
to rot.

It didn't matter to the woman whether it was
this side or that side
homicide or suicide . . .   *Pakeha Yu'. Sa' håfa na ti ma cho'gue esti gi
    tano'-niha? Dalai na bidan-niha gi tano'
    hagå-hu!*[8]

Whatever energy put it there
didn't belong there—
the land she settled on
thirty-three years ago

---

6. family
7. I was scared, then I called my son.
8. It's not my concern. Why didn't they do this on their own land? What they did on my
daughter's land—that was too much!

the land she and he built their first home on
the land their daughter later inherited.

When the hanging thing was finally removed
after hours of
questioning
deliberating
she decided
the tree must come down.

No man could hoist his cross high enough
say the right words
sprinkle water here and there
to drive the poison out of soil and air. Twice over, for that matter.

Only the buzzing sound of 2 1/2 horsepower against the trunk of
the tree
could lull
the woman
to sleep.

mechikung

Tutii Chilton (Belau)

bapa, where do you want to go eat?
longshoreman? furusato?
eh? you want to go to church tomorrow?
okay.

every sunday morning
we'd take the cold showers
using a japanese washcloth
my father would say,
scrub hard, your face, behind your ears
I still smell the soap and feel the cold water
my father would get dressed in black pants
and white shirt, always tucked in.
his hair would be neatly combed with pomade
I would wear the same, just a smaller version.

we'd head off to see mr. hiroshi
the local barbershop owner
and I'd get the weekly trim
short on the sides,
clean lines with a straight razor
the smell of lather on my neck
the oil in my hair as mr. hiroshi
parts it left to right
then we are off to church
in our yellowish-green datsun.

sitting in the pews next to him
listening to minister kuartei
just wishing it would soon be over
so we can go to peleliu club
eat udong with chicken and eggs
then play in the sand or catch fish with friends

while my father and his friends talk story
we'd stay there until 2 pm
then head home.

every sunday morning
my father and I
until july 8, 2007
our last sunday
no church, no haircut
no udong
mechikung[1]

---

1. farewell; goodbye

Rubak

Valentine N. Sengebau (Belau)

He reclined against his half-finished canoe
massaging his stiff right arm and aching back
from dressing the drift wood log
with axes and adzes all day.

It'd been a Herculean ordeal from the beginning,
towing and dragging the log from the reef far away
during the full moon tide; it taxed him three full days.
Now the three full moons had come and gone
and the canoe was still half finished
a bad sign for him these days.

The people called him Rubak.[1]

During his prime, Rubak could finish a canoe in two-moon time
and start working on the new one.
He had lost count of all the canoes he had made
which brought him fame far and wide.
His people spoke of him with deep respect and admiration.
Rubak married the daughter of the island chief.
But that was a long, long time past gone
when he was young, agile, happy and strong.
He stood straight like a proud tall palm tree
with its leaves and fruits conversing with the stars.

Alas for the last several years, Rubak's life had ebbed
to its lowest point like the low tide in the lagoon.
His dearly beloved spouse had passed away
like water seeping through the sand

Previously published, *Microchild: An Anthology of Poetry,* Northern Marianas Islands Council
for the Humanities, 2004.
1. titled male in the family, clan, or village.

and his children had gone to schools far away
and married through their heads and lived that way.

Rubak reached into his tet[2] searching for betelnut
and began preparing it with long experienced skill.
He also took out pictures of his children and grandchildren
and strained his eyes to examine them clearly.
He caressed each photo with paternal tenderness
while his heart swelled with pride and love.
He spat out his betelnut, and as he gazed beyond the reef
a lazy smile slowly stole across his wrinkled face
and his eyes became misty.

That's how his people found him the next day
lying beside his unfinished canoe
his left hand clasping the treasured stained photos
and his right grasping his favorite adze
with a radiant smile painted across his face.

It was three days before the foreigners' holiday
a birth called Christmas Day.
All his children had just flown in
with their children to see Rubak.

---

2. bag

Red Shoes

Kisha Borja-Quichocho-Calvo (Guåhan)

In 1976, Auntie Maria and Uncle Juan
    danced the cha cha for the first time.
She was in her red shoes;
    he was in his yori.

Every Friday,
even after their shoes wore out,
Auntie Maria and Uncle Juan still danced.

Red shoes are dancing shoes.

But Uncle Juan died last week.
People at the funeral,
in their black clothes and their black shoes,
couldn't stop crying over the man—
    who made them chicken kadu,
    taught them how to use a kamyu,
    and told them stories:
        how the two lovers jumped off the cliff,
        how Sirena turned into a mermaid,
        how the flame tree got its flames.

Red shoes are dancing shoes, not funeral shoes.

At the burial,
Auntie Maria danced her way up
to the casket
in her red heels.
They watched her

take off her red heels
and place them
    on top of the red roses
    that covered Uncle Juan's casket—

"Until we dance again," she said,
"Hu guaiya hao."

Sky Cathedral

C. T. Perez (Guåhan)

Nåna lives
in jewelled nights,
stars
like candles
lit
in a sky cathedral
as she prays with angels
in the sound of wind,
she prays for me.

"Abe, Nånan Yu'os
sen gåsgås Maria
ma'okte minaolek
yan gråsia siha."

Did you see that shadow pass
and pinch me on the cheek?
She misses me
and calls me
from my sleep.
"Nora, Nåna,"
I whisper
with waiting watchful eyes.

I find her
in gualåffon
dancing light
in a field of Latte
singing dreams
to me.

Gently then,
she strokes my hair

with moonbeam fingers
lets each strand
unfurl
and glisten
in the wind
cascading to
my shoulders
bare
that greet
this kiss
of Nåna's hair,
shining
silver streams
that drape me
with my past.

I am Nåna's daughter
born of earth and sky
scented breath
of salted breeze
surrounding seas
receive my soul
as Nåna takes
my hands
to pray.

"Åbe, åbe,
åbe, Maria,
Åbe, åbe
abe, Maria."

Nåna lives
inside my poems
in the dusk-to-dawn
of life.

Nåna lives
in mornings
when I wake
before
the light.

Ngedeloch

Valentine N. Sengebau (Belau)

You look very familiar
to me
like an old acquaintance.
I wonder
where did we first meet?
Was it in my dream
Or in your dream?
Or was it during your time
or mine?
Or whether I met you
in the books I read.
Strange . . .
You sure look very familiar
to me
Yet you're so fathomless.
You seem to be everything
to me
and yet you're none
of the things I know.
But somehow I can see your face
dancing all over
the recesses of my mind.
Perhaps we did meet
in some distant age
in some remote time.
Then again,
perhaps not.
But still you look very familiar
to me

Previously published, *Microchild: An Anthology of Poetry,* Northern Marianas Islands Council for the Humanities, 2004.

and it feels good
indeed
to know
that I feel
I know you
and that's very comforting
you know.

Food Thoughts

Teresia Teaiwa (Kiribati and Fiji)

"The tyranny of food," my mother called it, this culture that insists on an abundance of food. At the table, on the stove, in the fridge, in the pantry. This culture that insists that everyone must be fed. And that there must be food left over (for visitors, or relatives who just might drop by . . . and especially for the men who creep home while you are sleeping). This culture, in which time is measured by breakfast, morning tea, lunch, afternoon tea, dinner, and maybe even Milo and bread before bed.

Her mother had hated cooking. Her mother's mother had hated cooking, too. They emancipated themselves from the slavery of the kitchen.

"McDonald's and the Hot Shoppe were my grandmother's salvation," she tells me. "A coffee and pastry from the neighborhood McDonald's did the trick for breakfast. One square meal a day, courtesy of Hot Shoppe. My grandmother hated cooking, but loved food."

While I scribble in my notebook, she describes the way her grandmother would lick her lips after sipping her coffee, before she closed her eyes to lift the pastry to her lips. The way it disappeared into her mouth. The way she chewed, savoring each morsel with her eyes closed. Coffee and pastry from McDonald's.

"My grandmother made this breakfast look divine," she sighs.

My pen pauses over the irony.

"On the other hand," she continues, "my mother did not know how to love food. She ate if she was hungry, but she hated being hungry. You would have thought the food was going to bite her, the way she pushed it away from her place at the table! All the time." The memory clearly agitates her.

"Mother hated other people's hunger, too," she adds, telling me about the time her mother hit her for opening the fridge when she'd come home after school. While over at their homes her friends might have been enjoying biscuits and tea, or leftovers from lunch, rice and chop suey, tavioka, pie, or even some coconut ice, she would have nothing to eat after school. Nothing until dinner.

"And then there was just enough for whoever was at the table. And there were never any leftovers. And there were never any visitors. Or relatives." She sounds almost petulant.

Once, she reveals, her father threatened to beat her mother with a pot. It was empty, of course. So her father took up cooking.

"He loved it," she says, her face softening. "He loved food, so he grew to love cooking, and came to love shopping."

I want to interrupt her there.

"But Mother hated it." The hardness comes back. "She hated the way he shopped. More greens than the fridge could hold. More chillies than they could pickle. More fish than they could store in the freezer. More coconuts than Mother could stand. More food than we could eat. Mother didn't have to cook anymore, but she still complained."

Her father had had a garden. With taro. Tavioka. Kumala. Bananas. Pawpaw. Lemons. Sugarcane. Soursop. Her mother would give it all away.

"She liked giving food away (so it wouldn't oppress her at home)."

I marvel at the way she manages to convey the need for parentheses in that sentence.

As we draw the interview to a close, I decide it's time to name the inevitable.

"I'm not going to inherit any family recipes from you or Grandmother, am I?"

"No family recipes, love." My mother shakes her head without regret. "Not for food, anyway."

The Boys

Charissa Lynn Atalig Manibusan (Guåhan)

They roll down the streets of the vill like they own those strips of cracked pavement. Tape decks strapped to handle bars, bumpin NWA, The Beastie Boys and LL Cool J, sportin LA caps, NY Jerseys, Baggy jeans and zories. Talking bout "Fuck the Police!" like they gangsters or something. Thinking they scary, but really only scaring the chickens from the streets if they lucky.

They be passing by my house like five times a day acting like they the best thing I ever seen. But I know, you know and they know that they nothing but a bunch of wannabes, victims of pre-fab creativity and theft of identity, from way too many hours of watching that Americano MTV!

Previously published, Michael Bevacqua, Victoria-Lola Leon Guerrero, and Craig Santos Perez, eds., *Chamoru Childhood*, Achiote Press, 2006.

Auntie Lola's
Champion Chalakiles

Charissa Lynn Atalig Manibusan (Guåhan)

The pungent smell of garlic and onions floated out from the campus cafeteria, breaking off Isa's concentration from her Bio101 study guide and transporting her thousands of miles away from the wintry Boston weather into her Auntie Lola's worn outside kitchen on her beloved island of Guam.

If there was anything she missed badly since moving to Boston for school, aside from family and the warmth of a tropical sun, it was her darling Auntie Lola's culinary magic. The frying garlic and onion fusion summoned forth the homesickness she had managed to suppress that day, and the more-than-occasional cravings she had for Auntie Lola's Champion Chalakiles. Chalakiles is a chicken-and-orange creamed rice stew that can chase away the blues from the broken-hearted, or complement a cold day spent indoors in front of the tube, or, in Isa's case, a cold day spent studying for finals in an empty college cafeteria thousands of miles away from home.

One more day, just one more day till I'm leaving on a jet plane! she thought.

Dear Auntie Lola was the oldest child of ten and surrogate mother to all in her family. But most of all, she was Isa's closest confidant. Standing a mere five feet tall, this jolly round spirit forever wore a comical gap-toothed grin and exuded a warmth equal to that of her signature dishes. Isa had tried futilely to replicate Auntie Lola's Chalakiles—with its perfect balance of flavors—since moving away. It was the little piece of home that she knew would heal the woes of her homesickness. But there was always something missing; she could never pinpoint exactly what. It was almost a year since she had been home. She planned to make the most of this trip and to learn to make her auntie's Chalakiles or die trying!

🌺 🌺 🌺

Continental Flight 205 touched Guam ground at approximately 4 a.m. The thirteen-hour (plus some) flight should have tired Isa, but she was more awake and excited than she had been in months. Tears soon streamed from her round amber eyes and down her face, pale from a long sunless winter, as she exited the arrival gate and found herself greeted with hugs and kisses from her nana, tata, brother Joey, and dear Auntie Lola, who carried a thermos full of Chalakiles in her waiting hands as Isa had requested.

"Ai, nene,[1] let's get some color in you, adai. You're looking pretty haole! This should do the trick!" Auntie Lola joked as she handed Isa the thermos.

"Si Yu'os, Ma'ase Saina-hu! Hu Guiya hao!"[2]

"Come to my house when you get over your jet lag, baby, and I'll teach you how to make it! Ai adai,[3] I would have thought you would've figured it out by now, after being my number one cook's helper growing up!" Auntie Lola teased as they left the airport for home.

🌸 🌸 🌸

Isa returned from New Morning Mart with all the necessary ingredients Auntie Lola sent her to retrieve: a bag of achiote seeds, garlic, salt, black pepper, two yellow onions, a can of coconut milk, chicken broth, and cream of rice. Her dear aunt already had the chicken parts cut up and sitting in a Tupperware bowl, awaiting their delicious transformation. Isa was thrilled that Auntie Lola was willing to teach her her culinary secret, but not the least surprised. Auntie Lola had always been such a generous spirit. In fact, everyone knew that she was the rock that had held the family together ever since her Grandma Banki and Grandpa Ben died. Her nana had told her on the day of her grandpa's funeral a year after Grandma Banki's passing that he had never really been able to take being apart from Grandma for too long.

🌸 🌸 🌸

Isa could smell the love of many a comfort food made in her auntie's *kusinan sanhiyung*.[4] The aroma was embedded in the hut-like structure's ironwood posts, which held up its rusted tin roof. The old outside kitchen was just as Isa remembered it. Heavy silver cast-iron pots that had lost their shine years ago hung from the same nails hammered into the dark brown wood posts next to the makeshift sink. A timeline of family photos lined the concrete walls next to the main house's back door, which led to the outside kitchen. Isa spotted the picture of herself blowing out the candles of her tenth birthday cake with her cousins huddled around her. It hung in the same place it had for years, just below the picture of Auntie Lola's only daughter, Nona, at the baby shower they had thrown for Auntie Lola's first grandson, Frankie boy, ten years ago. She touched the numerous frames, overcome by nostalgia, and breathed in the scent of Auntie Lola's pink and purple orchids, which hung all along the sides of the outside kitchen.

---

1. baby

2. Thank you, my elder! I love you!

3. Ai, Adai – common Chamorro expression, similar to "Oh, my."

4. *kusinan sanhiyung* – an outside kitchen, a common and traditional attached extension to homes of Chamorro houses, usually made of wood and tin or concrete.

Auntie Lola motioned her now to the tar-encrusted gas burner standing on the right side of the sink. Isa moved toward her auntie, anticipating the *Aha!* moment when she would finally discover the secret ingredients to her auntie's Chalakiles that had eluded her thus far. She pulled a wooden cutting board from the dish rack and stood beside her in anticipation.

"The key, *haga-hu*,[5] is to have all your ingredients prepared beforehand: chop your onions and garlic, prep your achiote, salt your chicken and all that stuff . . . Just makes for less hassle."

And that's where Isa came in as designated chopper, a role she remembered well from her runny-nose days. Although she had moved up the chain since then, Auntie Lola still obviously outranked her. So back to her chopping fate she went! She was thrilled. Heh! Isa had been a chopper since she could remember, since she was able to hold a fork in her hand.

You would think that a responsible, rational adult would be concerned about handing a little kid a knife, but oh no, not in my family, she thought as she reminisced on her beloved childhood role. *If you were able-bodied, you were put to good use*, she rationalized.

But sitting at the table, chopping away at the tons of vegetables and whatever else the elder women in her family threw at her, wasn't always a pain in the *dågan*.[6] It had its perks: the kitchen table was gossip central! As long as she sat there quietly chop-chop-chopping away, the elder women would almost forget that she was there and she could get the heads-up on all the secret family and political drama. When they finally remembered that she existed and had ears to boot, or when they had something highly top secret to tell, they would switch from English to Chamorro mid-conversation.

She giggled to herself now as she prepared to chop the onions, remembering how she would sit there watching their facial expressions and listening for words she could understand—trying to piece things together. It was like playing a game of charades.

She thought about the time she had overheard her nana and Auntie Lola talking about her godfather, Uncle Ben. Uncle Ben was their youngest and most handsome brother, and Isa's favorite uncle. He had the brightest dimpled smile and brown eyes she had ever seen, and always gave her ten dollars or more whenever they visited him. He was the "big" man at the bank where he worked and so was always dressed in what Nana called his Sunday best. He smelled sweet, like cigars and old spice.

Auntie Lola and Nana had whispered while they prepared the red rice for her cousin Matmat's christening about how he was cheating on Auntie Rita with his secretary. Matmat was Uncle Ben and Auntie Rita's first baby and Isa's godbrother. In a scornful whisper, the kind that Nana used to scold her when she was misbehaving in church, Auntie Lola called his secretary a "stinky sex-satary," and Nana followed by calling her a "fuckin' puta!"

---

5. my girl
6. buttocks

Isa had felt so sorry for her Auntie Rita, but she was angrier at her once-favorite uncle. She had contemplated telling on him, but she knew how much trouble she would be in if she did. Instead, she had decided to forever ignore him, even refusing to *ahmen* him when she was prompted by her tata at Matmat's christening party. She had stayed in the outside kitchen the whole night, refusing to join the celebration being held in the front yard of Auntie Lola's house.

That night, Uncle Ben had teased her for ignoring him, telling her that she was being jealous of the attention Matmat was getting from him. As he turned his back and walked away from her, , Isa had wiped the tears of scorn from her eyes and called him a "stinky fuckin' puta," using the same scornful tone Auntie Lola and her nana had used, but at a volume far from a church whisper.

After the party was over she had accepted, with her arms crossed and her lips tightened to muffle her cries of pain, the four lashings her tata had administered with his thick leather belt.

Auntie Lola, having more than a hunch of where she'd picked up the dirty words, quickly came to her defense, telling Tata and Uncle Ben, "She learned it from her elders! Don't punish her for that! And it's not like she's lying either, Ben, so don't you have my girl punished for telling the truth!"

Tata had never spanked her in front of Auntie Lola again, and Isa, in turn, had never accepted anything from Uncle Ben again. He had tried to shower her with gifts and money for a whole week after, explaining to her nana that he had just felt really bad and didn't want his goddaughter to hate him. But Isa believed that it had more to do with him being worried about what she might have discovered about him.

❦ ❦ ❦

After washing the onions and garlic and dampening her knife to soften the sting of onion spray (a lesson learned after many years of chopping), Isa diced through a whole clove of garlic and two onions. Auntie Lola took great care to wash the chicken parts, scraping away as much of the fat as she could.

"You don't want your soup too oily, babe, and it's just not healthy. You know your Uncle Ben—boy, does he love that fat. Look at him now—fat as a cow, and his heart . . . Sus-Marion-Jose!"

Karma, Isa thought as Auntie Lola furiously rubbed salt and pepper into the chicken, as if to resuscitate the dead bird. Isa tried to observe just how much spice she added, but it was a fruitless endeavor. Auntie Lola didn't measure her ingredients—she never did. Her explanation of the process didn't help much either.

"Nene girl! You just make a Z-like motion over the chicken with the salt and shake the black pepper about six times and then massage it all in really good!"

Auntie Lola washed her hands of that task and started to prepare the achiote water, rubbing the red out from the tiny seeds under warm, running water into a ruby-stained plastic bowl while a pot of boiling water waited on the gas stove.

"That water's for the cream of rice," she said, motioning to it. "Let it boil and then slowly stir in half a box, okay?"

Auntie Lola watched over Isa's shoulder as she obeyed her command, lamenting meanwhile about how it was done in the old days.

"Ai girl, you know, the *antigu*[7] way is to grind the rice and roast it over the fire. If you ever tasted it the way Great-Grandma made it, you would know the difference. Nowadays we choose the easy way for everything. Lazy nai!"

Isa was surprised by this bit of information. She had always assumed that Auntie Lola's way was as traditional as it got. Her Chalakiles was better than any others Isa had ever tried.

After that task was completed, it was time to brown the chicken. In a medium-sized stew pot, Auntie Lola heated about three tablespoons of canola oil and threw in the chopped garlic and onions. Isa closed her eyes and breathed in as the aroma of the garlic and onion infusion filled the air. Her mouth watered.

She remembered how, after she had been helping in the kitchen all weekend long, the smell would get stuck on her fingers, in her hair and her clothes. She would scrub her hands constantly, trying to get the smell out. If the smell wasn't out by Sunday night, as a last resort she would soak her fingers in bleach and water. It was a choice between going to school smelling like onions and garlic or like the school cafeteria floor after the lunch ladies had mopped it. Either way, she would get teased by her classmates, particularly a boy named Jose Cruz, who often called her *mutung*[8] *finger girl*. Years later in high school, he confessed to having a big crush on her. She showed him her *mutung* finger, particularly the middle one.

❧ ❧ ❧

"Mmm—the smell of love!" Auntie Lola giggled as she stirred the mixture, throwing in the chicken as the onions turned clear. She stirred until all the chicken parts were browned on both sides and then added the achiote water and chicken broth into the mix. She immediately covered the pot as the ingredients danced in the simmering water. "Come sit now, babe, and let it boil. You want your chicken to be tender, falling off the bone almost."

They sat and transitioned naturally from cooking mode to conversation. Auntie Lola opened up the bag of sweet bread sitting on the table and offered it to Isa along with a cup of warm calamansi tea that she brewed herself. She usually had her bread with coffee, but had given that up about two years before Isa left for college.

"So, how are you, nene? How's school?"

"Fine. Just really missing home."

"Ai Haga-hu, I know you're *mahalang*[9] right now, but just hang in there. You'll be fine. Ai, I'm so proud—you were always a smart girl. *Aguguat*,[10] but smart!"

---

7. ancient
8. stinky or smelly
9. lonely
10. naughty

They both laughed, and Isa's eyes started to water as she struggled to hold back from confessing the utter loneliness that had accompanied her since leaving for school.

"Man, darn onions." Auntie Lola placed her hands on Isa's, giving them a reassuring squeeze.

❧ ❧ ❧

After about thirty minutes or so, it was time to add in the cream of rice. Auntie Lola lowered the heat of the chicken and slowly stirred in the creamy concoction.

"We stir it in really good and then let it simmer on low heat for about fifteen minutes," she stated matter-of-factly. She then pulled out three boonie peppers from the outside fridge and cut them up finely, taking great care to wash the seeds out, and then threw them into the pot.

"How many peppers you want to add is up to you, baby. But be careful adai! If you put too many, it's going to be *Chilli-kill-us*, not Chalakiles!"

They both laughed, and Isa realized just how much she missed her auntie's company.

The final step to completing the hearty homesickness elixir had arrived. Auntie Lola shook the can of coconut milk frantically before pouring it into the aromatic soup. She turned off the burner and made a point of emphasizing not to add the coconut milk until the end or until it was time to serve the food.

Auntie Lola grabbed two bowls from the dish rack and filled them to the rim from the pot of culinary gold. Isa retrieved the *finadenne*[11] from the fridge, setting it on the table alongside two glasses of iced calamansi tea and two spoons. She sat thankfully as Auntie Lola offered a prayer. This was the moment that Isa had craved for almost a year, and Auntie Lola did not disappoint. In fact, Isa could not recall a time when she had.

The food was utterly delicious, more so than she remembered: a perfect infusion of spices, vegetables, and chicken. She poured a spoonful of *finadenne* into her bowl for extra kick, while Auntie Lola ate hers with chili peppers on the side.

"Sainan Ma'ase,[12] Auntie. It is beyond delicious!"

"No problem, nene. I'm just glad that you are so willing to learn. Now when I die, I know that at least my Champion Chalakiles will live on!" she said jokingly.

"You know, Auntie, it's funny 'cause I really thought that maybe there was a secret ingredient that you added that made it so good. But there really isn't. I thought I was being privileged because I'm your *kirida*!"[13] she teased.

Auntie Lola laughed. "Ai haga-hu, you are my *kirida* and also a very perceptive girl. I think you already know what makes my Chalakiles champion."

---

11. dipping sauce made of vinegar, soy sauce, and hot peppers
12. Sainan Ma'ase – term of gratitude meaning "the elders are grateful."
13. favorite

what urohs say

Emelihter Kihleng (Pohnpei)

e katik?
right smack in the middle of her thick thighs
nei dama
kedeh toai
kedeh kasaformihe
masamwahu
lien Pohnpei
serepein en Pohnpei
kaselehlie
sakau en Pohnpei with a pohndal underneath
lih tohrohr

my friend sends me a bright green urohs[1] that says
kedeh tehk
but I can't help it.

English semi-translation

is it bitter?
right smack in the middle of her thick thighs
my favorite
don't hate
don't ruin my "form"
beautiful
Pohnpeian woman
Pohnpeian girl
kaselehlie (formal greeting)

---

1. Pohnpeian applique and machine-embroidered skirts, some of which have words and expressions sewn into the fabric.

Pohnpeian kava with a coconut shell (for sakau drinking) underneath
a real woman

my friend sends me a bright green urohs that says
ignore it
but I can't help it.

Beloved Sumay

James Perez Viernes (Guåhan)

The soil our fathers once
nourished gave birth to the sweet gifts
that sustained us
And the sapphire sea once kissed
the golden shores that encompassed
us.

Now Big Navy's
barbed wire fences embrace
what we once called home
And the waters that meet
the sand are now stained by
the entrails of your
passing aircraft carriers.

When the skies turned gray
that December day we ran towards
the refuge of the forest canopy
never knowing that
we'd never look back.
Then bayonets and treaties
pushed us up into the hills
looking over the home that once was
never to be again.
Our bitter tears spilled
in silence.

Now orphans stolen from
the only mother we knew
a new home we had to adopt.

Previously published, *Storyboard: A Journal of Pacific Imagery* 8, 2001.
For all the sons and daughters of Sumay, most especially Maria Sablan Pangelinan Perez and
Guadelupe Sablan Santos Viernes.

Decades later
an orphan passes
as each day becomes night.
Faint memories
are laid to rest.

Out of sight
far beyond the sentry's gate
in the hills accepting defeat
your red white and blue
can fly proudly now.

But never forget
that as your flag pole
pierces the ground we once
cherished
forever in our soul flies
only the spirit of
Beloved Sumay.

Fino' Gualåffon/Moonlight Talk

Mary Therese Perez Hattori (Guåhan)

On the seashore
in moonlight encounters
we share sunlight in our kisses
starlight in our breath

bodies are palimpsests
onto which beauty is registered
again and again
and again.

We are tåsi
the ocean
an infinite source of ink
with which we pen poems of love.

We are langit
the heavens
via lactea
the milky way galaxy

flows between us
our passion creates
constellations of pleasure
in secret skies.

On Guam, fino' gualåffon was an allegorical language, a language of secret love songs that was lost over time. This poem is a tribute to that lost language, shared in the spirit of love.

Portrait of Grandmother Eating Mango

J. A. Dela Cruz-Smith (Guåhan)

It is a hot bowl of volcanic sediment.
The waters anointing its depths

like machete to bush. If the wind could hold iron or steel
the jungle kisses the sky full with ambient possibilities. My grandmother

recalling fighter jets so high like vultures. And the breathless
quiet escapes the foliage. And a colony of jellyfish pumping in a tide pool.

Have you heard of the jellyfish? There are missiles waiting to nuke them all,
even though the jellies are non-stinging kinds, that is, harmless and
    floating,

if harmless had a body that could take the shape of any container. It greets
    everybody
who visits with smiles, water, and food (there's always food).

The colonizers didn't see it coming when we
looted their ships. We, Island of Thieves

We, Islands of Inexperiences. We, Islands of Dead Birds, of Bodiless
    Wings
of Shell-less Coconut Crab Things, of Diabetes, of Gout-thick Ankles. We,
    Islands of Soldiers

We, Islands of Mixed Races. I am a creature-kind to think things
in terms of prayers and I'm in a cathedral, a ritual looking at Spanish faces.

You can tell by my size and translucence and my ability to swim in rough
waters that I often get stuck between rocks and simply wade in the residue
    of dead fathers

like pews. Yea, they are my pews, where I pray some. Come. Come in, sit.
    The water is warm
because of lava flowing beneath us. Because of friction. Plate tectonics.

Imagine less people, now. Consider this an intimate, applicable exercise.
Pretend my hands are the air, the force that brings water to motion.

I open my palms toward the sky, release my fingers away from each other
and bring them together again. I waft the space between us as if I'm
     actually

grasping what is invisible here. I'm holding it, carrying that payload
and at any moment I drop it in our little cathedral of tiny, bright, darting
     fish.

Risks. I took the risk in showing you my power and all the life in our
water, among all the stones like islands scattering all the way across the
     horizon.

Always yield to the bodies that shatter—Oh.
Look at that. The water is settling, it's boiling down to a slow rumble.

Something bubbles toward the surface. Think, years. Think, moons
sliding in and out of view. Think, trees. Think, light gathering on the
     backs

of beetles, their polished wings bouncing back a day's breaking eyelid,
     open.
Think, about these tide pools! Pouring in with lived and living things.

Think sand below the currents, which complete the partial
sounds coming from utterances. The shifting over and under each other,
     all the time.

The swell sucked us right down and fashioned us into sea water (once)
     among those jellyfish,
the souls pulsing. The cliffs rise

out the frothy sea. My grandmother sitting on a fixture
of coral whose bodies were left blue and whose tombstones were carved
     out

of their own bodies. This is a long time. Like this, she's been waiting.
Reparations for the fighting, the war. The peeled mango. She peels a
     mango's skin

as she reenacts her time in the concentration camp, always beginning
     with her hand
up and down, up and down . . . While coconut crabs crawled beside her
     feet I asked,

What did you concentrate on? To keep her sane, she laughs.
Wipes seawater from the crevices under her eyes.

She remembers how the achiote shrubs shook, how right before
the beheading, her and her friends were playing. Blouses billowing,

believing they were gowns and hermit crabs abandoning their shells.
    Those shells,
jewel inlays for crowns. The little royalties sitting at the sandcastles they
    stacked.

I think of my grandmother and these thin girls on a strip of beach. What
    is a line?
The entire ocean at their little feet, fins pushing water somewhere out
    there. They stand

out because nothing looks more human than that horizon devouring the day
and with it, my grandmother's grief. After all, if you detonated something,

in its shadow even the horizon looks to have disappeared.
How she said that man was her uncle.

How she was so close, she could smell him, like, if the soldier's hand was
    as clumsy
as the wind, it could have let loose the machete like a plane and its roar

and the explosives dropping out of the atmosphere. Just like a
    disembodied head, she said
the blade. would have. her hurt, but. at least—   What? I couldn't hear.

Looks like so long. And the tourists ask her about it
while eating her kudo, while feasting on what took so long to prepare.

The tides came steady and she says, Thank god though.
That it wasn't the wind's doing, that a man had his heavy grip

on what he was ordered to take that day. My grandmother kneels,
scoops me up from the ocean by my arm, limp like ingredients

stewing for hours over a fire that warms the whole kitchen
and over and over again, I get back in the water.

Funny how water makes fish look larger than what they really are.
    I compare
them to the chunks of mangos she hands me, inspecting their sweet

boundaries bleeding; each piece as if it were the last thing I take from her. Of course, I tried to keep it from dropping into the water.

Of course, I tried to catch it in my mouth. But I'm slippery like fish against
   liquid
and the sand

was so fine it plumed and curled over the mango like a mushroom cloud swallowing the ocean after the bombs explode.

Hineksa Anonymous

Desiree Taimanglo Ventura (Guåhan)

I stare at the chipped dinner plate in front of me. To some, it will look full. All they see is a healthy meal. There is protein. There are vegetables. There are healthy carbohydrates. I stab the chicken with my fork, breaking off a small piece that I gently slide toward the whole-grain pasta sitting sadly on its left. The food doesn't taste bad, but the meal feels wrong. Broken. Incomplete.

There is no rice.

Rice, I am now being told, is bad. No one wants me to eat it anymore. The glossy magazines with toothpick-armed women suggest sweet potatoes and quinoa instead. My midwife, the haole with the nasal voice, reminds me that "my people" eat far more rice than we should. She also reminds me that "my people" eat too many canned foods. When she told me this, I contemplated reminding her that it was "HER PEOPLE" who brought canned food to "my people." She handed me a little pamphlet with a white woman on the front eating salad and laughing. Women from the States always smile and laugh in pictures of them eating salad. I stare at it. Ladies from the States really love salad. This pamphlet is filled with healthy options.

This meal is one of those options; and I don't feel anything like the laughing blonde on the cover. I have been struggling to view rice as something that is not "good" for me and my family. But I have always associated the presence of rice in my kitchen as a sign that we would be okay, that our meals would be satisfying.

I love rice. Even the act of preparing rice is soothing to me. I stare out my kitchen window, watching chickens walk by as I run my fingers through the wet grains, letting the clouded water drain into the sink. It calms me. I wash the rice with my son, smiling as his little hands cross paths with mine as we make circular motions. My mother did this with me. My grandmother did this with me. Rice is the first thing I learned to cook, and it has become the first

Previously published, *Local Voices: 12th Festival Pacific Arts*, 2016.

thing I have taught my child to cook. My mother once told me that as long as I knew how to make rice, I would be okay. If I could make rice, I'd always have something to eat.

When I was a little girl, trips to the States to visit strange relatives who had left Guam always resulted in awkward trips to restaurants. I would demand "regular rice" from waiters who stared in confusion, insisting the strange piles of yellow or brown grains scooped beside my meat were "rice."

At the end of the hallway, where I keep my towels and other linens, a blanket is folded gently on the top shelf. It was made by my paternal grandmother, Vicenta. She made many like it after the war, enough for all her children. The blankets are made of old Calrose sacks sewn together. They are perfect blankets for Guam's weather, providing the security you want when slipping into bed without making you uncomfortable in Guam's heat. When I look at that blanket, I think about how important a sack of rice was for a Chamoru family during different periods of our island's history. Somehow, even now, I feel an odd kind of panic when the rice supply runs low at our house. We could have a ton of other things in the pantry or in our refrigerator, but when I see the rice disappearing, I get a little weird and make sure that, as soon as possible, I get to the store and purchase rice to refill the container.

My maternal grandmother, Lola, also left behind stories reminding me of the strange power of rice in Chamoru history. She explained that when American priests came to the island, they wanted Pale Roman, a Spanish priest who was very close to many of the Chamoru families, gone. American businessmen on the island helped to circulate a petition that insisted he be removed.

My grandmother explained that her mother really didn't want Pale Roman to go; she liked him a lot. He spoke Chamoru to the people and prayed in Chamoru, which the Americans did not like. But she ended up signing the petition, because when the American men showed up at the house with the paper, they also brought a sack of rice. My grandmother told me that they never questioned Tan Maria (her mother) about signing. They understood that they could not turn down rice. My grandmother told me her mother was very sad when the men left with the petition. She served them rice silently that night.

Stories of rice also come down to me from my father's side. My father tells me that some of my "mother's relatives" were more influential than his in the past. She had uncles who knew the value of rice and used it to exert power over poorer Chamoru families. One of my maternal uncles was tasked with distributing WWII food rations. When he went to my paternal grandfather's home to hand out food, he would make a point of scattering the rice on the ground, knowing that he could act this way and still be allowed back during the next visit. That uncle was an American. My grandfather hated this uncle and refused to drop to the floor and gather the rice in front of him. But when my uncle left, my grandfather and his wife would gather the rice up anyway. Each time my American uncle visited with the rice, my grandfather suffered this humiliation.

These are just some of the family stories that have been handed down involving rice. Rice, for my family, was something that symbolized getting by and making it through even the toughest days. By the time my generation was born, rice had become a way to provide comfort. Every meal served by my mother and grandmother included rice. Those meals were made with love and a desire to provide for their children.

But it is 2013 now. The war is over. And now, rice makes you fat. You should only eat a tiny little scoop of it once a day (according to the stateside midwife with the nasal voice). I have been serving less rice since she gave me the pamphlet. This disappoints my father and son. My dad claims he NEEDS white rice. He argues that he might get a "stomach ache" if I make brown rice. He tells me (again) that when he was a young boy, traveling to the States for a baseball tournament, he had to be transferred to a Filipino host family. The Caucasian family kept giving him potatoes. He claims he got "very ill" and this is proof that he NEEDS rice.

I stare at my chicken and whole-grain noodles, trying to convince myself that this is better for me. Suddenly, I feel myself trying to claim I NEED rice, too. These whole-grain noodles might give me a stomach ache. After about ten minutes, I look around the kitchen. I am alone. I stand up and walk guiltily toward the rice pot. I open the lid, letting the steam waft over my face. I stare at the beautiful mound of fluffy white rice, untouched in the pot.

Just a little.

I am from . . .

Lynnsey Sigrah (Yap)

I am from chewing betelnut, from eating fish and taro.
I am from dry hills and small streams, with the fresh smell of morning
 gardenias.
I am from rows of orchids and big coconut trees, whose long-gone limbs
 I remember as if they were my own.

I am from late nights and family time and singing old evangelical songs.
I am from respect and humility and spending time with grandma, listening to her stories of old.

I am from being quiet, from listening to every single word of the old
 people talking.
I am from long women meetings.
I am from Arngel and dolphins are my taboo, from drinking coconut and
 eating guava while still in the guava tree.
From combing grandma's long white hair, and listening to her story of
 how she met grandpa.
From laying down on the mattress thinking about what will happen tomor-
 row, and holding on to the memories of today.
I am from putting family first, and cherishing every moment together.
I am from a loving, caring and traditional place, where life is the most
 important thing, and time always runs out.

A NEW MICRONESIA

Pohnpei Outer Space

Emelihter Kihleng (Pohnpei)

Nahn! I saw you on the MySpace
noumw space o songen lel![1]
I tried to IM you, but it wouldn't work
I requested you to be my friend
you have so many friends!
100 plus! and all mehn Pohnpei
in GA, SC, Kansas City, Hilo, Honolulu . . .

my policy is that I'll accept you as my friend
as long as you're Pohnpeian
if you're not, then I have to know you personally
I don't want just anyone showing up on my profile
you know what I mean?

Nahn! why do all these Pohnpeians write like they're Black?
posting "holla back"
"I'm out"
"peace out"
when we all know they went straight from
Kolonia to Tennessee
never even met a real Black person in their life
don't even speak good lokaiahn wai[2]
after all, when they get to the States they only
hang around with other Pohnpeians
other Pohnpeians from the same part of Pohnpei too!

I'd rather have them write me in Pohnpeian
than in broken, fake Ebonics/English

Previously published, *My Urohs*, Kahuaomānoa Press, 2008.
1. Your space is so nice!
2. English

i pahn kohwei pirapw mwangas nan sapwomwen[3]
is better than wassup homie, where you at?
Ohiei.

I know, I gotta work on my profile
it's so boring
I gotta add more pictures
pictures of me and my friends
holding tequila shots
drinking straight from the pwotol en sakau[4]
eyes half-closed from intoxication
so that I look popular, cool
but then if I make it too nice
with all the moving photo albums
and graphics
it'll look like I have no life
and spend all my time
pimping my space
and not doing my homework

3. I'm going to go steal coconuts from your land
4. bottle of Pohnpeian sakau (kava)

Development

Katerina Teaiwa (Kiribati and Fiji)

1999   *Development Part I*

Thursday, Friday and Saturday nights in Suva:

After a good pump at the Rabuka Gym
And a good scrub with Protex
Anti-bacterial soap
Energized by a good dose of Fiji One TV
I surveyed my Wai Tui Tavarua shirt
Adjusted my Stolen Pig Pants
Climbed into my Mitsubishi Pajero DE007

Feeling fine
Fair and Lovely
With the plot of *Melrose Place*
And *Party of Five* on my mind
Stopped at the Bank of Hawai'i
With more ATMs in the country
Listening to Barbie Girl
On Fiji's Number One thanks to YOU

Pass Village Six-In-One-Cinemas
And the Downtown Boulevard Mall
And McDonald's on Victoria Parade
And Lucky Eddie's on Victoria Parade
And O'Reilly's on Victoria Parade
And the Bad Dog on Victoria Parade
And Bourbon Bluez on Victoria Parade
And Signals on Victoria Parade
And Traps on Victoria Parade

Where I stay and drink the rest of my paycheck
And shout six rounds of Fiji Bitter

With Taki Master Rob: Number One All Blacks Fan

And my mate Jone, straight here from work

2009   *Development Part IV*

Thursday, Friday and Saturday nights in Suva:

After a good pump at the Gym Formerly Known as Rabuka
And a good scrub with Protex
Anti-bacterial soap
Energized by a good dose of Sky TV
I surveyed my Polo shirt
Adjusted my J. Crew Pants
Climbed into my BMW EF007

Feeling fine
Fair and Lovely
With the plot of *CSI*
And *American Idol* on my mind
Stopped at the ANZ
With more ATMs in the country
Listening to Mr. Grin and Red Child
On Fiji's Number One thanks to YOU

Pass Village Six-In-One-Cinemas
And Morris Hedstrom's City Centre Complex
And Liquids on Victoria Parade
And McDonald's on Victoria Parade
And O'Reilly's on Victoria Parade
And the Bad Dog on Victoria Parade
And Bourbon Bluez on Victoria Parade
And Signals on Victoria Parade
And Traps on Victoria Parade

Turned up
To Kahawa on Gordon Street
For a mochaccino and half chicken salad roll

With Simone from UNDP
And Pierre from the Alliance Française
And Charmaine from the Fiji Women's Rights Movement
And Elizabeth from the Forum Secretariat
And Mosese from the *Fiji Times*
And Richard from BULA FM
And Sheetal from Munro Leys

And Suzy from femLINK
And Helen from the New Zealand High Commission
And Conrad from AusAID
And Dinesh from USP

We eat our half sandwiches

And drink our mochaccinos

And head to Traps

And there we stay

Map Gazing

Marianna Hernandez (Guåhan)

Dots
In a wide blue expanse.
They seem to need all those lines and words
To box them in
With that ever-present Other contained
Inside innocuous parentheses.

Those curved lines and their masters within,
They're like a cushion, a safe harbor
To protect those little helpless dots
From all the horrors of the world
Closing in on them from all sides.
But I see something different on

My little dot.
I see the lines and curves and words not shown.

The line between inside and outside
Defined by guns and uniforms.
The curve of an arching back
As it is bent over backwards.
The words of newspapers and signs and talk
That all say one thing.
"This little dot
Is not your little dot anymore,"
And underneath it all
The sly question,

"Was it ever?"

Yes it was.
Yes it is.
It always has been.

It always will be,
No matter how many lines and curves and words
Suppress my little dot,
Colonize my little dot,
It will always be my dot
And the dot of my people.

So while others star gaze,
Against the backdrop of the night sky
I map gaze
against
lines
curves
words.

Look at It This Way

C. T. Perez (Guåhan)

When you're born
On an island,

You
Don't
Know   you're   on

An island

Until   someone

Tells you.

They say,
"How
can you
live   on such
a   sma-a-all
island?"

I ask,
"How
can you   not?"

and,

"Sma-a-al, as compared
to
What?"

My island is as big
As the sky,
flowing to where
All waves crest and fall.

My island reaches
Beyond my breath
And from
Before all time.

Where birds fly,
My island lies.

I could be Miss Guam Tourism

Kisha Borja-Quichocho-Calvo (Guåhan)

I could be Miss Guam Tourism
if I were 5'3"
and looked good in a bikini.

It doesn't matter
if I know Guåhan's culture and history,
how Chode Mart sells the crunchiest empañada on the island,
or that the best pickled mango can be found in the village of Talofofo.
It doesn't matter
if I know that before one enters the jungle,
    she must say, "Guella yan Guello"
    to show respect for her ancestors.
It doesn't matter if I know that "going around the island" with family
    means only going around the South.
And if I said that every Chamoru's childhood
    included going to Ipao Beach and capturing duk-duk crabs in the sand
    and playing with the thickest black balati,
it still wouldn't matter.

I'm not 5'3".

My dågan can barely fit into a bikini.

Previously published, *Storyboard: A Journal of Pacific Imagery* 10, 2009.

Well, we're all eating chå'guan now

Evelyn Flores (Guåhan)

From barbecued short ribs
teriyaki-glazed, bubbling
in the heat of the fire
smelling of ha'iguas

we're all eating chå'guan[1] now

We wrap our pride around us bravely
and wander—we hope unnoticed—
into Simply Foods[2]
where we'd never have been caught
dead
a year ago

Now that being dead
is a distinct possibility
not just a metaphor,
according to the mild-mannered doctor
with tragic eyes,
we're
looking at rows and rows
too many rows of
definitely not meat
Big Franks without the frank
Prime Steak without the steak
FriChik without the chik

and we're all eating chå'guan now

---

1. grass
2. Simply Foods is a popular vegetarian restaurant and the only vegetarian grocery store on Guam. Many Chamoru elders find their way there after being diagnosed with diabetes or heart disease and told by their doctor to make radical changes in their diet and lifestyle to save their life.

The mild-mannered doctor
with tragic eyes
says
"You've been poisoned
by good old American gluttony
and mass food production
that puts steroids where steroids
have never been before
and feeds chickens
the excrement of cows."

we need to return
to the food of our ancestors
he says

So leathery Tun Juan, *familian Månok,*
who was the master barbecuer
and fisher
back in the day
he's dragging his feet into Simply Foods,
he says it's gout
but I suspect there's a certain huge undertow
that starts in the belly
and creeps up the memory
pulling him back to Sunday
at Ipan Beach with
those spare ribs
bubbling and those soy sauce–sweetened
juices dripping down into the fire
and oozing out
over the edge of flank steak

This is a tortured path back
is all I can say
through diabetes and what Chamoru call "heart."[3]
definitely not as in "have a heart"
or in "I give you my heart"
but as in
"Don't break my heart, my achy, breaky heart"

One way change comes
is through necessity

---

3. Elderly Chamoru say "heart" for short when talking about heart disease of any kind.

and that's where we are
with one of the highest diabetes rates in the nation
and lots of heart,
maybe the most heart per capita
in the magnificent United States
plus its territories.

Between the sugarless jams and
the frozen bolono (without the baloney)
we hear this conversation:
"Do you have heart?"
"Yes, aiaday, diabetes and heart!"
and the mild-mannered doctor
with the tragic eyes says,
"Returning to the past is
moving into the future."

Currents, cross-currents, returning currents
present, past, future
where is our star-map?
here in meatless Simply Foods,
how do we track the birds?

Can you hear the breathing of the ancestors
in Aisle 1 where the
rows and rows of whole grain flour, nuts, and legumes
threaten our food supply?

Can they, who ate the food of paradise,
tell us anything about
hearts and grass-eaters
that will guide us into a future
that we're told is our past?

Row 3 there
looks in its gnarled complexity
like a Banyan Tree
perhaps we should ask,
"Guela yan Guelu
Kao sina yu un hasgayon?"[4]

---

4. *"Guela yan Guelu, kao sina yu malofan"* is the traditional way to ask permission of the ancestors when going into the jungles. Literally, it is translated, "Grandmother and Grandfather, may I pass through?" I've adapted it to mean, "Grandmother and Grandfather, please help us survive this trip through Simply Foods."

My life is a poetry reading

C. T. Perez (Guåhan)

And I search for the word
To express what I feel
Tell what I see

When my eyes are closed
It is when I see best
When the words come pouring

From thoughts
I didn't know I had

I share what I know
I write words for the pleasure of writing
For the pleasure
Of saying
Word by word
A word over and over
To think it,
To say it,
To feel it, to love the word
As it is given
As I breathe it
In billows
And hollows
Never knowing
If another
Will come again

I move in faith

I speak the word
In many languages
The language of my mother

Of my friends
Of my travels
Of my heart
Of my mind
Of my knowing
And unknowing

See the curves and lines
In billows
And hollows

In fiery gesticulation
In soothing caresses

And love the word

I see them floating in the air
Dancing around me

I hear them singing
In everything that moves
And doesn't

They come the loudest
When I am
Trying to sleep

Calling me by name

And my life like a poem
Is never done

Hiking

Leiana San Agustin Naholowaʻa (Guåhan)

my hikes on this island
valleys and mounds sprout shrubs and trees
just rained—soft like clay
slip and fall
shoes covered in dirt
legs traced in red
stained skin.

sword grass sharpens
moments need
to grip
hold on, life
slide down this mountain
to the river.

March in mantras
rhythmic air swirling hot kisses
keep moving, dig deeper
hands in earth's iron
straight upward
to the next decline
don't stop.

baseball cap soaked through salt and sweat
and water
beneath the coconut forest
by the river, near the shrimp in
the pool's waterfall, mossy stones deceive
Reeboks worn cracked weary
stabbed feet in currents and paths
smoothed by her
ghost
the white lady—

singing mourning
lost heart of a
faceless lover—and a never wedding—she
breathes, crying through the water
wait staying
do not find her.

over passages and lanes of sorrow
readied joys of a
sandy promise—to the pacific, I wait
for you there.

The floating world

Terry Perez (Guåhan)

She rolls over on her back. Sunlight hits her hard in the face. Is it noon? Her body lies flat on a futon. The tatami's sweet grassiness revives her somewhat. Her companion also lies basking in light and then turns over to meet her. Methodically, in an exhalation, the two become entwined—an innocent mess of feet, legs and arms. A slow coiling.

They haven't "slept" together; she is almost sure. It's too difficult to think just yet. She opens her eyes. His body shifts. Her mouth stuck, she mumbles "hello" to her companion.

"Umm," he moans, eyes closed.

They lie in her apartment: white walls with unpacked boxes atop a makeshift nylon closet. No real furniture besides futon and tatami, a kotatsu on loan from her school, a decent TV set she found in a neighbor's trash pile, and some mis-matching pillows good-naturedly propped against one wall for visitors. Nine long months have gone already.

Half an hour of silence later, they're lying on their bellies; his arm and leg graze her. He's reading the paper. She shifts. Propped on one elbow now, she watches him for a long stretch of time.

"Must be nice to understand Kanji."

He continues his downward glance. Long straight hair half hides his face, his cocky half-Japanese eyes, and skims his pale brown skin much like hers. His nickname around town is *Keanu*. And so he is. A sawed-off, less cinematic version. A well-known cad whom, her hostess friends have urged, she needs to . . . .

No longer half-asleep now, she remembers the alley: She sat there outside the bar jammed in with other expatriates, campfire-style, like drunken boy scouts. A rush of liquor bottles encircled her, traveling from unidentifiable mouth to unidentifiable hand. Her vision clouded. Very soon the world faded out for her. At dawn, her stupefied senses awoke to yelling. She looked up, dimly saw police-men in front of her. They were hurling foreign threats at her, verbally pinning her to that one lonely spot she had kept all night—utterly alone—until she heard a voice speak in a whiskey blur, in the tones of both angel and hero:

"Come on. Get up. They want us to leave."

He had been sitting there holding her hand.

And just now lying with him, gazing at him through his long hair lit by the mid-morning sun, she can quickly recall in succession the cab ride and their catnap; nothing sloppy was exchanged between them—nothing awkward or even situational, although Japan can be such a whore sometimes. She sighs and wonders how warm his lips might feel.

I Will Drink the Rain (For Toma)

Teresia Teaiwa (Kiribati and Fiji)

Ko na moi? I ask.

    Moi n te ra? He asks.

Te ranibue? Te maitoro? I offer a choice.

    His face is blank. He appears unimpressed.

Coke? I suggest, with bated breath.

    He shakes his head. And slowly says, N na moi te karau.

So I get him a glass. For the rain.

Flip Flops

Teresia Teaiwa (Kiribati and Fiji)

Suck
in the rain
flipping leaves
and mud
up your legs
on your shorts
or skirt
sometimes right up
your shirt

Suck
if you slip
on tiles
or wood
landing
on your butt
that sucks

In the sea
a hassle
they sink
into sand
like whales
(whales sink?
in sand?
when they're beached,
I guess)

In the sun
on land
they're excellent:
flip flops,
I mean

Unless
they're not
yours,
which is likely

So friendly
they'll go walking
without you

Black Coral

Maya Alonso (Guåhan)

Standing three vinyl checkerboard tiles apart in the narrow hallway of my parents' apartment, my mother and her younger brother face each other, arms stretched towards each other. My uncle, tentative and halting; my mother, agape, anticipating an accident. Before I notice he is holding something, a flame explodes in my uncle's hand, between their expectant faces. My mother *whoops* in the way she always does, even now: without a shred of self-consciousness. My uncle is not injured; in fact, both are pleased with the result, which appears to be a branch, still burning. I am four years old and watch unnoticed from the pile of quilts on the living room carpet, where their whispered commiserating has roused me. This is my earliest memory in Tumon village.

Shaking cocktails and uncapping beer behind the bar of a strip club in Guam's tourist district, I cringe silently while listening to exotic dancers from the U.S. try with the best of intentions to educate tourists or military personnel on Guam's geography, culture, history. I know from the confidences we have exchanged that, without adequate transportation, many of these young women, here on contracts typically lasting no more than two months, never leave the now-metropolitan village of Tumon. Much of their perception of Guam is limited—skewed by their isolation. I am sympathetic to what amounts to me as their indentured servitude but can barely contain my annoyance over how little they know of the rest of the island; I am further incensed by its disproportion to the heaps of misinformation they are more than happy to dispense. More maddening still is their assessment that the Tumon in which they live—in which "adult entertainment," luxury goods, and hotel resorts have virtually restricted public access to the beaches on which they sprawl—is the actual heart of the village.

Before Tumon developed into the entertainment capital it has become, fueled by retail sales, sex tourism, and food and beverage consumption, it was a narrow, two-lane stretch, lined on either side by skinny *tangantangan* and their confetti leaves, its sandy shores overlooked by potential investors in favor of the Hagåtña Bay etched out of our island's capital. As the village grew and roads were paved, a handful of hotels went all but unnoticed as my mother, her sisters, and their girlfriends raised us children, baking in the sun, on the beaches of our barely inhabited Tumon.

In the same presumptuous way that my auntie pierced my ears with a needle and an apple, I was, at the age of five, led away from my sandcastle and hoisted onto the front end of a windsurf board by my mother's best friend. She then hefted herself onto the board, raised the sail by its cord, and gripped the bar.

At once, we were off, swept across the shallows and out toward the reef by a steady wind. Gravity my only restraint, I squatted on the board's point the entire ride, rapt and intrepid, as coral skeletons, *balate*, and the orange daubs of triggerfish streaked beneath us, disappearing. I must have been too young to know to be afraid, because I remember clearly that I wasn't. Never did it occur to me that I might fall over or be knocked in the head by the corner of the triangular sail. Her assured stance, her feet firmly planted—only once did I look back up at my pilot and was comforted.

I don't remember when fear crept into my life, when I began to imagine man-eating fish in water too deep to see to the bottom, or when exactly I began to restrain myself in the adult-ish way most of us eventually do. Even at eight years old, when I positively identified a *duendes* that years of higher education, skepticism, and Catholic scoffing still cannot deny, I was not afraid. The dwarf of local legend did not at all resemble the illustrations in *Myths of Guam*, or the descriptions spoken of by elders threatening its impish wrath.

It stood the height of a tire on a midsized sedan, not nearly short enough to while away its days beneath a mushroom cap. I remember because it stood beside such a tire as we made eye contact. And instead of the childlike and playful creatures from the drawings, the duendes looked like a greenish-gray menacing old man. Though I was looking down on it from where I lived on the second floor, it maintained its stare long enough for me to assess the situation and leave my room to tell my mother. When we returned to the window together, I could still see it—she could not. Trusting that I did indeed see the creature and worrying over the safety of my newborn brother since, legend has it, duendes steal babies, she ordered me to shut the blinds and not look out again. Still, I was not afraid.

There was a wantonness to the children of Tumon. Japanese tourists fawned over us, asking to be photographed in cheery groups, two fingers held upright: Peace. Often, we went unsupervised, or were trusted to supervise each other. While young parents nurtured relationships veering toward tedium and ambitions just within their grasps, they were at least allowed a little bit of comfort in the safety of their children, afforded by the isolation of our beach community. And so it is difficult to pin down: When? When exactly, did this childish bravado begin to recede into mature caution?

Despite the Guam Tourist Commission's vision of concentrating the visitor industry in Hagåtña Bay, foreign investors found Tumon all the more appealing for their purposes, and we soon found shops and restaurants obscuring the views from our apartments, beaches suddenly interrupted by the swimming pool/koi pond expanses of resort hotel grounds. All too soon, the children of Tumon, who once hiked through the jungles later cleared for the construction of P.I.C. (Pacific Islands Club), who were allowed to walk all the way to Fiesta Villa to moon over the '50s kitsch so popular in the early 1980s, whose parents didn't worry over the whereabouts of their children until well after sunset, were unwelcome in the posh hotel lobbies, were trespassing in resort water parks, were turned out with a literal "Shoo!" when seeking nothing but shelter on a rainy July afternoon. Shame is what I might now call the feeling we didn't name at the time. And without a name, how could we talk about their contempt? How could we fully grasp our exile? And so we didn't. And we kept our bikes in our hallways and confined ourselves to the parking lot. And our parents made other plans.

The last memory I have of our apartment in Tumon was playing with my brother on the living room floor. *Magnum P.I.* was blaring from the television when he swallowed a Lego and began to choke. A near eight-year gap divides us and so I might have handled the situation better, but even today, hysteria manifests itself in squeals and giggles. My father, who stitches his own wounds and consults professionals only to confirm whether or not a layer of epoxy might be a suitable replacement for tooth enamel, reached into my brother's throat and saved him. The memory of the panic all but faded as we prepared to move to our new home, six villages away, in Nimitz Hill.

Hours previously spent on the shores of Matapang or the Seahorse, floating on our backs or mastering the underwater summersault *without* getting water up our noses, were replaced with solitary days, overlooked amid bustling, eager tourists on our boat. Gone were the workdays when, left unsupervised in our apartments, the children of Tumon, fearless and proprietary, walked to the beach, stopping at Uncle Pito's Ypao Beach Store to plunk nickels and dimes on his counter in exchange for the junk our parents forbade. Those of us who left Tumon young were spared much of what we well considered our indignity; those who stayed, I assume, learned to cope.

Remembering Tumon, returning to it dreadfully, squinting at the too-bright (and too-frequent) signage, and narrowly missing an errant tourist or eager taxi driver, I pass the brick apartments in which I grew up. And I recall the morning I woke to my mother and uncle, setting branches alight to some mysterious purpose. Though the process of heating black coral, to shape for jewelry or the sort of tropical-bohemian home décor my mother then favored, was explained to me shortly thereafter, the spectacle remains as mystical to me as it did that morning. Each time my eyes fall on the petrified, thinly gnarled twigs, bereft in a dusty old crystal vase at my parents' house or forgotten in a cloisonné one, sticky with the close humidity of my grandmother's home, I remember the surprise, the wonder, the awe of my mother and uncle, not simply two siblings burning a rare and prized bit of reef to preserve, but practitioners of some esoteric ritual.

On the Occasion of the Quarter Century

PC Muñoz (Guåhan)

On the occasion of the quarter century,
synchronicity
steam from your coffee
my wanderlust
the death of a loved one
some spiteful injustice

In chambers,
I'll smile sideways
and offer mechanical help

The choir will sing
"we've come this far by faith"

Children will snooze during the lecture.

This, the passing of time.

The romance of reality.

Archery

PC Muñoz (Guåhan)

I did rope tricks for a dollar at the yearly carnival
YOU sculpted a bust of Hemingway in the parish parking lot

I made great escapes from vilified carnage boxes
YOU performed a one-woman play behind the neighborhood Lucky's

I filled six dough-boy pools with the fat of a three-toed sloth
YOU sold handmade earrings at a friend's garage sale

I did somersaults onstage in Wichita
YOU published an essay on vaudeville comedians

I stuffed my socks with cotton candy
YOU had an elegant meal with C. Delores Tucker

I snuck into an underground bar to watch videos of university professors
    defiling nubile aliens
YOU had a walk-on part in a Gregg Araki film

I winced when the tobacco boy didn't finish his job
YOU painted your dad's name in nail polish on the side of your building

I drilled holes in oversized encyclopedias
YOU dipped yourself in olive oil as a thesis

I slipped and fell through the feathery mess my lover had made

YOU sighed

and made a decision.

Tidepools

Evelyn Flores (Guåhan)

Then

the air smells like death

                                               here

                         sometimes

plastic burning

                    drifts

                        across   green hills   blue ocean whispering

exhaust from a thousand cars
slides on the back of the hot wind into our lungs

      in the wrinkles of our toes the moist sand lingers
                    the waves sigh into the soft shoulders of the dark

I remember
the kid walking along a beach
with a bunch of other kids
you know, just kids, out for a beach walk one early sunday morning
picking up stuff, just stuff that had washed onto the shore,
                   hey, look at this cool dukduk[1]
                 look over here an old float—take it home
who picked up a grenade and almost blew himself up with it
PDN said, "WWII undetonated explosive"

I remember
walking down Asan beach
finding a black, oblong metal thing
          crouched between the sand crabs scuttling into dark tunnels
              their morning's work
            bulging singular eyes peering into our shadow

Previously published, *Amberflora* 1, 2017.
1. small hermit crab

and my dad saying don't touch it
let's call the explosives detonation team

children
                        holding leftovers from the bloody cannibal feasts of WWII
on our island
                japanese blown up
                                american guts spilled on the shores of the bay
each side pointing their guns and blasting away

                    Gera! Gera! Gera!
                War! War! War!
my grandmother screamed as she fled the burning village with a baby in her arms
a toddler dragged along, the others   *running running running*
            away from the street flowing with liquid fire

13 days of bombing, strafing, riddling
        28,761 shells bombarding
        houses, churches, coconut trees, plumeria
                                        fleeing villagers

the island left
                razed, flattened, blackened, scraped clean

                        simple as that

Now

over Litekyan,
        where our grandmothers' and grandfathers' bodies are buried
            and theirs and theirs and theirs for thousands of years

over Litekyan, they want to put a live firing range

they say it will be just occasionally that they will
            shut those ancient beaches down to us
those sacred sites that are home to our ancestors' bones
    and bear our history on the walls of caves

"our guns will protect the site from pilferers"
they say—

who will protect the site from them, pilferer enough—

            our children will walk the beaches picking up empty shells
                    bullets that have missed their target
                        maybe one of them will get hit by stray lead

haggan[2]
in the dark, the infant turtles struggle out of their shells
and make their way to the ocean,
following an ancient route that has outlasted invading
diseases and wars and war games
above them the guns of a live firing range loom leering

don't swim in this beach   or that beach

or that   and that   and that
in the black jagged rocks of the shoreline, we stumble across a massacre site
blood, intestines everywhere
balati[3] death

The seductive appeal of béche de mer
who would have done this?

hunters with no hearts
who want only one part

and to leave the rest

the moon is full
the ocean is silver
the coral is breathing

---

2. turtle
3. sea cucumber

Afterword

Indigenous Literatures from Micronesia is a vessel carrying our stories across the vast distances of silence. Within the multilingual hull of this book, the established and emerging authors form a diverse kinship network from across our archipelagoes and our diasporas. The editors, after years of voyaging, have guided us safely to our destination: here, upon the shore of your attention.

This anthology is historic because it is the first compilation of twentieth- and twenty-first-century Micronesian writers. It is significant because it changes the perception that our literature is lacking. It is significant because it introduces our literature to an international audience. This anthology makes visible what was once invisible.

Micronesian literature descends from oral chants, genealogies, songs, and tales passed down through memory and voice. If you listen closely, you can still hear the sonic textures, rhythms, and tongues of our spoken words vibrating on each page of this anthology. Our literature also descends from visual arts. If you look closely, you will see narrative patterns analogous to storyboard carvings, housing architecture, weaving, canoe design, and tattooing. Our literature also descends from a global web of literary influences. If you read closely, you can map an interwoven and international literary genealogy.

Today, Micronesia is threatened by climate change, colonialism, militarism, and global capitalism. Our islands have become endangered, and our people are migrating in record numbers. At the same time, we continue to protest these violent forces and protect our sacred lands and waters. We continue to revitalize our cultures and languages, both at home and abroad. We continue to write our stories in order to understand the past, navigate the present, and imagine the future. We continue to author a new Micronesia.

We hope this anthology has inspired and empowered you. We hope you will value and remember our stories. We hope you will gift copies of this work to your friends and relatives. We hope you will teach this book in your classrooms, share it in your communities, and catalogue it in your libraries.

We hope you will carry this book with you and pass it down to future generations.

Craig Santos Perez

About the Contributors

Baltazar Aguon is a Chamorro writer born and raised on Guam. He received his MFA from the American Film Institute's Center for Advanced Film and Television Studies (CAFTS) and has been published in numerous Guam publications. He has also had key roles in the production of significant documentaries and film pieces about Guam, including co-directing *I Tinituhun* and co-producing *War for Guam*. As a producer for PBS Guam, he wrote, produced, and directed *I Know Guam*, a five-episode series that explores Guam history.

Julian Aguon is a writer, activist, and attorney who specializes in international law, human rights, and Pacific Islands legal systems and political development. He is the author of numerous books and law articles including *Just Left of the Setting Sun, The Fire This Time, What We Bury at Night*, and *On Loving the Maps Our Hands Cannot Hold: Self-Determination of Colonized and Indigenous Peoples in International Law*. He currently teaches international law at the University of Guam and works as an attorney in private practice.

Maya Alonso is a graduate of the Academy of Our Lady and the University of Guam. She has taught at Southern High School and been an editor of *GU Magazine*. Maya's nonfiction includes "Guam's Top Five Environmental Problems," "Inside DOC," and "The Cult of Virginity." More recently, she has prepared official responses to the U.S. Navy's Environmental Impact Statement and helped in the production of cultural events, including the Guam Micronesia Island Fair and the 2016 Saipan exhibition of Paul Jacoulet in Micronesia. She now lives in Monterey, California, where she cares for her manåmko.

In her writing, Belauan author and educator, **Isebong Asang** explored issues of Belauan identity both at home and abroad. Her 1999 book *Searching for a Palauan Identity with an English Accent: Language with an Attitude* examines negotiations of diaspora identity in an alien, sometimes hostile environment. Her doctoral dissertation, published in 2004, focuses particularly on Belauan culture. Dr. Asang served on the faculty of Palau Community College until her death in August 2017.

Monica Dolores Baza finds constant inspiration in Guam's natural environment and its culture. Her paintings, drawings, linoleum block prints, and linoblock mixed media are expressions of her awe and admiration of the beauty that surrounds her island. Pride in her Chamorro heritage also filters through to her art in the form of cultural motifs and her use of color and symbolism. She creates her art primarily in her home studio in Talofofo, Guam.

Michael Lujan Bevacqua (familian Kabesa/Bittot) is an assistant professor in Chamorro studies at the University of Guam and a longtime blogger, artist, writer, and poet. His academic work deals primarily with the effects of colonization on Chamorros and their islands and theorizing the possibilities for their decolonization.

Joseph Borja is a Chamorro who was born on Guam and has lived there all his life. He attended the University of Guam, and his work has been published in the university's literary journal, *Storyboard*.

Chamoru writer **Kisha Borja-Quichocho-Calvo** is from the village of Mangilao. She received a BA in English from Hawaiʻi Pacific University, an MA in Pacific Islands studies from the University of Hawaiʻi–Mānoa, and an MA in teaching from the University of Guam. She has taught at both the secondary and post-secondary levels. She most recently taught in the School of Education at the University of Guam and served as editor for the Micronesian Area Research Center Publications. She is pursuing her doctoral degree in political science, specializing in indigenous politics, at UH Mānoa.

Jacob Camacho is a Chamoru writer, educator, mentor, poet, and activist. He has an MFA in creative writing from Rutgers University, Camden, and is an alumnus of the University of Guam and UCLA's Extension Writers Program. He is an academic coach at YMCA of South Jersey and lead facilitator of Move-Mountains in Colorado.

When **Tutii-Elbuchel I. Chilton** was six years old, he left Koror in the Republic of Belau to live with his mother on the U.S. mainland. His next twenty years were spent growing up and going to school in California and New Jersey before finally returning home in 1994. He has served as dean of academic affairs at Palau Community College and is presently the president and CEO of the Learning Institute for Everyone (LIFE) Schools. He and his family live in Belau.

Nikkie de Jesus Cushing lives in Puyallup, Washington, with her family. She graduated from the University of Guam with a bachelor's degree in linguistics and currently works as an intelligence analyst. Her passionate dedication to volunteering at organizations that support children and families, music education, and endangered species highlights her emphatic desire to effect positive social change and global sustainability.

Ruby Dediya was Nauru's first female MP elected to parliament. She was elected in 1986, and over the course of her eight-year career as a member of parliament she has held positions as speaker of parliament, minister for health, and minister for finance. She was born on Nauru; educated in Victoria, Australia; and attended university in Christchurch, New Zealand, where she graduated as a midwife.

J. A. Dela Cruz-Smith is a Chamorro Filipino poet living in Seattle, Washington. His family is from Guåhan. He is pursuing an MFA in the Rainier Writing Workshop. His work has been published in *The Good Men Project* and in *Assaracus: A Journal of Gay Poetry.*

Christine "Tina" Taitano DeLisle is a Chamoru author and an assistant professor of American Indian studies at the University of Minnesota. She has published articles in leading journals in Pacific studies and in gender, women, and sexuality studies, and is currently completing a book manuscript on the historical and cultural relations between Chamorro women and American Navy wives in Guam. She was born and raised on Guam, and she has collaborated with Humanities Guåhan (HG) on community conversations about the U.S. military buildup on the island, served as curator for HG's I Kelat/The Fence exhibit, and was a consultant to the Guam Museum.

Vicente (Vince) M. Diaz, a Filipino-Pohnpeian scholar and writer from Guam, is an associate professor of American Indian studies at the University of Minnesota. He received his undergraduate and master's degrees in political science from the University of Hawai'i at Mānoa, and his doctorate degree from the interdisciplinary History of Consciousness program at the University of California at Santa Cruz in 1992. He is the author of *Repositioning the Missionary: Rewriting the Histories of Colonialism, Native Catholicism, and Indigeneity in Guam* (2010).

Canisius Tkel Filibert has served as president of the Micronesian Community Network and as program director, Pacific Resources for Education and Learning (PREL). His poems in this anthology were first published in the University of Guam's literary journal, *Storyboard.*

Evelyn Flores (familian Cabesa yan Yaman) is an associate professor of English and Chamorro studies at the University of Guam. She earned her doctorate in English from the University of Michigan, Ann Arbor, and has published three children's books, a genealogy of a Chamoru family central to the introduction of Protestantism to Guam, and a number of poems in various journals. Her research focuses on oral histories, Indigenous and women's studies, and Pacific Island literatures. She and her family reside in Windward Hills, Guam.

Jan Furukawa is a Chamoru writer, editor, publisher, educator, and entrepreneur. She earned her BA in journalism from the University of Hawai'i at Mānoa. She has worked in radio, and public television in Guam, Saipan, and Belau. As an educator, she has taught English, language arts, and Chamorro courses in both public and private schools, at Guam Community College, and the University of Guam. She is presently working with the *Pacific Island Times* and pacificislandtimes.com, a regional newsmagazine and website.

Maria Gaiyabu is secretary for education in Nauru. She received her doctorate from the Faculty of Education, University of Cambridge, UK, in 2008. Her publications and presentations since then have been numerous, focusing on education and the status of women in Nauru.

Anne Perez Hattori is a Chamorro writer and a professor of Pacific history and Chamorro studies with the University of Guam. She is the oldest of nine children and is of the clan familian Titang. Her doctoral research, entitled *Colonial Dis-Ease: U.S. Naval Health Policies and the Chamorros of Guam, 1898–1941*, was published in 2004. She also has a list of published essays in key journals that focus on the complex linkages between colonial policies and practices in Guam and the everyday lives of Chamorro.

A native of Guåhan, **Mary Therese Perez Hattori** is one of nine children of Paul Mitsuo Hattori and Fermina Leon Guerrero Perez Hattori. She is a Chamoru scholar, author, educator, mentor, and public speaker. Her areas of interest and teaching include educational technology, culturally sustaining leadership, indigenous research, digital leadership, and digital wisdom.

Marianna Hernandez is a proud Chamoru daughter from the island of Guam. She currently teaches at Tiyan High School and is a PhD student in the University of Alaska Fairbanks Interdisciplinary Studies program. Her interests lie in the political history of her homeland and the revitalization movements that have empowered her people.

Chamoru writer **Angela Hoppe-Cruz** was born and raised on Guam. Her career, which began in the field of domestic violence advocacy, has heightened her consciousness of the violence against women and minority communities in Oceania, specifically in Micronesia. She currently resides on the Waianae Coast of Oʻahu with her family, where she is a program counselor for a local nonprofit, the Institute for Native Peace Education and Culture, which supports individuals working towards their academic goals. She is also an instructor at Leeward Community College, Waianae.

When **Chris Perez Howard** returned to Guam, he sought out information not only about his mother but also about his "mother culture," from which he had so long been separated. He joined the struggle for self-determination and at one point served as chairman of the Organization of People for Indigenous Rights, a group that strove to bring Guam's unresolved status into the limelight. His groundbreaking *Mariquita* is a re-membering of his mother's story and of her death during WWII.

Josie Howard is from Onoun, a small island in Chuuk. Drawing on her island background, her BA in anthropology (UH-Hilo), and her master's in social work (UH-Mānoa), Josie continues to advocate for the overall health and well-being of her people, with strong respect for her culture and the cultures of others.

Today, Josie serves as director/founder of We Are Oceania, empowering Micronesian communities in Hawaiʻi to navigate success while honoring their diverse heritage.

Leonard Z. Iriarte, Mark A. Santos, and **Jeremy N. C. Cepeda** were all involved in I Fanlalaiʻan, a significant oral history project based at the University of Guam. In 1998, Leonard (familian Yǻyi), the leader of the group, founded Guma' Pǻlu Liʻe'–I Fanlalaiʻan (The House of the Seeing Mast—The Place for Chant), a Chamoru chant group. In 2007, the I Fanlalaiʻan project was officially inaugurated, focusing on the group's vision of creating chants that would preserve a traditional art form and that would revitalize the use of endangered indigenous words.

Nauruan author **Lucia Itsimaera** wrote "Egade" for the *Stories from Naura* (1991) anthology. She was part of the University of the South Pacific's (USP) series of workshops in creative writing and drama held in 1990. The workshops encouraged Nauruans to write and publish their oral literatures and myths. The anthology was the first to publish primarily Nauruan voices, and a second edition was published in 1996.

Yolanda Joab was born and raised on Pohnpei. She helps run the Climate Change Adaptation, Disaster Risk Reduction and Education Program (CADRE) in schools and communities in the Federated States of Micronesia and the Republic of the Marshall Islands, and the International Organization for Migration in Micronesia. She lives in Chuuk with her husband, son, and family.

Kathy Jetñil-Kijiner is a poet, spoken word artist, and environmentalist. She received international acclaim through her poetry performance at the opening of the United Nations Climate Summit in New York in 2014. Her first collection of poetry, *Iep Jāltok: Poems from a Marshallese Daughter*, was published in 2017. Kathy also co-founded the youth environmentalist non-profit Jo-Jikum. Kathy was selected as one of thirteen Climate Warriors by *Vogue* magazine in 2015 and was named the Impact Hero of the Year by Earth Company in 2016. She received her master's in Pacific Islands studies from the University of Hawaiʻi at Mānoa.

Emelihter Kihleng completed her PhD in Vaʻaomanū Pasifika/Pacific studies from Victoria University of Wellington in Aotearoa, New Zealand. She was the fall 2015 Distinguished Writer in Residence in the English department at the University of Hawaiʻi at Mānoa. Emeli's collection of poetry, *My Urohs*, was published in 2008, and she has continued to publish in international journals and magazines since then. Most recently, she served as the cultural anthropologist for the Pohnpei Historic Preservation Program in Pohnpei Island, FSM.

Myjolynne (Mymy) Kim is Chuukese and of the clans Ráák and Enengeitaúw. She received her BA in philosophy and theology from Mount Mary University in Milwaukee, Wisconsin, and her MA in Pacific Islands studies from the

University of Hawaiʻi, Mānoa. She is currently living in Australia as she works on her PhD in Pacific history at the Australian National University but returns frequently to Chuuk to be with her son. She further identifies herself in terms of the many places she's lived and from which her ancestors came.

Ronald Laguana and **Rudolph Villaverde**, experienced chanters from the island of Guåhan, have presided at almost two hundred ceremonial events. Villaverde is the webmaster of http://ns.gov.gu and a systems programmer at the University of Guam. Laguana is a retired administrator of the Chamorro Studies and Special Projects Division in the Guam Public School System. He currently serves as a language translator for the courts and is the elected chair for the Northern Soil and Water Conservation District for Guam.

Born and raised in Nauru, **Alamanda Roland Lauti** graduated from the University of the South Pacific in Fiji with a major in management and public administration and tourism studies. Today, she is the campus director of the University of the South Pacific Nauru Center. Alamanda is one of the authors of a groundbreaking report on women's parliamentary representation published in 2006, titled *A Woman's Place Is in the House—The House of Parliament*.

Selina Neirok Leem is from the Republic of the Marshall Islands. She is a graduate of the international UWC Robert Bosch College in Freiburg, Germany. Leem is a youth advocate for the Marshall Islands against climate change and the abuse of women. She spoke at the COP21 in Paris, France, where she addressed world leaders and urged them to participate in the fight against climate change.

Victoria-Lola M. Leon Guerrero is the managing editor of University of Guam Press. She teaches women's and gender studies and has taught creative writing and other writing courses at the University of Guam, Mills College, and Southern High School. She has a master of fine arts degree in creative writing from Mills College and a bachelor of arts degree in politics from the University of San Francisco. Victoria has published a children's book, short stories, and essays; has co-edited an anthology of Chamoru writers; and was the editor of *Storyboard: A Journal of Pacific Imagery* for three years.

Chamoru writer **Arielle Taitano Lowe** began writing spoken word poetry in 2011 with Sinangån-ta Youth Movement, Guam's official spoken word arts organization. She earned a spot on Guam's National Poetry Slam team, performing with them from 2012 to 2014. Since then, she has written various works addressing indigenous rights, island ecology, and cultural identity, and has published in *Storyboard* and *Local Voices*. She is currently working on her master's in English at the University of Guam.

John Mangafel was a much-revered leader not only on his home island of Yap but across Micronesia. He was the first Yap State governor, served as a driving force behind the Federated States of Micronesia (FSM) Constitution, and was later an FSM senator. He passed away on April 11, 2007. He is remembered for his lack of pretension and his satiric humor.

Charissa Lynn Atalig Manibusan is a native Chamoru from the island of Guåhan. She is a former member of Ginen I Hila I Maga' Taotao Siha (From the Tongues of a Noble People), an association of artists who perpetuate the Chamoru language and culture through the mediums of theater, music, and writing. She represented Guåhan as a Literary Arts delegate at the Festival of the Pacific Arts held in American Samoa in 2008 and again in 2016 when the festival was held in Guåhan.

Chamoru writer **Clarissa Mendiola**'s work has been published in *As Us, Literary Hub, Omniverse*, and *The Offending Adam*. Clarissa has an MFA in writing from California College of Arts, was a 2011 Hedgebrook Writer in Residence, and teaches creative writing summer camps for junior high school students. She lives in San Francisco with her husband and two sons.

During the 1970s in Belau, **Elicita "Cita" Morei** fought alongside her mother, Gabriela Ngirmang, Mirair (women's leader) of eastern Koror, for the world's first nuclear-free constitution, which was passed in 1979. They led a group of women known as Otil a Beluad ("anchor of our land") to keep the Pacific nuclear free. In 1988, Otil a Beluad was nominated for the Nobel Peace Prize.

PC Muñoz is a mestizo musician, producer, and poet based in San Francisco. His diverse body of work includes Grammy-nominated contemporary classical music, CMJ-charting funk music, an award-winning haiku CD, and avant-garde compositions for film and dance.

Leiana San Agustin Naholowaʻa received her master's degree in English from the University of Guam and her bachelor's in literature and writing studies from California State University, San Marcos. Her research interests focus on the figure of the maternal in Chamorro mythos and historiography. She recently completed an oral interview project about Guam's maternal tradition that resulted in a documentary film entitled *Mothering Guåhan*.

Raised in the sprawling hills of Talisay, Agat, in Guam, **Sandra Iseke Okada** was dramatically changed by several trips she took to Bali in 2007 and 2008 as part of her sociology program at the University of Guam. She passionately spearheaded the production of two documentaries based on the trips, *Casting Our Net: Rediscovering Community in the 21st Century* and *Symbols of Survival*. She co-founded Traditions Affirming Our Seafaring Ancestry, Inc. (TASA), and remains a passionate member of the seafaring community in Guam. She is presently pursuing a master's degree in international business.

Chamoru writer **Peter R. Onedera** is best known for the historical plays he has written and produced and for his persistence as an outspoken Chamoru language advocate. His earliest work, *Nå'an Lugåt Siha gi ya Guåhan: Guam Place Names* (1989), recovers forgotten place names, while his latest production, *Gi I Tilu Gradu (In the Third Grade)* (2009), highlights nonstandard English and the socio-political changes that toppled Chamoru from its key position as the language of the majority of the Chamoru people of Guam.

A respected journalist and historian, **Antonio "Tony" Palomo** made it his life's work to tell the Chamorro version of history. In 1954 he earned a bachelor of science degree in journalism from Marquette University, Wisconsin. He worked as a journalist with the *Pacific Daily News* and *Pacific Stars and Stripes*, and also served three terms as a senator, twelve years as an administrator in the Department of Interior, and eleven years (from 1995 to 2007) as museum director/administrator for the Guam Museum. In 1984 he published *An Island in Agony*, one of the most complete accounts of the Chamorro people's experience during World War II. He passed away on February 1, 2013. In recognition of his efforts to preserve Guam's history, the newly constructed Guam Museum was named in his honor.

An indigenous Chamorro writer, **C. T. Perez** has been published in *Indigenous Women: The Right to a Voice* (1998) and in *Storyboard 5: A Journal of Pacific Imagery*. Perez earned an MA in Pacific Islands Studies from the University of Hawai'i at Mānoa. She resides in Guam.

Craig Santos Perez, a Chamoru writer from Guåhan (Guam), grew up in the village of Mongmong and lives in Hawai'i. He is the co-founder of Ala Press, editor of three anthologies, and the author of four collections of poetry. He is the first Pacific Islander author to receive the American Book Award. He received a master of fine arts degree in poetry from the University of San Francisco, and his PhD in comparative ethnic studies from the University of California, Berkeley. He is currently an associate professor at University of Hawai'i, Mānoa.

Terry Perez has published in *Storyboard* and in *Kinalamten Gi Pasifiku: Insights from Oceania*. She has served as lead editor for *Local Voices: An Anthology*, published for the Festival of Pacific Arts in 2016, and is currently working with the University of Guam Press to curate and rewrite an anthology of legends from Guåhan.

Fred Quinene began writing poetry as a boy and continued writing even during his twenty-one years of teaching and his many years as an administrator. In the 1980s, Governor Ricky Bordallo named him Guam's first poet laureate in recognition of his outstanding achievements in capturing Guam's experiences and emotions through his writing.

Vidalino (Vid) Staley Raatior is a proud Chuukese parent, educator, citizen blogger, and social entrepreneur who lives in Northern California with his wife, Desha, and children, Keala and Keoni. He earned a bachelor's degree in communications from University of Guam, a master's degree in private school administration from the University of San Francisco, and a doctorate from the University of Hawai'i at Mānoa. He currently works at the University of California, Santa Cruz.

Hermana Ramarui was born in Belau. She completed her undergraduate studies in English at the University of Guam in 1970. After returning to Belau, she taught and worked with the government's bilingual program, which produced reading materials in the vernacular for elementary school teaching. Hermana's poems of protest were first published as *The Palauan Perspectives* in 1984.

Tereeao Teingiia Ratite is I-Kiribati from the islands of Nikunau and Beru, both in the southern island group. She is currently working at the University of the South Pacific, Kiribati campus, as a continuing and community education manager. She has published in *Mana; Saraga-Pacific Contemporary; Education for Sustainable Development: Pacific Stories of Sustainable Living, Vol. 2; VASU-Pacific Women of Power; Dreadlocks;* and the Kiribati Writers' Union magazines.

Alex Rhowunio'ng recounts the moment that fueled his determination to write. It was when he opened up a voluminous History of Micronesia series looking for his island and found only its location, shape, and what the explorers named it. Since then, he has written for *Pacific Daily News, Marianas Variety,* and *Kaselehlie Press,* among others, and is currently a broadcaster with Joy FM @91.9, a Christian radio station.

Johanna Salinas was born in Tamuning, Guam. She is currently a teacher for the Guam Department of Education. She hopes one day to travel and write a novel.

The late **Valentine N. Sengebau,** a Belauan poet, traveled from his birthplace, Peleliu, to Chuuk and then to Berkeley, California, for college. He spent his final years in his adopted home, Saipan, in the Northern Mariana Islands. During a prolific four-year period, from 1976 to 1980, he composed dozens of poems that were published in the *Micronesian Reporter,* the official quarterly magazine of the Trust Territory of the Pacific Islands government, and in the *Marianas Variety.* He died in 2000, leaving behind a body of work that speaks to the impact on ordinary Micronesians of the dramatic changes in the region during the latter half of the twentieth century.

Jelovea (Jenny) Seymour is from Kosrae and Chuuk in the Federated States of Micronesia. At the time she wrote the two poems in this anthology, she was not accustomed to speaking English fluently. Frustrated in her English classes, she wondered if there was no place where what she and others like her had to say would matter more than the errors on her page. Her two poems were inspired by a fellow islander's book of poems, Emelihter Kihleng's *My Urohs*, which empowered Jenny to try to capture her own experiences in poetry.

Lynnsey T. Sigrah is from the State of Yap in the FSM. She is currently a student at the College of Micronesia-FSM (COM-FSM) in Pohnpei and is studying to become an elementary school teacher. She started writing at a young age, inspired by her love of reading. COM-FSM gave her the privilege to be able to speak her mind through poems and other writing, and now she writes often.

Nedine F. Songeni is a daughter of Udot éfékur Fanapanges with Fanapi roots. Guam has been her adopted home for the past 13 years. She graduated from Guam Community College, created a growing family, and has continued to work towards helping other Micronesian families improve their lives through the power of the humanities and literacy.

Innocenta Sound-Kikku is from the island of Lukunor in Chuuk State, FSM. She is the founder of Pacific Voices and Kokua Kalihi Valley, and vice chair of the Micronesian Health Advisory Committee. She lives in Hawai'i.

Lehua M. Taitano, a native Chamoru from Yigo, Guåhan (Guam), is a queer writer and interdisciplinary artist. She is the author of two volumes of poetry: *Inside Me an Island* (WordTech Editions, 2018) and *A Bell Made of Stones* (TinFish Press). Her chapbook, *appalachiapacific*, won the 2010 Merriam-Frontier Award for short fiction. She has two recent chapbooks of poetry and visual art: *Sonoma* (Dropleaf Press) and *Capacity* (Hawai'i Review). She has served as an APAture Featured Literary Artist via Kearny Street Workshop, a Kuwentuhan poet via the Poetry Center at SFSU, and as a Culture Lab visual artist for the Smithsonian Institute's Asian Pacific American Center. Taitano currently serves as the Community Outreach Coordinator on the executive board of the Thinking Its Presence: Race, Literary and Interdisciplinary Studies Conference.

Artist and poet **Teweiariki Teaero** was born on Nikunau Island in Kiribati. In addition to his publications in various literary journals, he has published two collections of his work, *On Eitei's Wings* (2000) and *Waa in Storms* (2006). Teaero is an educator and artist as well as a writer. His works are held in both private and public collections, and his illustrations have been featured in various literary publications. He began teaching at the University of the South Pacific in Fiji in 1992 and also served as head of the School of Education. In 2012, he retired to return to Kiribati, where he is now a private consultant in art, education, and culture.

Katerina Teaiwa is an associate professor in the School of Culture, History and Language in the College of Asia and the Pacific, Australian National University. She has also been a consultant with UNESCO and the Secretariat of the Pacific Community. She was president of the Australian Association for Pacific Studies 2012–2017. Katerina is of Banaban, I-Kiribati, and African American descent and was born and raised in Fiji. Her research revolves around family history, the loss of their Banaban homeland to Australian and New Zealand agriculture, and the displacement of her people. The result has been several scholarly pieces and a book, *Consuming Ocean Island: Stories of People and Phosphate from Banaba* (2015). Katerina and her family live in Canberra.

Teresia Teaiwa was of Banaban, I-Kiribati, and African American heritage. She was born in Honolulu, Hawai'i, raised in the Fiji Islands, and lived in Wellington, New Zealand. She has one collection of poetry, *Searching for Nei Nim'anoa* (1995), and her writing has featured in a number of venues, including the spoken word CD *Terenesia: Amplified Poetry and Songs* with Sia Figiel (2000). In 2008 Teresia launched her solo CD of poetry *I can see Fiji*. She was director of Va'aomanū Pasifika, the Pacific and Samoan Studies programs, at Victoria University of Wellington (VUW) in New Zealand, where she taught Pacific Studies beginning in 2000. She received the Pacific People's Award for Education in 2015, the VUW Teaching Excellence Award in 2014, as well as the Ako Aotearoa Tertiary Teaching Excellence Award in 2014. Teresia authored numerous journal articles and book chapters and edited several special topic collections. She passed away in 2017 and her legacy as a prolific scholar and poet of Oceania lives on.

Chamorro writer **Stephen Tenorio Jr.**, an attorney by profession, for many years worked on an ambitious project, a historical fiction that dramatized life during the waning years of the Spanish empire on turn-of-the-century Guåhan. In 2012, he published *An Ocean in a Cup*.

Dickson Dalph Tiwelfil was born and raised in Topwat Village in Wottegai Woleai, Yap. He comes from two clans, Geofaliuwe and Sauwefange, with his cultural inheritance derived primarily from his mother's Geofaliuwe clan. Like many of his peers, he left home when he finished high school to pursue a degree at the College of Micronesia in Pohnpei.

Desiree Taimanglo Ventura has been published in the *Aulama Literary Journal* and the *Storyboard Journal of Pacific Imagery*. Her website, *The Drowning Mermaid*, regularly publishes creative entries and short essays regarding life within a non-self-governing territory. She earned her bachelor's degree in English from Chaminade University in Hawai'i, and a master's in rhetoric and writing studies from San Diego State University. She is a full-time instructor of English and communications at Guam Community College. Desiree lives with her family in Yigo, Guam, on her ancestral land, the subject of much of her work.

James Perez Viernes (familian Ginza, Kotla, and Miget) is from Santa Rita, the village built by those Chamorro displaced from Sumay village at the end of WWII. The stories of sorrow and longing told by his displaced elders fueled his research to pursue a more critical understanding of the American military presence in Micronesia. He has his doctoral degree in Pacific Islands history from the University of Hawai'i at Mānoa. He has served as program coordinator of the Chamorro Studies program at the University of Guam and is currently outreach director of the Center for Pacific Islands Studies at University of Hawai'i at Mānoa.

Melvin Won Pat-Borja is a writer, teacher, poet, raptivist, and father from Malojloj, Guam. He received his bachelor's degree in secondary education and his master's degree in Pacific Islands studies from the University of Hawai'i at Mānoa. Melvin represented Hawai'i in the National Poetry Slam in 2004, 2005, and 2006. He was the Hawai'i Grand Slam Champion in 2005. He co-founded Pacific Tongues and the Sinangån-ta Youth Movement. He also coached the Youth Speaks Hawai'i Slam Team from 2005 to 2007 and the Guam Slam Team from 2009 to 2010 in the Brave New Voices International Teen Poetry Slam Festival.

Born and raised in Yap, **Dolores Yilibuw** has traveled for her education as far east as Kentucky and Florida and as far west as the Philippines. She received her master of divinity degree from Asian Theological Seminary in the Philippines. She then returned to Yap, where she was hired by the United Bible Societies to translate portions of the Old Testament into Yapese and to assist in coordinating other Bible translation projects throughout Micronesia from 1988 to 1991. Her article, "Tampering with Bible Translation in Yap," was published in *SEMEIA*, a biblical studies journal. She currently serves as the library director at Lexington Theological Seminary in Lexington, Kentucky.